Knoxville, Tennessee

Knoxville, Tennessee

A Mountain City in the New South

♦ SECOND EDITION ♦

William Bruce Wheeler

THE UNIVERSITY OF TENNESSEE PRESS / KNOXVILLE

Copyright © 2005 by The University of Tennessee Press / Knoxville.
All Rights Reserved. Manufactured in the United States of America.
Second Edition.

First cloth, 2005.
First paperback, 2005; second paperback, 2008.

Frontispiece: View of "The Hill" at the University of Tennessee, 1902.
From *The Volunteer*, vol. 6 (1902).

This is a second edition of *Knoxville, Tennessee: Continuity and Change in
an Appalachian City* by Michael J. McDonald and William Bruce Wheeler,
published by the University of Tennessee Press in 1983.

This book is printed on acid-free paper.

Library of Congress Cataloging-in-Publication Data

Wheeler, William Bruce, 1939–   Knoxville, Tennessee : a mountain city
in the new South / William Bruce Wheeler.— 2nd ed.
         p. cm.
Rev. ed. of: Knoxville, Tennessee / Michael J. McDonald and William Bruce
Wheeler. 1st ed. c1983. Includes bibliographical references and index.
ISBN 1-57233-335-9 (hardcover)
ISBN 10: 1-57233-336-7 (pbk.)
ISBN 13: 978-1-57233-336-9 (pbk.)

1. Knoxville (Tenn.)—History.
2. Knoxville (Tenn.)—Economic conditions.
3. Knoxville (Tenn.)—Social conditions.
4. Knoxville (Tenn.)—Politics and government.
 I. McDonald, Michael J., 1934–2002 Knoxville, Tennessee.
II. Title.

F444.K7W47 2005
976.8'85—dc22   2004026000

Contents

Illustrations

Figures

Maps

Preface

James Gatz reinvented himself. In order to escape from a drab, plebian past and later in an attempt to win the elusive—and married—Daisy Buchanan, James Gatz had become Jay Gatsby, the "Great" Gatsby, as it were, of F. Scott Fitzgerald's hauntingly tragic 1925 novel. As Gatsby himself told it, he had been born to great wealth, had been educated at Oxford University ("a family tradition"), had inherited the family's fortune and lived "like a young rajah in all the capitals of Europe," had become a much-decorated ("even Montenegro") hero of the Great War, and then had come to West Egg, where he lived in conspicuous opulence and stared across the water at the woman he would never have. As one critic put it decades later, James Gatz presaged how "the cult for self-improvement becomes the craze for self-invention, which ends in self-delusion."[1]

In a way, Knoxville, Tennessee, is the Great Gatsby of American cities. In order to explain to themselves as well as to newcomers why Knoxville is the way it is, Knoxvillians, like Gatsby, have invented a past that, while it holds within it great explanatory power, is essentially like Jay Gatsby's autobiography: an exercise in self-invention and self-delusion. And yet, instead of inventing a past that would give them energy, optimism, and strength, Knoxvillians fabricated a history that portrayed the city as the almost impotent product of historical forces that it could neither alter nor control. Such a history, of course, tends to paralyze those who create, relate, and believe it, thus sapping energy rather than providing it. To many Knoxvillians, the city's collective mentality can be explained by its citizens' history of near-helplessness against the forces of isolation, poverty, and fear of change.

Undoubtedly much, although by no means all, of Knoxville's collective mentality can be explained by the fact that it is, as part of this book's subtitle suggests, a city of the *mountain* South, an Appalachian city, a city in a subregion of the American South whose transition to the modern age frequently has been painful and where change often is *not* beneficial but sometimes terrible, frightening, and unwelcome. On those ridges and in those coves, overpopulated farms often gave way to massive logging and later to mining, in many cases leaving the sturdy men and women little better off than they had been before the intrusion of extractive industries and modernization. Many abandoned the ridges and coves for the "shotgun houses" of Knoxville, leaving their farms but bringing with them their kinship ties, their religion, their values, and their culture. Thus while accents and diets and musical tastes may make

Knoxville *seem* to be a southern city, in fact it is not: it is a city of the southern mountains that, like all cities, has been shaped in part by its surrounding hinterland as well as by the ideology and culture of those men and women who have migrated to it. In some ways Knoxville has absorbed the Appalachian South's view of the past as the story of immutable, powerful historical forces against which human will and effort are impotent. As we shall see, it was a belief system that had enormous power.

And yet, if the cultural conservatism of Knoxville's Appalachian in-migrants has explicable origins, that of much of the city's socioeconomic elite is less so. The commercial barons of post–Civil War Knoxville merged, in time, with an infusion of mill owners and industrialists who in turn eventually had to make way for the developers. Groups that had at one point constituted the cutting edge of change fell back on conservatism and often on political lassitude. What could be termed the civic-commercial elite of the city was constantly changing, both in composition and attitude. The conservatism of the city's older elites and that of its laborers stamped Knoxville, to many, as a dreary little mill town, and there were many in these two groups who liked it that way, preferring constancy and the familiar over change in any form. The culture of mill hand and mill owner, then, made a rather odd but effective alliance that opposed new people, new enterprises, and new ideas. Hence the other part of this book's subtitle forewarns the reader that this also is the story of a *New South* city that, like other such urban clusters, boomed after the Civil War and carried on a fierce and almost continuous battle between the forces of change and those of resistance.

Of course, those bulwarks against change could not last forever. Fresh waves of newcomers and native Knoxvillians who had "made good" and ascended the social ladder embraced economic and political reforms that might be slowed but not stopped. Growth-oriented boosters quickly recognized that the demographic and economic currents of the 1950s and 1960s moved to further their designs. Industrial retardation in Knoxville coupled with spreading industrial locations on a regional basis helped to make the city increasingly oriented toward service and government (federal and municipal), which in turn attracted newcomers from outside and caused many industrial workers to seek employment elsewhere. For the development mentality, the conjuncture of an influx of the upwardly mobile with a hemorrhage outward of the temporarily displaced was favorable. It balanced the development-progressive forces against the elite and Appalachian conservatives in favor of the developers, setting Knoxville on a new path.

For much of its history, Knoxville's conservative elites had left politics to the representatives of the Appalachian and black poor because they were unthreatening most of the time; they, too, resisted change. The coalition of newcomers and native boosters broke what they saw as an unpleasant and unwarrantable deadlock and set about changing the city's image. For good or ill, the city is, at least temporarily, on that path.

And yet Knoxville's invented history remains, even as the city itself changes. And as more and more newcomers move to the Knoxville area and as an increasing number of long-time Knoxvillians begin to probe their collective past, that Gatsby-like, self-invented past continues to exercise its hold on Knoxville's present. This book offers old and new Knoxvillians alike an alternative interpretation of the history of the city and its people, one that, it is hoped, owes less to Jay Gatsby than it does to the historical record.

This study begins roughly at the end of the American Civil War, with the alternately sleepy and wild river town of just over 3,000 people occupied by Federal troops and about to experience the influx of northern businessmen and investors, Appalachian whites, and former slaves. These groups, as well as the men and women who already were here, acted to change the town profoundly, until within a few decades Knoxville was barely recognizable as the frontier town founded in 1786 by James White. For the early background of Knoxville, this author recommends Mary U. Rothrock, ed., *The French Broad–Holston Country* (1946) and Lucile Deaderick, ed., *Heart of the Valley* (1976).[2]

The first edition of this book ended with the 1982 World's Fair. Many trends that were not so evident then are clearer now, allowing a general reassessment of many of the principal trends and events in Knoxville's past. Moreover, in the two decades since the World's Fair many scholars, not a few of them former students, have filled in many important gaps in the story and, even more important, have caused this author to change his mind about some things that appeared in the book's first edition.

My former colleague, coauthor, and friend Michael McDonald died on May 19, 2002, before we could undertake this edition. Even as I worked in solitary sadness on this edition, I tried to keep in mind what Mike would have wanted to say had he been given time to say it. Hoping that he would not have been disappointed, I dedicate this work to him.

1

The New South
Comes to Appalachia

The Emergence of Knoxville, 1850–1940

In his introduction to a pictorial review titled *Progressive Knoxville 1904,* local publisher Russell Harrison explained that Knoxville, Tennessee, "had grown in importance in spite of herself, to shake off her moss and become a giant of the mountains . . . and a leader in southern progress."[1]

Harrison's statement is particularly curious, since by the turn of the century Knoxville was the third most important wholesaling center in the entire South (behind only New Orleans and Atlanta) and during the first five years of the twentieth century the city more than doubled the value of its manufactured goods. Knoxville's post–Civil War businessmen had merged fairly smoothly with the city's prewar aristocracy until by 1904 the two were very nearly indistinguishable. The Panic of 1893 was but an unpleasant memory, and even the devastating fire of 1897 was offered as proof of Knoxville's regenerative powers.

What, then, did Harrison mean when he wrote his odd but laudatory statement, one that partially contradicted all the contemporary booster tub-thumping about Knoxville's boom times?[2] Although Harrison never clarified what he wrote, one can imagine that he believed that Knoxville's road to

progress had not been a smooth one and that efforts by some to introduce innovations, growth, and change had been opposed by people who preferred to cling
to the traditional and familiar. Hence Knoxville was more an Appalachian city
than it was a southern one, a city that was a product—and beneficiary—of its
region even as some of its citizens tried to free themselves from its forces. Thus
Knoxville was—and in some ways is—a product of the struggle between innovators and traditionalists, between those who embraced change and those who
were threatened by it.

Yet this struggle was barely perceptible in 1904. Like water running
through the limestone caverns under parts of the city, these forces were not recognized or appreciated by most Knoxvillians until much later. Instead,
Knoxvillians seem to have been caught up in the infectious dream of building
a major city of the New South. After all, hadn't a fortuitous combination of
accessible natural resources, investment capital, good rail connections, and the
heretofore virtually untapped labor pool of the surrounding hinterland already
made Knoxville a major commercial and industrial center? Wasn't Big Lick,
Virginia, soon to become Roanoke? Hadn't Atlanta once been Terminus,
Georgia? In such an exciting spirit, Russell Harrison's veiled warning was
almost totally ignored.

And yet it soon became evident that such progress exacted a high price,
both from those who embraced it and from those who fought against it even
as they were caught up in the wheels of change. Rural whites and blacks who
moved from the agriculturally overpopulated and increasingly troubled hinterland in search of employment soon learned that urban life threatened to cut
them off from the culture and institutions they valued so highly. Bankers and
businessmen who had been the original architects of Knoxville's version of the
New South Movement increasingly found themselves—or their children—
resisting some change, fearful of the political excesses of those who purported
to speak for the restive working-class whites and blacks. Some of these members of the elite abandoned the city for new and sanitized residential developments on the outskirts. At the same time, however, they sought to alter
Knoxville's political institutions so as to give themselves more power to achieve
their vision. And as the city grew, it simultaneously lost whatever sense of unity
it previously had possessed, dividing into mutually suspicious socioeconomic
and political camps that sporadically attacked one another but were not powerful enough to control or direct Knoxville's institutions to solve the city's
mounting problems. Entering the modern age ambivalent and divided, Knoxville appeared either unwilling or unable to alter its physical or spiritual environment. The New South had come to Appalachia, but that dream had its
darker side.

Knoxville in Peace, War, and Recovery

Ellen Renshaw House was an unreconstructed rebel. A native of Savannah, Georgia, she moved to Knoxville with her family in late 1859 or early 1860 when she was sixteen years old. When a Union army under Gen. Ambrose Burnside took control of the city in 1863, she ministered to wounded Confederate prisoners of war, occasionally acted as a spy, and at war's end was unwilling to put the war behind her and get on with her life. On September 1, 1865, she mourned, "[N]ow we are slaves—slaves to the vilest race that ever disgraced humanity." And on November 1, she confided to her diary, "I am glad Lincoln was killed."[3]

Ellen Renshaw House was not the only Knoxvillian who carried wartime grudges and hatred into the postwar period. Several former Confederate families either left the city, were expelled by federal authorities or local Unionists, or refused to return to Knoxville for fear they would be flogged or worse. Writing to a Miss Canny, Father Abraham Ryan commented that Knoxville was "worse in scenes of blood and acts of violence than even Nashville was. Scarcely a day passes but some man or family is either beaten almost to death, or driven from the country."[4]

And yet, although violence continued sporadically for up to two years after war's end, the vast majority of Knoxvillians were anxious to get on with the business of building a great city as well as their own personal fortunes. For them, Knoxville's past was but a prelude to the wonderful things that lay ahead.

For both good and ill, Knoxville's early history had been intimately linked to the economic, political, demographic, and social history of East Tennessee. The mountains that residents and tourists alike now admire were initially great barriers, preventing the region's significant population growth in the antebellum years. Moreover, the area's climate and terrain seem to have made it inhospitable for the rise of large plantations and of slavery. Those men and women who did arrive in Knoxville prior to the Civil War usually were but travelers searching for better land and opportunities westward. Knoxville earned a reputation as a comparatively wild town, boasting of (or embarrassed by) an abundance of taverns and tippling houses (far outnumbering churches), gambling and prostitution, riverboat men, and the seemingly endless trickle of passersthrough. Efforts by the town's citizens in the 1830s to wipe out liquor sales and prostitution were quixotic and generally unsuccessful.

Economics, cultural characteristics of the population, and physical isolation led the East Tennessee region into different political paths than those of the western and middle parts of the state, creating an intrastate political rivalry that has not disappeared. Like the mountain areas of Virginia and North Carolina, East Tennessee fought running political battles with other regions of the state over legislative appointments, taxation, internal improvements, slavery and, finally, whether Tennessee should join other southern states in secession. Such conflicts helped to create the stereotype of East Tennesseans as a provincial and suspicious lot, wary of government (which many were convinced was corrupt and conducted solely for the benefit of someone else), lawless, fiercely loyal to kin and clan, and wary of all outsiders, a stereotype that was less false than overdrawn.[5]

Knoxville's ruling class in the prewar years was homogeneous. Composed mostly of merchants, professional men, and owners of large real estate holdings descended from some of the town's original settlers (when Knoxville, prior to 1792, was known as White's Fort), this elite group was growing progressively wealthier as secession approached. A large proportion were Presbyterians, most belonging to the socially acceptable First Presbyterian Church. A majority owned few if any slaves, mostly house servants.[6]

As early as the 1830s Knoxville's elite group recognized the benefits rail connections would bring both to the town and to themselves. Endless meetings, subscriptions of private monies, and even voting of public funds (once even taking $50,000 supposedly set aside for a new waterworks) brought extremely slow results, due largely to difficult topography and shaky financial backing of the proposed lines. By the time of the Civil War, however, Knoxville had full rail connections as far as New York City, although economic ties with Virginia, South Carolina, Georgia, and other southern states via those rail connections clearly marked the town's commercial economy as southern oriented, selling enormous amounts of foodstuffs to the cotton and rice plantations of the Deep South. Indeed, largely for that reason, most of Knoxville's merchants, bankers, professional men, and owners of large real estate holdings would support the Confederacy while the region all around them displayed marked anti-Confederate sentiments. Thus local attorney William Gibbs McAdoo was not exaggerating when he wrote that Knoxville must cast its lot with the South because the "laws of trade compel us." So strong was the pro-Confederate feeling among the Knoxville elite that the First Presbyterian Church (where most of them worshiped) was taken over by the Union Army when it occupied Knoxville in 1863 and was not returned to the church's elders until a year after the war ended.[7]

Ostensibly, Knoxville's city government was democratic, at least after 1839 when the mayoralty became an elective office. But for all practical purposes the town's elite continued to preside over local affairs almost unchallenged. In 1860 fewer than a third of the eligible voters cast ballots in the mayoral race, and other election statistics (with the exception of the ballots on the question of secession) reinforce the impression that most Knoxvillians deferred to the town's mercantile and professional nabobs. Simultaneously it appears that the citizens simply ignored ordinances and regulations that they felt impinged on their individual rights or personal liberty. Hence, one can say that Knoxville's elite had great power and at the same time was essentially powerless.[8]

Although rail linkages had done little by the Civil War to benefit the town economically, those same linkages made Knoxville a strategic objective of no little importance. For the Confederacy, the railroad was vital for moving men and supplies to the Virginia theater. For the Union, the capture of Knoxville would break the Rebels' supply lines, serve as a wedge for future offensives into the heart of the Confederacy, and provide an uplift in morale for East Tennessee Unionists (an important consideration in the eyes of President Lincoln). Thus, in 1863, when the Confederacy suffered the dual defeats of Gettysburg and Vicksburg (losing over 28,000 at Gettysburg and an additional 40,000 at Vicksburg), the Union Army in Tennessee felt free to move eastward from Nashville to brush Bragg away and take Knoxville. Indeed, Knoxville, once having sworn allegiance to the Confederacy, in 1863 embraced the Union occupation of the town, very likely because under Rebel administration business had nearly ground to a stop, and food and clothing shortages had been severely felt.[9]

U.S. troops continued to hold Knoxville until the end of the Civil War, in spite of Confederate efforts in late 1863 to recapture the town and thereby reopen rail traffic to Richmond. That Confederate effort, culminating with the southerners' unsuccessful attempt to carry out an ill-conceived assault on the Union's hastily completed earthworks at Fort Sanders, was described by one historian as "the most bungled, inept and ill-fated campaign in Confederate military annals," not only wasting troops that the Confederacy could ill afford to lose but keeping the town essentially out of the war after 1863.[10]

As noted earlier, after the war some Knoxvillians with Unionist sympathies urged wholesale proscription and persecution of former Confederates. The vast majority of ex-Confederates and Unionists alike, however, seem to have believed that their modest town stood on the brink of profound changes and that they would need one another to make those changes as beneficial to themselves and to the city as possible. Indeed, some may even have recognized that two years of Union occupation actually had been good for Knoxville in terms of money flowing into the city as well as the fact that the city was spared the devastation suffered by other cities of the South.

Examples abound of Knoxville's general desire to put hostilities behind it and move forward. Of the fifty former rebels from Knox County who applied for pardons between 1865 and 1867, Tennessee governor William G. "Parson"

Brownlow (who had renamed his Unionist newspaper *The Knoxville Whig and Rebel Ventilator*) opposed only eight of them, and six of those eight were granted by President Andrew Johnson anyway.[11] At the same time, one hundred Unionists took an oath to eschew violence against former Confederates. Many former southern sympathizers were able to return to Knoxville, regain their property after wartime confiscations, and even cooperate with Union men in business dealings and civic affairs. And while the Ku Klux Klan was creating havoc in other parts of Tennessee, in Knoxville it was comparatively inactive. Finally, by 1867, when a serious flood threatened the town, former Confederates and Unionists worked together to save the Cumberland Avenue Bridge (by removing all of its planking) and provide assistance to over two hundred people whose homes had been washed away.[12]

The New South Comes to Knoxville

Although the Civil War carved deep and painful wounds in the body of the republic that even today have not completely healed, in actuality at the same time that bloody conflict was a comparatively brief interruption in the important trends and forces moving in and affecting the American South. Once the Confederacy fell at Appomattox Court House, those trends and forces reappeared, in many cases stronger and more insistent than they had been in the antebellum era.

For years the antebellum South had seen the gradual rise of a group of businessmen, merchants, bankers, and attorneys who held a different—and competing—vision for what journalist Hodding Carter over a century later called "Uncle Sam's Other Province." Concentrated mostly in the towns and larger commercial centers of the South, this rising nonplanter elite envisioned a section where bounteous natural resources, a virtually untapped labor pool, and investment capital (from foreign and northern speculators) could be brought together to build a southern railway system, urbanize and industrialize the South, make it less dependent on northern and European manufactured goods, and even sidestep the mounting sectional crisis. Dubbed "Southern Yankees" by historian Susanna Delfino, these men hoped to imitate the successes of their northern counterparts. Indeed, these men had been present in the South for most of the nineteenth century, but the weakening by war of the plantation aristocracy gave them both opportunity and power to put their ideas to work. Bolstered and reshaped by a host of ambitious would-be entrepreneurs from outside the South, members of this nonplanter elite attempted to create what they referred to as a "New South," in fact a variation on the rising commercial and industrial triumphs of the North.[13]

Knoxville as seen to the north from the Tennessee River.

McClung Historical Collection. Knoxville–Knox County Public Library.

Gay Street, 1869.

McClung Historical Collection. Knoxville–Knox County Public Library.

The most articulate spokesman for the New South Movement was Atlanta editor and booster Henry Grady. In an address to the New England Society of New York in 1886, Grady unveiled his New South vision to a delighted audience:

> We have sown towns and cities in place of theories, and put business above politics . . . and have . . . wiped out the place where Mason and Dixon's line used to be.
>
> Never was nobler duty confided to human hands than the uplifting and upbuilding of the prostrate and bleeding South—misguided, perhaps, but beautiful in her suffering. . . . In the record of her social, industrial, and political illustration we await with confidence the verdict of the world.[14]

In many ways Knoxville was in a perfect position to take advantage of the New South Movement. Rail connections, natural resources (especially coal and iron), and a potential labor pool in the rural hinterland all were abundant; strong Unionist sentiments and the erosion of Civil War hostilities made the town attractive to northern entrepreneurs and investors; the black population was, by southern standards, comparatively small; the populace appeared to show little interest in politics, thus making control by the elite easier. Indeed, to Knoxvillians and interested outsiders, it seemed that the once-sleepy town possessed all the ingredients necessary to become a major city of the New South. By 1868, one visitor from Virginia described Knoxville as "perhaps the widest awake and livelist [*sic*] town of its population, not only in Tennessee, but in the Southern States."[15]

But as Don Doyle has persuasively argued in his analysis of post–Civil War Atlanta, Nashville, Charleston, and Mobile, these ingredients, while critical, could not by themselves build or revive a city of the New South. What was more important was the presence of an elite with the vision and energy to take those ingredients, mold them together in creative and innovative ways, and use them to the advantage of their respective cities and themselves.[16]

The elite that gradually coalesced in Knoxville in the decades following the Civil War was just such an energetic, dynamic, and visionary upper class. It was composed of members of an old commercial elite (many of whom could trace their ancestors to the origins of the town in 1786), transitional figures who arrived in Knoxville prior to the Civil War but who generally did not become prominent until after that conflict, and new men, most of them from outside the South, who saw in Knoxville a place to make their fortunes. By the 1880s these three strains had melded into one socioeconomic elite whose business ties were reinforced through intermarriage, being godparents to one

Knoxville Iron Company, founded in 1867.

McClung Historical Collection. Knoxville–Knox County Public Library.

Old Catholic Church, 1876.

From *History of Knoxville*, edited by W. M. Goodman (1907).

another's children, working together in philanthropic societies as expected of the "better sort," and serving as pallbearers and honorary pallbearers carrying their neighbors to their final resting places—usually in Gray Cemetery.[17]

Sam House certainly was exaggerating in the late 1850s when he wrote from Knoxville to his family in Georgia that "[m]ost here are parvenus." To be sure, Knoxville's pre–Civil War business elite was small and only recently possessed of impressive wealth. But it certainly had ambition, vision, and energy. Perhaps most typical of Knoxville's antebellum commercial elite was James Hervey Cowan (1801–1871). Born in Knoxville, Cowan began his career as a salesman in a store owned by his stepfather, but in 1820 he opened his own retail establishment with his brother-in-law Hugh A. M. White (a relative of Knoxville's founder James White). In 1830 he married Lucinda Dickinson, a native of Massachusetts who arrived in 1830 (one year after her brother Perez Dickinson) to teach at the Knoxville Female Academy. In 1832 Cowan entered into a partnership with Perez Dickinson, which later expanded into the prominent wholesaling firm of Cowan, Dickinson, and McClung. By 1867 Cowan, McClung and Company was the state's largest taxpayer. Cowan served as an elder in the Second Presbyterian Church from 1836 until his death, was a trustee of East Tennessee University (with Dickinson, Oliver Perry Temple, Edward J. Sanford, Charles McClung McGhee, and Samuel B. Luttrell), and was on the board of directors of the Knoxville Female Academy (with John Hervey Crozier, Hugh Lawson McClung, Edward J. Sanford, and William W. Woodruff) and the Tennessee School for the Deaf (with Crozier, Woodruff, and Calvin Morgan McClung). He was related (through his mother's second marriage) to Thomas W. Humes (1815–1892), a member of Cowan, Dickinson and Company, later rector of St. John's Episcopal Church, and tenth president of the University of Tennessee until he was forced out in 1883. Small, compact, and increasingly wealthy and ambitious, this elite of Cowans, McGhees, Whites, McClungs, Croziers, Humeses, and others controlled the economic life of the awakening city.[18]

Prior to the Civil War, this small business elite was augmented by a number of individuals who moved to Knoxville before the war and by the end of that conflict had merged into the native elite. Two of the most interesting transitional elite figures are Perez Dickinson (1813–1901) and Oliver Perry Temple (1820–1907). As noted earlier, Dickinson was a native of Amherst, Massachusetts, who arrived in East Tennessee in 1829 (at the age of sixteen) to teach at the Hampden Sidney Academy (he became principal the next year, at the age of seventeen). In 1833 he abandoned the schoolroom for the mercantile house and by the Civil War had made a fortune as a partner in Cowan and Dickinson and later in Cowan, McClung and Company. He also served as president of

The mother of Knoxville's elite:
Margaret Russell Cowan
Humes Ramsey.

McClung Historical Collection.
Knoxville–Knox County Public Library.

Perez Dickinson.

Knoxville–Knox County Public Library.

James Hervey Cowan.

McClung Historical Collection.
Knoxville–Knox County
Public Library.

the First National Bank and was the first president of the Knoxville Industrial Association, founded in 1869 and a forerunner of the Chamber of Commerce. As noted above, he was the brother-in-law of James Hervey Cowan and was a member of numerous philanthropic organizations. In 1869 he purchased the six-hundred-acre Williams Island (later known as Island Home), on which he built a fabulous mansion, where he entertained lavishly. Although born in Massachusetts and never having seen military service, he often was called "Colonel" by associates and acquaintances, a sobriquet he enjoyed. He was regularly seen riding in his extravagant carriage with matching horses and liveried footmen (before the war they were slaves).[19]

Considerably less ostentatious but no less influential was Oliver P. Temple. Born near Greeneville, Tennessee, Temple moved to Knoxville in 1848 after having been defeated in a congressional election by Andrew Johnson. Similar to almost all members of the native and transitional Knoxville elite, Temple was a self-made man and an extremely successful one (by 1869 he had the second highest taxable income in Knox County and averaged over $10,500 per year in income from his law practice). A friend and ally of Parson Brownlow, he was a firm Whig and Unionist, although (like Brownlow) he believed that slavery was protected by the Constitution. He was influential in bringing the railroad to Knoxville and for several years was a director of the East Tennessee and Georgia Railroad. Temple was an important advocate of modern agricultural methods but was also (with Dickinson) a founder of the Industrial Association and a member of its successors, the Board of Trade and the Chamber of Commerce (established in 1887). In the 1870s Temple retired from his law practice and began living off the dividends from his several investments. When his widow died in 1929, her estate was valued at over $300,000.[20]

Although this transitional group melded with the native elite, they displayed some interesting differences. To begin with, almost all of them were from outside Knoxville. Most were Whigs and strong Unionists. And while they formed numerous business contacts with members of the native prewar elite and served together on several philanthropic boards (including the University of Tennessee, the Deaf and Dumb Asylum, the Knoxville Female Academy, the public library, etc.), close personal relations appear to have been rare. Some intermarriage did occur and some prewar elite men and women served as pallbearers, godparents, etc., but decidedly less often. For example, honorary pallbearers for Perez Dickinson and Oliver P. Temple contained no prominent members of the native prewar elite. Finally, when the Rev. Thomas Humes was forced from the presidency of the University of Tennessee because he refused to be swayed by the trustees' calls for modernizing the university, it was Temple who led the charge. Except in the boardrooms, perhaps the native

Peter Kern immigrated to Knoxville from Germany in 1865 and built a successful bread company on Market Square.

McClung Historical Collection. Knoxville–Knox County Public Library.

Oliver P. Temple.

McClung Historical Collection. Knoxville–Knox County Public Library.

Thomas W. Humes.

McClung Historical Collection. Knoxville–Knox County Public Library.

prewar elite and the transitional elite were closest to one another in eternal repose, in Old Gray Cemetery.[21]

Yet for all their energy and vision, the native prewar and transitional components of Knoxville's business elite would never have been able to thrust the city into the midst of the New South Movement without the addition of numerous *new* men, most of whom arrived in Knoxville after the Civil War to carve out their respective futures in the modest but growing and increasingly self-confident city. Less hospitable Knoxvillians might call them "carpetbaggers," but in many of those carpetbags there were ideas—and money.

One of the most visible members of this new group was Edward Jackson Sanford (1831–1902). Born in Connecticut, he arrived in Knoxville in 1853 to ply his trade as a carpenter. After serving in the Union army during the Civil War, in 1864 he established E. J. Sanford and Company, a pharmaceutical firm (one of his enemy's referred to him as a "bottled poke-juice financier"). In 1872 he combined with Andrew Jackson Albers (1844–1910; born in Ohio, served in the Union army, and came to Knoxville in 1865) and William P. Chamberlain (1840–1917; born in Ohio, served in the Union army, and came to Knoxville with his brother Hiram in 1865) to form Sanford, Chamberlain and Albers. He invested in railroads, iron manufacturing, coal mining, and textile mills, and at one point was president of the Mechanics National Bank and vice president of the East Tennessee National Bank. One of his sons married a daughter of William Wallace Woodruff (1840–1926; born in Kentucky, served in the Union army, came to Knoxville in 1865, established a successful hardware firm, and invested in real estate, bank stock, a fire insurance firm, and iron manufacturing). A prominent figure and contributor to the Republican Party, Sanford's son Edward Terry Sanford was appointed by President Warren Harding to the United States Supreme Court. At his death in 1902, E. J. Sanford's active and honorary pallbearers read like a "who's who" of the Knoxville business community, including several men from the native prewar, the transitional, and the new elite (his obituary referred to antebellum elite member Charles McClung McGhee as Sanford's "bosom friend").[22]

Together these three components of Knoxville's socioeconomic elite controlled much of the business life of the city. For example, Samuel Luttrell (1844–1933) was the president of twenty-nine local business concerns and held stock in over a hundred other firms. As president of the Mechanics Bank from 1883 to 1922, he owned 55 percent of the bank's stock and approved unsecured loans from the bank to twenty-two companies of which Luttrell was either president, director, majority stockholder, or stockholder. And yet Luttrell's banking practices were hardly unique, as the other men who were major stockholders in the Mechanics Bank did the same thing, so much so that

William P. Chamberlain, Edward Jackson Sanford, and Andrew Jackson Albers.

Courtesy of the East Tennessee
Historical Society.

in 1891, 20 percent of the total amount of the bank's loans went to companies controlled by this same group.[23]

This is not to say, however, that this control meant that Knoxville's elite was a closed circle. New faces continued to appear in the boardrooms of the city's companies. Innovators and hard workers like Max Arnstein (1858-1961; born in Germany, came to Knoxville in 1888, and became a successful mer-

William Woodruff House, c. 1880.
McClung Historical Collection. Knoxville–Knox County Public Library.

chant and generous philanthropist) or Peter Kern (1835–1907; born in Germany, came to Knoxville in 1865, and transformed an ice cream parlor on Market Square into a large and successful bread company) always were welcomed, if not always admitted into the inner circle with the McClungs, Cowans, Temples, Sanfords, etc. Or one might invest the coalescing elite with status and "class," as did Lawrence D. Tyson (1861–1929), who came from the North Carolina planter elite, graduated from the United States Military Academy, was sent to Knoxville in 1891 to be professor of military science at the University of Tennessee, graduated from the university's law school, resigned from the army and joined the law firm of Lucky and Sanford (with Edward Terry Sanford, son of E. J. Sanford), married a daughter of Charles McClung McGhee (who was related to Knoxville founder James White), and became a successful businessman with virtually every door open to him. McGhee Tyson Airport was names for his son, who died in 1918 when his plane went down in the North Sea.[24]

And so a New South elite was created in Knoxville, composed of antebellum, transitional, and new strains. And if Knoxville's New South elite was composed of three principal groups, ideologically it was almost homogeneous. All of its members embraced the postwar spirit of economic expansion, unrestrained capitalism, and unfettered urban growth. As the *Knoxville Daily Chronicle* exulted, "Our merchant princes are increasing in number, and fortunes that a few years back would have been considered fabulous are now undoubted facts." And the word about the reawakened town had spread so far that in 1871 a Richmond, Virginia, newspaper announced that "no city of the South except Atlanta" had "improved more rapidly since the war than had Knoxville, Tennessee."[25]

As Oliver P. Temple and others had predicted, the railroad was the key to Knoxville's growth. The city could serve as a commercial hub for the Appalachian region, bringing in goods manufactured in the Northeast and Midwest and distributing them to the towns and rural general stores of East Tennessee, Southern and Eastern Kentucky, Southwest Virginia, Western North Carolina, and Northern Georgia. Literally hundreds of traveling salesmen ("drummers," of whom there were over six hundred by 1906) representing Knoxville wholesalers scoured the landscape taking orders for their respective company's commercial goods. In the 1880s, drummer John P. Carter, representing C. M. McClung Company, had a territory that took four weeks to cover—from Bearden to Concord, Lenoir City, Friendsville, Maryville, Townsend, Sevierville, and then north through Jefferson, Hawkins, Claiborne, and Union counties.[26]

At the same time that Knoxville jobbers were importing and distributing manufactured goods, they also were shipping the region's extracted natural resources (principally coal, marble, and lumber) throughout the country and also collecting the region's agricultural products (wheat, corn, livestock, etc.) to send to the Deep South, mainly to Louisiana, Georgia, South Carolina, Florida, and Texas. By 1890 there were twenty-eight marble quarries in Knox County alone and six lumber companies with capital investments over $100,000. Abundant coal was being mined, some of it with convict labor, approximately thirty miles from the city. By 1882 the city could boast of forty-four wholesaling firms, over half of them established since 1870. Groceries, dry goods, boots and shoes, hardware, marble, and coal led the list of products being shipped by rail through the burgeoning city. And in Goodspeed's 1887 history of Hamilton, Knox, and Shelby counties, it was conceded that "no other city of equal size in America has so large a wholesale trade as Knoxville. . . . Nearly all the firms are backed by abundant capital, and are controlled by competent, progressive and practical men."[27]

The results were nothing short of astounding. By 1885 Knoxville was the fourth leading wholesaling center in the entire South, surpassed only by New Orleans, Atlanta, and Nashville, with an annual volume of business of between $15 million and $20 million (three times that of manufacturing). Goods arrived in the city by rail from nearly everywhere. For example, Daniel Briscoe and Company, a notions wholesaler, bought 86.3 percent of the goods he distributed from outside the South, over half of it from New York City but also from Chicago, Baltimore, and Philadelphia. In 1884, wholesale grocer H. B. Carhart purchased items from 142 towns and cities, some of them from as far away as Georgia, Virginia, and Kentucky. So impressive was the city's wholesale trade that by 1896 Knoxville was the South's third largest wholesaler, with an annual volume of over $50 million, a striking figure, since at that time the nation was only beginning to emerge from the depression that had followed the Panic of 1893.[28]

Barely noticeable at first in the thriving commercial center was the rise of a new industrial order that surfaced soon after the Civil War but was not fully appreciated until several years later. Relying on technological proficiency from outside the region as well as on investment capital from the city's merchant princes and northern speculators, the industrialization of Knoxville served to supplement the healthy commercial sector and thus acted to pull more labor out of the hills and coves of Appalachia.[29]

At the end of the Civil War, Knoxville had little that could be called industrial activity. The town could boast of only a few flour mills, small furniture shops, saddleries, foundries, and other assorted modest enterprises. Indeed, when Oliver P. Temple addressed the newly founded Knoxville Industrial Association and asserted that many things that the town imported "could be profitably manufactured" in Knoxville, it seems as if his message fell mostly on deaf ears.[30]

Probably the first significant manufacturing establishment in Knoxville was the Knoxville Iron Company, founded in 1867 by Hiram S. Chamberlain. A native of Ohio and Burnside's chief quartermaster during the Union occupation of Knoxville, Chamberlain was mustered out of the service in Knoxville and decided to remain in the awakening town. Using borrowed capital, he established the Knoxville Iron Company, which by 1900 employed around 850 workers, mostly Welsh immigrants and African Americans. The racially mixed workforce lived close to the factory and to each other in the area soon known as Mechanicsville. Chamberlain spoke in glowing terms of the blacks he employed, praising their good work habits, their eagerness for education, their abilities to take on responsible positions, and their penchant for saving money to purchase their own homes. There is some evidence, however, that he actually used black workers to discourage labor unions.[31]

The Knoxville Iron Company set patterns others would follow in the industrialization of Knoxville. Most enterprises were located on the northern and northwestern fringes of the growing city, where land was generally inexpensive and where access to the important railroad lines was easy. Housing was constructed around the factories and mills either by the industrialists themselves or by private developers. By the 1880s Knoxville's downtown commercial center was ringed on the northern and northwestern fringe by a collection of mill villages such as Mechanicsville and Brookside Village that continued to maintain characteristics of individual neighborhoods long after they had grown together as one city. Skilled labor usually was imported from other areas, whereas the semiskilled and unskilled jobs went to black and white in-migrants from the nearby countryside. Coal was almost invariably the source of power.

The 1880s witnessed Knoxville's greatest manufacturing boom. Between 1880 and 1887 alone, ninety-seven new factories were built. In addition to iron mills and machine shops that processed iron into a multitude of finished products, cloth mills and furniture factories sprang up and prospered. And once the cloth mills came to Knoxville, it was only natural that a thriving apparel industry would follow. One of the most significant was the Knoxville Woolen Mills, incorporated in 1884 and by the turn of the century one of the largest clothing manufacturers in the country, shipping its goods to commission agents in New York, Chicago, St. Louis, San Francisco, Cleveland, Louisville, Cincinnati, and elsewhere. Its principal stockholders included several members of the city's commercial business elite, such as E. J. Sanford,

James D. Cowan, Charles J. McClung, C. M. McGhee, William P. Chamberlain, A. J. Albers, Oliver P. Temple, and Lawrence D. Tyson. From 1884 until 1904, stockholders received dividends averaging 12 percent per year, as high as 40 percent in some years.[32]

Other important manufacturers included Brookside Cotton Mills (1,200 employees by 1900), William J. Oliver Company (mining equipment, the largest privately owned machine shop in the United States), Post and Company (wagons), White Lily (1885, flour), and Dempster Machine Shop (1886, engines, pumps, drills, mill machinery). Coal companies were founded to provide power for the mills and factories as well as heat for residences (Knoxvillians having virtually denuded the outskirts of the town by the Civil War in their search for firewood). Apparel mills were nearly everywhere, as Knoxville by the turn of the century led all southern cities in the manufacturing of ready-made clothing. Little wonder Minnesota native John Wesley North, president of the Knoxville Foundry and Machine Shop, observed that Knoxville was "very much a northern city."[33]

By 1900 heavy manufacturing and related enterprises had become a significant factor in Knoxville's economy. Capital investment in manufacturing had multiplied sixfold between 1870 and 1890, rising from $449,915 to $3,045,661, while the number of men, women, and children employed in manufacturing had risen even more dramatically, from 436 to 3,113. Indeed, by 1900 more Knoxvillians were engaged in manufacturing (30.6 percent of the labor force) than in commerce (29.5 percent), which had been the city's initial stimulus to economic growth after the Civil War. The value of goods manufactured annually in Knoxville had jumped from $923,211 in 1870 to $6,201,840 in 1899. Although the commercial sector still led in dollar volume, the percentage increases in manufacturing and the rising proportion of the labor force employed left little doubt that industrialization was Knoxville's wave of the future. Between 1900 and 1905 alone, manufactured goods had increased by over 100 percent.[34]

Although the Panic of 1893 temporarily blunted the city's impressive economic growth, by the early years of the twentieth century the frenetic commercial and manufacturing activity of the preceding three decades was affecting other sectors of the city's economy. Bank clearings in 1905 were up 120.48 percent over those in 1900, having gone from $28,834,248.48 to $63,576,086.17. Those increases testified to the health of the city's ten banks, all of which had been organized after 1870, with four founded since 1890. Construction of new homes (over 5,000 built between 1895 and 1904, most of them in the latter years) was so impressive that as late as 1939 a Knoxville housing survey found that over 20 percent of all the city's houses had been built during that

William J. Oliver.

McClung Historical Collection.
Knoxville–Knox County
Public Library.

Gay Street, c. 1900.

McClung Historical Collection. Knoxville–Knox County Public Library.

ten-year period. Forty companies were distributing coal by 1905; sales of shoes manufactured in the city totaled $4 million annually by 1908; cloth manufacturing was highest among any southern city; and dry goods and hardware sales were equally impressive. Truly, it appeared that all the optimistic prophecies of Knoxville's postwar boosters had come true.[35]

The creation of major commercial and manufacturing centers acted as powerful magnets to attract people to the awakening city. Between 1860 and 1900 population increased almost ninefold, from 3,704 in 1860 to a robust 9,693 by 1880 and an extremely impressive 32,637 by 1900. To be sure, some of that increase can be explained by the annexations in 1883 of McGhee's Addition (later Mechanicsville) and in 1898 of the adjacent town of West Knoxville (earlier White's and Ramsey's Addition and later known as the Fort Sanders area) and the working class neighborhoods north of Baxter Avenue. The West Knoxville area was an especially welcome addition to the city, for during the latter years of the nineteenth century the wealthy postwar elite had increasingly abandoned its older residential neighborhoods in favor of newer, more opulent suburbs near the old Civil War redoubt of Fort Sanders. Here, magnificent late-Victorian residences were constructed, many of which, graced by wide porches and decorated with profusion of then-fashionable gingerbread, compared favorably with the most luxurious in the nation.[36]

While Knoxville boosters trumpeted the fact that people moved to the city from virtually every state in the Union, the vast majority of in-migrants came from the rural hinterlands of East Tennessee. And these men and women merit further examination, since it was they who helped to shape the new city as much as did its elite, perhaps more.[37]

Of particular interest was the dramatic rise in the city's African American population. Of Knoxville's 3,704 residents in 1860, only 752 (20.3 percent) were black, most of them house slaves or free men and women. When Union soldiers took Knoxville in 1863, however, African Americans began to arrive in large numbers in search of freedom and opportunity. The end of the Civil War did not halt this flow, even though the recently formed Freedmen's Bureau advised newly freed blacks to remain in the rural areas and not to glut Knoxville's then-small labor market. But commercial and then industrial expansion in the postwar years did provide jobs for African Americans, many of whom found employment with the Knoxville and Ohio Railroad; the East Tennessee, Virginia and Georgia Railroad; the Knoxville Car Wheel Company; the Knoxville Iron Company; and Burr and Terry's Saw Mill. And, of course, those increased economic opportunities attracted still larger numbers of blacks, until by 1880 they numbered 3,149, or 32.5 percent of Knoxville's population.[38]

The burgeoning numbers of black customers and clients gave rise to a local black professional and business leadership, and by the 1880s a complete class structure could be seen among African Americans parallel to that of the white population. Knoxville's blacks moved quickly after the war to organize their own churches (nine by 1875, the largest of which was the Greater Warner Tabernacle AME Zion Church), fraternal orders, self-improvement societies, and fire companies. Educational opportunities were expanded, in part because of the assistance of white benefactors such as Emily Austin of Philadelphia (who used money raised in the North to found schools for African Americans) and the Presbyterian organizers of a school for blacks that was established in 1875 and eventually became Knoxville College. But blacks such as Laura Ann Scott Cansler, the first black schoolteacher in Knoxville, played active roles as well. Indeed, by the 1880s the city could boast of African American police officers (not seen in Atlanta until 1947), city aldermen, county commissioners, and occasionally jurors. With blacks representing 35.6 percent of the total registered voters in 1894, they surely were hard to ignore. Hardly a Garden of Eden, for African Americans Knoxville appeared to offer much of what previously had been denied them.[39]

Despite these advances, however, some local black leaders were disappointed with what they saw as the pitifully slow progress being made. Since black voters represented over one-third of the city's voting population throughout the late nineteenth century, the potential existed for blacks to make their disappointment felt at the polls. Some black leaders proposed that the people do just that.

After their enfranchisement, most southern blacks had voted Republican, seeing that party as the party of Lincoln, emancipation, and the Freedmen's Bureau. But by the mid-1870s, the national Republican Party had turned in a different direction, a direction dramatized by the barely successful presidential campaign of Rutherford B. Hayes in 1876. To Republicans, it was a matter of political necessity, for as southern states one by one returned to the Union, the Republican Party feared that it would become again a minority party to be regularly trampled on by the Democratic majority. Thus Republicans began to change political direction, hoping to embrace the new businessmen of the New South. With that goal in mind and less willing to stand at the deteriorating forefront of social and political reform (especially with regard to the freedmen), the party of Lincoln and emancipation became the party of business and business conservatism.[40]

Many black leaders in Knoxville, as throughout the South, sensed the Republican Party's change of direction. Republicans, they reasoned, might still

be eager for their votes but less willing to alienate New South business interests by trading those votes for political support of Negro economic and social
objectives. The only solution, black leaders felt, was to declare their independence of both major political parties, and, with Democrats and Republicans
alike, to barter ballots for programs in the interests of the freedmen.

This revised approach by blacks has been labeled the "New Departure."
In Knoxville it was signaled in 1876 when black attorney William F. Yardley
announced that he would run for governor of Tennessee as an independent.
Yardley was thirty-two years old in 1876, a free mulatto who had been born in
Knox County in 1844, read law on his own, passed the bar examination and
became a respected criminal lawyer and local political figure. Yardley had no
chance of victory, and very likely he knew it. But the Knoxville lawyer used the
gubernatorial campaign to dramatize blacks' declaration of independence from
the Republican Party. Yardley spent most of this time attacking the Republicans. Blacks had naïvely and patiently voted Republican, he asserted, and had
received little in return for their political fealty. Not surprisingly, Yardley was
swamped.[41]

William F. Yardley.
Courtesy of the Beck
Cultural Exchange Center.

To many black leaders in Knoxville, however, Yardley's campaign was less a realistic political battle than it was the cannon signaling the New Departure. In 1877 Yardley again stood at the forefront of Knoxville's blacks, urging them to move independently of the Republican Party in their efforts to secure the right to sit on juries. In addition, blacks began regularly to form committees in the 1870s and 1880s to interview candidates for local offices. For example, in 1888 a committee of black leaders met separately with both Democratic and Republican candidates for mayor. The Reverend Job Lawrence, a black minister of the Shiloh Presbyterian Church and probably a member of the committee, subsequently attacked Republicans for ignoring blacks except at election time. "We are," Lawrence asserted, "no more free than in the days of bondage."[42]

Black support of mayoral incumbent James C. Luttrell Jr. undoubtedly was an important factor in the Democrat's reelection. In return for that support, Luttrell pressured aldermen under his control to appoint Lawrence to the Knoxville Board of Education. The appointment was greeted by an immediate public explosion. The board itself was loath to let Lawrence sit as a member, never informing him of meeting dates and once ejecting him from a meeting. One local editorialist fanned the fires by commenting that Lawrence's behavior in forcing himself on the previously all-white school board "may be an indication of what he [Lawrence] might do should he take a notion to visit the Girls' High School." Ultimately the board sued to remove Lawrence, who lost an appeal to the state supreme court. Subsequently Lawrence probably left the city; at any rate, he was not in Knoxville in 1893. But Yardley's rout and Lawrence's departure did not mollify white political leaders. In 1894 and again in 1912, leaders from both parties quietly gerrymandered Knoxville's African Americans into virtual political impotence, and the so-called "New Departure"—at least in Knoxville—was dead. From 1912 until 1969, no African American served as an alderman or city councilman.[43]

While the number of African Americans in Knoxville quadrupled between 1860 and 1880, the influx of whites was even more impressive. And although some came from other states as well as from Europe (especially from Germany and Ireland), the vast majority of this tidal wave came from the hills and coves of Appalachia.

At first they came not because they wanted to but because they *had* to. For example, the population of neighboring Sevier County (southeast of Knoxville) increased an alarming 70 percent between 1870 and 1890, due almost exclusively to one of the highest fertility rates of any county in the state. With so many sons among whom to divide the land, the number of farms burgeoned from 920 in 1860 to 3,193 in 1900, with a corresponding decline in average size from 270.1 acres to 78.1 acres.[44]

Life for many mountain farmers was hard and short. In 1881–82, of the 61 people who died in Sevier County, 17 (28 percent) were children under 1 year old, and 34 (56 percent) were under 21. Average life expectancy was but 41.5 years. By 1917–18, when the United States began calling up men for military service in the Great War, 57.1 percent of Sevier County's draftees were disqualified on physical grounds.[45]

After 1900, the growing chasm in standards of living between the city and the Appalachian countryside continued to draw people out of the rural counties, although by this time an increasing number were beginning to seek opportunities farther afield, in cities beyond the region. For example, at the turn of the twentieth century, education in rural Appalachia was an inadequate hodgepodge of underfunded public schools (that usually met for less than

Adelia Lutz's painting class.
McClung Historical Collection. Knoxville–Knox County Public Library.

three months a year), mission schools, and private schoolmasters. In 1900 in Sevier County, of the 548 students in the fifth grade the previous year, *none* passed on to the sixth grade. And of the county's total school enrollment of 6,876 in 1900, the majority attended school for only one year, only 25 students were enrolled in the seventh and eighth grades, and until 1922 no classes were even offered beyond the eighth grade. Education as a way out of the discouraging cycle of overpopulation, decreasing farm size, and comparatively low life expectancy simply was not available.[46]

Contrasting lifestyles continued to lure people out of rural Appalachia. By 1926, Knox County had 19,520 residential electricity customers, whereas Fentress, Grainger, Hancock, and Union counties had no electricity users. In 1929, Knox County had 21,947 automobiles, but Hancock County had only 211. By 1928, Knox County had 25,753 telephones, whereas Fentress, Grainger, Johnson, Cocke, Hancock, and Sevier counties *together* could boast of but 2,399. And in 1900 Sevier County had only twenty-five physicians, but by 1927 that number had shrunk to twelve, six of whom were over fifty years old. Little wonder that, even with astounding rates of natural increase, the rural population of the entire Tennessee Valley between 1900 and 1920 grew by an anemic 14.7 percent, whereas the valley's urban population mushroomed by 243.6 percent. By 1930, 48.4 percent of the people of the Tennessee Valley lived in towns or cities with a population of 10,000 or greater.[47]

Hence Knoxville became not so much a southern city as an Appalachian urban enclave. Unlike their black counterparts, most of the white in-migrants initially came to the city less in search of opportunity than to escape the devastating demographic and economic forces that were increasingly crushing them under their inexorable weight. Similar to black in-migrants, however, they arrived with only marginal education and skills and hence also took low-wage jobs in the factories, wholesaling houses, and transportation facilities of the mushrooming city. Few had left behind their Appalachian mores, their suspicion of government and authority at all levels, their rough-and-tumble democratic politics, their belief in the superfluity of education, their fundamentalist religions, or their hatred of those who possessed more then they did. The once-sleepy town turned into an increasingly violent and crime-ridden one, and the area from the Central Avenue Wharf to Sullivan's Saloon became littered with pool halls, gambling dens, saloons, "cocaine schools," and houses of prostitution, a neighborhood in which "the color line is very lightly regarded . . . and all men are equal, so long as they have the price of a drink." The dour *Knoxville Chronicle* warned that visitors and inhabitants of the "outside world" increasingly viewed the area as "inhabited by wild semi-barbarians who had no part nor lot with other portions of the South."[48]

Rhetoric and Reality in the New South

And yet the growth of commerce, manufacturing, and population gave Knox-ville's boosters all the evidence they needed that they lived in the "new jewel in the crown of the New South." Large retailers, merchants, bankers, factory owners, and real estate holders were never without statistics that seemed to prove the city's great progress and even greater potential. As noted earlier, even the great fire of 1897 (which destroyed a number of businesses on the east side of Gay Street, roughly north of Union Avenue) was proudly dubbed the "Million Dollar Fire" to trumpet the fact that Knoxville's central business section was valued at over $1 million. In 1900 local journalist and civic tub-thumper William M. Goodman suggested that the local Commercial Club organize and host a "grand exposition" to showcase the city's progress, an idea that by 1910 became the successful Appalachian Exposition under the leader-ship of Indiana native and prominent Knoxville manufacturer William J. Oliver, who had only arrived in Knoxville in 1905. The exposition was so suc-cessful that other expositions were held in 1911 and 1913, all of them at Chilhowee Park. Like the original 1910 Appalachian Exposition, its successors

The "Million Dollar Fire," 1897.
McClung Historical Collection. Knoxville–Knox County Public Library.

were designed to ape the earlier self-congratulatory expositions of Chicago, Buffalo, St. Louis, and Atlanta and were intended to dramatize the Appalachian city's economic vitality. Although regional agriculture maintained a prominent place at the most famous of these expositions, the Appalachian Exposition of 1910 (for which impressive buildings were constructed that ultimately became the principal buildings of the Tennessee Valley Agricultural and Industrial Fair), undoubtedly Knoxville's New South advocates were more interested in displaying the city's commercial and industrial prowess.[49]

Yet even as Knoxville's architects of the New South continued to boast of the city's progress and potential, evidence suggests that all was far from well. To begin with, the phenomenal growth that the city's boosters bragged about was at the same time the source of many of Knoxville's increasingly serious problems. The almost universal use of coal in both factories and homes not only gave the city a distinctly grimy, sooty appearance but also doubtless was the cause of health problems recognized as early as 1885. Beyond the downtown area, street paving was spotty at best, and brick paving and macadamization did not begin in earnest until 1893. Cows and hogs, accompanied by inevitable odors, roamed Knoxville's often muddy streets as Knoxvillians continually battled flies and disease resulting from foul streets and the lack of a sewer system. Knoxville residents of the period remembered dirt, coal dust, and unpleasant odors as the most conspicuous and ubiquitous characteristics of the city at the turn of the century. By 1904 the *Knoxville Sentinel* mourned that the "city is in a wretched state as regards streets, sewers," and other necessities.[50]

More important for Knoxville's future than the city's physical griminess was the residential segregation by economic class that was beginning to divide the city. In the early days of the city's industrialization, factory owners, foremen, and workers had lived close to one another. Indeed, one can still see the architectural vestiges of this residential heterogeneity in the East Scott–Oklahoma Avenue area as well as around the Fourth and Gill neighborhood. But the increasing deterioration of the air and streets as well as a desire to separate themselves from the flood of Appalachian whites and blacks—whom some feared even as they needed their labor—caused many of Knoxville's wealthier citizens to build fashionable enclaves like West Knoxville (Fort Sanders) on the fringes of the city. The extension of streetcar lines probably was the key force that uncorked the demographic bottle and allowed the "better sort" to escape to their more refined neighborhoods. Simultaneously, the demand for housing among the Appalachian newcomers meant that once-separated mill "villages" were beginning to grow together, merging into large working-class neighborhoods. In those neighborhoods, members of the elite might well be treated with great deference on a rare visit, but they were definitely traveling through areas that were no longer theirs. Increasing residential segregation became a fact of life that Knoxvillians would have to deal with for years to come.

Perhaps most symbolic of the business elite's apparent inability or unwillingness to deal with the unwanted by-products of the city's growth was the running battle to create a modern municipal waterworks. Until 1883, water had been brought to downtown businesses in wagons, and the Knoxville Water Company, a private firm, was not established until 1885. But cries of complaint were heard almost immediately, in part because of poor service but largely due to the poor quality of the water itself. And yet an attempt to get the city to purchase the company and deliver potable water was beaten back in 1893, mainly because the elite did not stand together in favor of the reform. In 1904, when the company asked the city's permission to sell around $750,000 worth of bonds in order to construct a modern water plant, again many elite businessmen were in opposition. Not only did the president of the Chamber of Commerce oppose the bond issue, but so also did solid elite business figures such as E. T. Sanford (son of the enormously powerful E. J. Sanford, who had died in 1902), Lawrence D. Tyson, former mayor Samuel Gordon Heiskell (mayor in 1896–97, 1900–1901, and later in 1906–7 and 1910–15), and current mayor William H. Gass. The bond issue was approved comfortably in a popular referendum (with low voter turnout), but Sanford and Heiskell charged that the vote had been fraudulently conducted (no surprise in Knoxville elections of the period, when many votes were purchased) and that numerous "no" ballots had not been counted by election officials. Less important than the referendum's outcome (the city ultimately bought the Knoxville Water Company in 1909) was the fact that a growing number of voters and elite business figures were resisting change, often for fear that taxes would have to be raised. Frustrated newly arrived businessman William J. Oliver complained that "the only thing which held Knoxville back was an attitude of greed and conservatism."[51]

There were other disturbing signs that Knoxville's elite was losing its postwar dynamism, growing increasingly conservative, and psychologically separating itself from the city that it had had such a large role in building. As noted earlier, the Knoxville Woolen Mills, chartered in 1884, was one of the largest manufacturers of woolen clothing in the United States. But the unwillingness to upgrade equipment and the insistence on paying only the lowest wages to its workers meant that the quality of the goods declined and, according to president Lawrence Tyson, the best workers drifted away "and only the poor and indifferent ones remain." In addition, the shift in tastes to worsted goods, which the mill equipment was unable to produce, meant that the company

Samuel G. Heiskell.
From *Southern Review*,
May 1898.

had to reduce its prices in order to sell any goods at all. And yet when officers of the corporation begged the stockholders to subscribe to a preferred stock issue of $150,000 in order to replace equipment and reverse the company's sagging fortunes, only $55,500 worth of the stock was purchased. The Knoxville Woolen Mills ceased operations early in 1911 and its real estate, buildings, and equipment were sold at auction on March 1–2, 1911. The fate of the once-proud company would have been tragic had the stockholders also lost their money, but while refusing to acquire new equipment, pay workers good wages, and bail the company out of its difficulties, from the founding of the company until its ultimate liquidation those stockholders had voted themselves dividends on their investments that averaged around 14 percent per year—as high as 40 percent in some years. Thus even as it trumpeted the accomplishments of their New South city, Knoxville's elite increasingly embraced the notion of exchanging long-term growth and vitality for short-term profits. At the same time, its exodus to newer enclaves to the west symbolized a general abrogation of responsibility for the city it had done so much to create. It was as if the elite's political conservatism, so typical of New South parvenus (as Ellen House's brother Sam had dubbed them), had infected their economic and social ideas as well. Critics like William J. Oliver, who accused the established elite of actually discouraging more growth and new businesses, were listened to but generally not heeded.[52]

One can only speculate on why Knoxville's once dynamic and vibrant elite (a mixture of pre–Civil War, transitional, and postwar arrivals) became so conservative. Clearly they seem to have been of two minds about the city they had created, at once embracing the wealth it brought them but also loathing the black and white in-migrants who provided the muscle in commerce and manufacturing—much as the northern industrial barons they yearned to emulate hated the peasants from southern and eastern Europe who, like Appalachian blacks and whites, provided the labor for northern commerce and industry. As they fled the city for their new aristocratic neighborhoods in West Knoxville and beyond, they left the running of the city to their lieutenants—and to the mob.

Knoxville College, probably the class of 1907.
Courtesy of the Beck Cultural Exchange Center.

Another likely explanation of the elite's growing conservatism was its recognition that Knoxville was finding it increasingly difficult to compete in the emerging, consolidating national economy. The railroad, once the key factor that ended the town's relative isolation and created opportunities for commerce and industry, by the turn of the century had swept the New South city into a national economy where it was at a comparative disadvantage. Small East Tennessee farms could not compete against the huge and increasingly mechanized farms of the Midwest. Once the railroad made it possible to ship enormous amounts of wheat into East Tennessee, the growing of that crop, once a regional staple, simply collapsed. At the same time, Knoxville manufacturers learned that hatchets made in Geneva, Illinois, could be shipped by rail to the city and actually undersell locally manufactured hatchets by three to five dollars per dozen. Similar savings could be had by purchasing handsaws made in Fitchburg, Massachusetts, which undersold Knoxville handsaws by seven dollars per dozen. As rural East Tennessee's economy was devastated by being swept into the national economy, so also the city's manufacturers were hurt by the very thing that had created them—the railroad.[53]

Many of these troubling strains came together in the prohibition issue. From the 1870s on, the conflict over the prohibition of liquor sales had been a central issue in Tennessee politics. Little by little the prohibitionists had triumphed until, by 1907, the whole state was dry except for the four largest cities. In that year the state legislature made it possible for these cities to redraw their charters of incorporation so as to eliminate the sale of liquor. The redrawn charters would have to be approved by the voters of the respective cities.[54]

Though campaigns were mounted by the Women's Christian Temperance Union (WCTU), the Anti-Saloon League, and other groups in all four cities, Knoxville was the only one that responded. In Knoxville the combined forces of the WCTU, the fundamentalist churches, and the Republican Party (which had embraced prohibition statewide as a vote-getting device) proved extremely strong. Yet the elite, while continuing to slake its own thirst in exclusive suburbs and private clubs, seems to have done little or nothing to stop the prohibitionists' rout. Some of the elite even welcomed prohibition as a way to prevent working-class whites and blacks from securing strong drink, believing as they did that whiskey only encouraged them to be more vicious than they already were.

Those who stood against prohibitionists' attacks and the elite's inertia were overwhelmed. Mayor Samuel Gordon Heiskell, along with most of his Democratic political comrades, opposed prohibition in Knoxville. Heiskell, a city and state officeholder since 1884, had been a longtime friend of education, African American rights, and the New South ideology. In spite of the obvious danger to his political career, he attacked the prohibitionists, asserting that the $30,000 brought in annually from the saloon tax was used to support public education and that the loss of that revenue would mean that property taxes would have to be raised to balance the loss. Such an argument had little effect on the prohibitionists. Religious excitement, Republican vote-getting tactics, and the determination to "dry out" the working-class white and black neighborhoods easily carried the day by a vote of 4,150 to 2,255. The charter revision was approved and Knoxville was dry—at least in name.[55]

The elite's growing unwillingness to become involved in the economic, social, and political life of Knoxville had almost disastrous results for the city. Racial hostility, never far from the surface, now ran virtually unchecked, as African Americans, their numbers having more than quadrupled between 1870 and 1920, competed with whites for the declining number of jobs in the economically troubled city while at the same time pressing against—and occasionally across—the boundaries of white working-class neighborhoods. And although most white and black leaders counseled peace and moderation, the city in fact was a virtual tinderbox that awaited but one spark to set it aflame.

To be sure, incidents had occurred, as in 1893 when whites protested the exclusive employment of African Americans on street paving crews, or in 1905 when black leaders called for a boycott of Knoxville's segregated streetcars (which ultimately was unsuccessful), or in June 1913 when a white mob attempted (also unsuccessfully) to lynch a black man accused of killing a white police officer. But most Knoxvillians were lulled into a false sense of security by men such as Lawrence Tyson, who in 1911 said of the African American that "the people here [Knoxville] understand him and are more sympathetic to him than our northern neighbors," or by Booker T. Washington, who visited the 1913 exposition, or as late as February 1918 by respected black educator, lawyer, and Republican political figure Charles Cansler (a son of Laura Ann Scott Cansler, the city's first African American schoolteacher) when he wrote that in "no place in the world can there be found better relations existing between the races." Indeed, in 1919 African American leaders and sympathetic whites established a local chapter of the National Association for the Advancement of Colored People (NAACP).[56]

In August 1919 the uneasy peace was broken. When police arrested Maurice Mayes, a mulatto who reportedly had shot and killed a white woman in an attempted burglary, many whites reacted with anger and alarm. Although Mayes had been quietly moved to Chattanooga, a mob stormed the Knoxville jail, freed several white prisoners, emptied the jail's whiskey storage room (where since prohibition confiscated whiskey had been kept), and demolished both the jail and the sheriff's adjoining home. From there the mob lumbered toward the corner of Vine and Central avenues, where it was rumored that armed blacks were gathering. On their way, the whites broke into several businesses, principally to acquire firearms. Even though guardsmen of the Tennessee Fourth Infantry had arrived on the scene, shooting broke out, with soldiers and white rioters firing at blacks and the blacks returning fire. Although the announced death toll was modest, there is some evidence that the true number was much higher. Some whites later boasted of "mowing niggers down like grass," stories continue to be told of bodies dumped into the Tennessee River, and even respected African American educator and leader Charles Cansler later admitted that there were many deaths "on both sides." The *Chicago Defender* reported that perhaps over 1,500 blacks fled the city until additional guardsmen eventually restored a semblance of order.[57]

The elite was stunned, shaken out of its complacency. Deceived by the assuring words of leaders like Tyson and Cansler, the elite had convinced itself

Maurice Mayes.
Courtesy of the Beck
Cultural Exchange Center.

that Knoxville was a model of good race relations in the New South. Hadn't Mayor John E. McMillan denounced the recently revived Ku Klux Klan? Hadn't Cansler himself been honored by the city? Hadn't blacks and whites lived and worked side by side for over a generation? All of a sudden, the elite felt that the city was falling apart.

But Knoxville's business and political leaders had badly misgauged the situation. Rural whites who had migrated from the Appalachian hinterlands had had a hard time adjusting to the city's regimented way of life. In industries like the Knoxville Iron Company and the Southern Railway, they had been forced into proximity with blacks, whom they already loathed. Residential segregation, a regular feature of American urban life, had been breaking down under the pressure of black population growth. Moreover, the early years of the twentieth century had been anxious economic times for Knoxville. Like the Knoxville Woolen Mills, many commercial and industrial firms had been forced to close because of poor management or because they could not compete with manufacturers in other parts of the nation. Those closings, and the fact that the city's working-age population had grown faster than the number of jobs, had caused a great deal of anxiety, frustration, and anger. Doubtless it was this frustration and anger that had found its vent in the heightened racial tension and the 1919 riot.[58]

In the face of all these realities, the rhetoric of Knoxville's New South spokesmen seemed hollow indeed. Physical griminess, economic slowdown, modest population growth, residential segregation by class and race, the growing conservatism of a large segment of the elite, and racial problems together signaled that if the New South had arrived in Knoxville, the benefits it brought to the city clearly had been mixed. For those so optimistic as to refuse to see reality, the city's 1917 annexation of approximately twenty-two square miles of Knox County (including the areas of Lonsdale, Mountain View, Park City, Oakwood, South Knoxville, and Looney's Bend [Sequoyah Hills]) masked the city's paltry population growth sufficiently to make booster rhetoric plausible, if not entirely believable. So self-deluded had some of the elite become that in the face of all these difficulties the local Rotary Club distributed a publication from the Chamber of Commerce that confidently predicted that by 1930 Knoxville's population would be an impressive 200,000, an outlandish estimate when one considers that the 1920 population was 77, 818.[59]

The Politics of Rhetoric and Reality

In many ways, local politics mirrored the city's economic and social problems. New South boosters had advocated a new commercial-industrial order that demanded a strong measure of economic and political control from above. But .

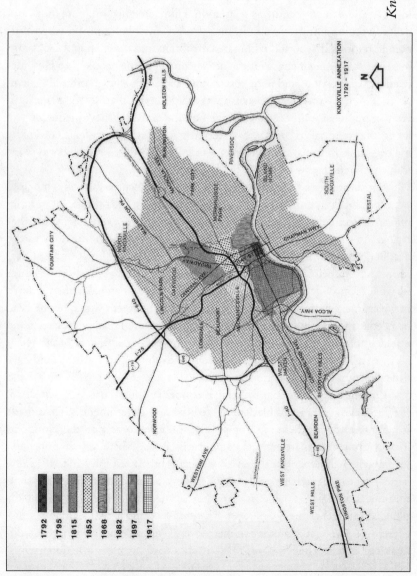

*Knoxville Annexations,
1792–1917.*

the influx of blacks and Appalachian whites not only presented severe economic and social problems but also strongly challenged this notion of political deference. Their traditional suspicion of their "betters" combined with their distrust of government and political authority in general caused them to resist political control and planning from the top.

Those still active among Knoxville's elite seized on the general philosophy of the nationwide Progressive Movement of the early twentieth century. Though generally—and correctly—labeled a major American reform movement (touching, as it did, issues of antitrust legislation, railroad regulation, pure foods and drugs, working hours and conditions), Progressivism also proposed governmental reforms that would eliminate corruption and undue popular passions by removing government from the direct control of the people through independent commissions and nonelective officials. Hence, though ostensibly democratic, in many ways Progressivism was anything but that. In Knoxville as in many if not most southern cities, those political and efficiency-oriented movements that were called "progressive" served essentially to perpetuate control by the elite or its lieutenants and to keep working class whites and blacks as politically impotent as possible.[60]

Not surprisingly, Knoxville's elite for the most part enthusiastically embraced this aspect of Progressivism—although they often frowned on some of its other reform objectives, such as regulation of private corporations. Believing that changes in the structure of the city's government would both bring forth businesslike efficiency and honesty and lessen the potential threat of a political uprising from below, in 1912 the business elite supported a new city charter by which Knoxville abandoned government by a mayor and aldermen in favor of government by five commissioners. Each commissioner would be the head of a department: public affairs, accounts and finance, public safety, streets and public improvements, and parks and public property. All were to be elected at large, virtually insuring that racial or economic groupings by wards could have little effect on election outcomes.[61]

But the commission form of government quickly proved ineffectual. Working-class whites and blacks resented the new government, since it made it more difficult for them to bring political pressure to bear on the "nonpolitical" commissioners in matters of political favors, jobs, and neighborhood improvements. Moreover, the 1917 annexation had not only added tax revenues to the city's coffers but also put such severe financial strains on the commissioners' ability to provide city services that the new government was rapidly plunged into debt. Finally, the combination of executive and legislative functions in the five-man commission made overseeing the city's government a difficult task at best. Graft was uncovered in the awarding of construction, paving, and garbage collection contracts as well as in the administration of the city hospital and waterworks.[62]

Blatant corruption and fraud (including election fraud) became so widespread that in 1923 the active portion of the elite and an aroused middle class demanded still another structural change in their local government. This time, the scandal-ridden commissioners would be replaced by the "incorruptible" city manager–council type of government. The city manager form of government was also popular among progressives, for it too emphasized businesslike efficiency, honesty, and the *appearance* of democracy while the real power resided in the hands of the nonelected manager. The office of mayor was reinstated, although the position was largely an honorary one that automatically went to the councilman-at-large candidate with the highest vote total. In theory the elected council set broad general policies and the city manager enforced those policies in a nonpartisan manner. All three Knoxville newspapers endorsed the reform, as did most of the local civic clubs and the newly organized League of Women Voters. The city manager form of government was easily approved by voters, and *Knoxville News* editor Edward J. Meeman crowed that it was "a revolution in the affairs of the city."[63]

The new form of government got off to a splendid beginning. Assuaging the citizenry, the first mayor and vice mayor were well-known businessmen with impeccable reputations. The mayor was Ben A. Morton (1875–1952), the son of a Blount County physician, who at age fifteen went to work for his brother-in-law Henry Tate Hackney in the latter's wholesale grocery business and took control of the company in 1899 upon Hackney's death. By 1923 Morton was one of Knoxville's leading business figures (he, Hugh Sanford, and William Cary Ross were the city's premier financiers and were nicknamed the "Three Musketeers") and was a man of peerless reputation. The post of vice mayor went to Weston Miller Fulton (1871–1946), who came to Knoxville in 1898 to work at the weather bureau but made a fortune by inventing a seamless metal tube that could be used as a bellows, which Fulton dubbed a "sylphon," after Sylph, the Norse goddess of air.[64]

As the first permanent city manager, the new councilmen hired Louis Brownlow, a professional city manager with a national reputation. A distant relative of William G. "Parson" Brownlow, Louis Brownlow had earned his national stature as the manager of Petersburg, Virginia, but was lured to Knoxville by a munificent salary of $15,000 and the promise of a free hand in appointing his department heads. With Morton and Fulton as the popular liaisons between the manager and the voters and with a man of vision and energy such as Brownlow, the new form of government had more than a fair chance of success.[65]

Brownlow wasted little time in instituting his ideas and arousing opposition. Having little patience with Knoxville politicians (whom he charged with being "corrupt, graft-ridden, dominated by personal considerations") or the voters ("freedom loving, highly individualistic, conservative, loyal to friends but suspicious of others"), the new city manager made no secret of the fact that he thought the city was ugly, its government "chaotic," and its people backward and provincial. Nor did he disguise his disgust with the elite who had withdrawn from the volatile and often nasty and sordid political arena ("citizens holding to higher standards in their private lives and in their private businesses deemed it almost indecent to engage in politics").

To blunt the influence of the politicians and the voters, Brownlow hired professionals from outside the city to administer the various departments, restructured the city's finances, consolidated several smaller (and possibly corrupt) agencies in a new Department of Public Welfare, started a centrally administered public improvements program, and moved municipal offices into new quarters in the buildings that formerly housed the Tennessee Deaf and Dumb Asylum. Thus, in spite of the fact that one volume of his autobiography was titled *A Passion for Anonymity,* Brownlow was anything but anonymous as he fought to overcome what he saw as Knoxville's lethargy and hostility to change as well as the people he considered to be the city's political Neanderthals.[66]

It is surprising although understandable that Brownlow, in spite of his many accomplishments, saw his brief stay in Knoxville as essentially a failure. In addition to his imperious manner and the fact that many working-class voters and their political spokesmen had no intention of allowing the city manager form of government to work as it was intended, perhaps Brownlow's Achilles' heel was his need to increase municipal revenue, an effort that had the potential of bringing the parsimonious elite and working class voters suspicious of any form of government together in an unholy alliance. To be sure, Brownlow's administration was a frugal one, as he was able during his first year to reduce municipal expenses by $620,000. But his ambitious plans were costly, and taxes would have to be increased. By 1926 Brownlow was being harassed almost continuously by political pressure groups and a city council that had turned against him. Driven to a nervous breakdown, he resigned in what he considered to be a crushing defeat of both himself and his efforts to bring good government to the Appalachian city.[67]

One should not, however, dismiss Brownlow's short stay in Knoxville lightly, for his failure is a key to understanding the politics of the New South city. By World War I the conservatism of the post–Civil War Knoxville elite had become so pronounced and pervasive that more energetic newcomers to its circles (like Oliver and Heiskell) seemed anomalous. Though members of the elite undoubtedly had the power, few had the inclination to become politically active in the rough-and-tumble Knoxville political arena. At the same time, those whites and blacks who had come to Knoxville seeking factory employment selected as their political spokesmen and champions men reminiscent of the rural Appalachian political styles they so fondly remembered. Fiercely democratic with a large streak of egalitarianism, these voters, through their spokesmen (whom the elite often characterized as demagogues), voiced their anger and frustration over their collective lot and their abiding suspicion of their "betters."[68]

Brownlow's principal antagonist during his brief tenure as city manager was Lee Monday, a city councilman who represented South Knoxville almost continuously from 1923 through 1939. Friend and enemy alike recognized that Monday was the voice on the Knoxville City Council of the white Appalachian workers, a man who articulated their fears. A sagacious politician, Monday became the most powerful person on the council less through his oratory than

Gay Street, c. World War I.
McClung Historical Collection. Knoxville–Knox County Public Library.

through political arrangements and deals made with some other councilmen, a kind of political horse-trading at which he was most adroit.

Of Monday, Brownlow recalled:

> He was a hillbilly and he gloried in it. He was a roughneck and he knew it. He dressed the part and looked it. He was an orator in the good old mountain fashion, and he knew that too. Most of the time nearly every council meeting was taken up by his oratorical displays. It was frequently difficult to understand exactly what he was talking about, but one knew, whatever the words, he instinctively was talking for the South Knoxvillians against all and sundry. He was the representative of his district and he was the representative of his clan, the East Tennesseans. He was representative of that top-of-the-voice screamology of East Tennessee mountain politics, and rarely in either his speeches or in the council or in the diatribes which my ears suffered when he called at my office did he ever depart from his own clear consciousness of his place in the scheme of things.[69]

As Monday saw it, his "place in the scheme of things" was to echo the thoughts and fears of the once-voiceless white working class against the city's "better sort." He was skeptical of Brownlow's concept of an active city government that, in addition to providing basic services for both the old city and the area annexed in 1917, sought to create recreation programs, regulate plumbers and electricians, and plan for future growth and development in the public sphere. He opposed the tax increases Brownlow demanded (a 16 percent increase during Brownlow's brief tenure), darkly warning of wasted monies and the city manager's reckless and extravagant schemes. More than once he accused Brownlow of heaping taxes on the working people so the elite could be better served and further enriched.

Louis Brownlow (far left) with his cabinet, 1926.

From *A Passion for Anonymity* by Louis Brownlow (University of Chicago Press).

Lee Monday.
McClung Historical Collection.
Knoxville–Knox County
Public Library.

Fighting back, Brownlow's allies on the city council censured Monday for his attacks on the city manager. At the same time they tried to blunt Monday's opposition to tax increases by declaring a 10 percent tax dividend. But Monday would not be silenced. Dubbing Brownlow "King Louis I," he pilloried the city manager for his proposal of a large bond issue to build a new water plant, mocked his acquisition of the Deaf and Dumb Asylum for a new city hall as shamefully wasteful, and kept up a withering barrage on Brownlow's friends in the Welfare Department and on the new planning commission. Monday campaigned beyond his district for anti-Brownlow city council candidates in a special recall election in 1926, the results of which deadlocked the council between pro-Brownlow and pro-Monday councilmen. During that election Monday distributed a graphic poster that showed Brownlow and his allies as baby pigs sucking the teats of their city government "mother." Sensing the recall election results as a mandate against tax increases, an active city government, and change, Brownlow saw the handwriting on the wall and resigned.[70]

Thus Knoxville's two attempts at governmental reform in the early twentieth century both ended in failure, although the city manager–council government limped along ineffectually until the 1940s. While most members of the business elite seem to have favored limited government, few changes, and low taxes, their lethargy was reinforced by the political ideology of Appalachian in-migrants for whom taxes symbolized urbanization and an attendant loss of independence. At the same time, spokesmen for these white working-class men and women opposed any efforts to make the city government less democratic by placing more power in the hands of nonelected officials. Therefore, while Knoxville's politics were often vicious, even occasionally corrupt, they were nevertheless democratic and reflected the conservative sentiments of both the elite and the working class.

Politically it was necessary to keep taxes as low as possible and to secure needed services or improvements through deficit spending and by issuing long-term bonds. Hence by 1930 Knoxville's net per-capita indebtedness was nearly twice that of any other Tennessee city, and debt servicing consumed increasingly large chunks of the city's operating capital. In 1930 the cost of city government was the highest among the state's major municipalities, even though some were almost twice as large as Knoxville. Therefore, as other cities in the nation and in the New South began considering schemes for improved services, urban renewal, and general beautification, a combination of conservative politics and poor finances kept Knoxville from responding to its own opportunities. Indeed, by the time John Gunther visited the city in 1945, Knoxvillians seemed incapable of bringing any such improvements to fruition.[71]

The Fragmentation of the 1920s

Students of the 1920s have recognized for a long time that the period between the end of World War I and the Crash of 1929 was considerably more than an epoch of flappers, movie idols, bootleg gin, and the lost generation of Fitzgerald and Hemingway. Beneath that surface of prosperity and gaiety were profound economic and social problems that lent an air of both fear and desperation to the decade. Urbanization, demographic changes, and economic problems created a kind of fragmentation of society, a fragmentation that even today has not been totally erased.

Knoxville was deeply affected by this fragmentation. As we have already seen, Knoxville in the 1920s was the scene of bitter political battles between those espousing opposing ideas of Knoxville's problems and of the role the city's government should play in addressing those problems. At the same time, residential segregation both by class and by race (a trend that had been going

The Regas Brothers Café opens in 1919.
Courtesy of William F. Regas.

on for some time) seemed to accelerate, further fragmenting the city both socially and culturally. Having witnessed Brownlow's fate, those who might have been inclined to offer Knoxvillians other options remained silent.

As did the nation in the 1920s, the New South city of Knoxville on the surface appeared to be thriving, a city whose glories were still in the future. In 1930 Knoxville's population reached 105,802, up from 77,818 a decade before—an impressive 36 percent increase. To give shelter to this mushrooming population, over 6,123 houses were built in the city between 1920 and 1929; building permits reached a peak in 1927–28, with over 1,200 new construction projects, averaging over $6 million in value, begun each year. If taxes were kept so low as to prevent the provision of basic services, that appeared to be the way most people wanted it, preferring instead to defer payments through deficit spending and bonded indebtedness. Even more noteworthy, a relatively high proportion of Knoxvillians and Knox Countians owned their own homes in 1930, and the city's population was young, with more than 30 percent under fourteen years old and 82.93 percent under forty-five. Indeed, every statistic—from the number of telephones installed to the number of civic club members to the county's impressively low illiteracy—seemed to add weight to the assertion that Knoxville finally had "arrived."[72]

Private developers sensed the elite's need for insulation from the city and responded accordingly. In the 1920s several plans were hatched for ostentatious suburban developments in the western sections of the city, those areas annexed in 1917. In 1925 an out-of-state developer bought a large tract in Looney's Bend, renamed the area Sequoyah Hills, and made plans to sell lots to affluent citizens fleeing the core city. Nearby developments like Talahi maintained the upper-class flavor of the area, with all house plans submitted for approval and with rigid restrictions on grounds and service courts. Parks, fountains, gardens, and impressive stone edifices were designed to give the area both natural beauty and exclusivity. "Today a great city is built close by," the Talahi developers boasted: "Near at hand is a busy artery of traffic [Kingston Pike] to and from that city, ten minutes away. . . . But in TALAHI'S virgin forest, as in long years past, nature rules supreme. Its charm has not been subject to ruinous exploitation. On the contrary, the creators of this community have preserved for all time its natural beauty, adding to it only splendid adaptations of the landscape architect."[73]

Beneath the surface of economic vitality and developing elite suburbs, however, lurked disturbing demographic and economic trends. Most striking was the massive exodus of whites, both elite and working class, from the center (pre-1917) city. They were replaced not by other white in-migrants, as had been the case previously, but instead by blacks who were moving into the center city both from outlying wards and from black agrarian settlements beyond the county and state. This white exodus accounted for absolute white population declines between 1920 and 1930 in the pre-1917 city, Wards One through Nine (from the central business district northward to approximately Moses Avenue). Ward Five (east of Gay and bordered on north and south by Commerce and Church streets, respectively) experienced a dramatic 77.88 percent drop in white population during this period. Simultaneously, black population increased in eight of the nine wards during the 1920s and by 1930 accounted for over half the population of wards Three and Five. Between 1920 and 1930, Ward One (east of Gay along the Tennessee River) recorded a 247 percent jump in black population, with four of the other eight center city wards experiencing an increase of more than a 32 percent.[74]

Why did so many blacks move into Knoxville so soon after the racial troubles of 1919? First, in the 1920s hard times were forcing many marginal farmers—white and black—off their traditional homesteads. Without land, the farmers had nowhere to go but the city. In addition, some of the blacks who migrated to the center city in the 1920s came from other city wards (Seventeen, Eighteen, Twenty, Twenty-One, and Twenty-Three all experienced absolute declines in black population during the decade). Made anxious by the 1919 incidents, blacks may have felt more secure in areas where they lived in larger numbers. For whatever reasons, Knoxville's black population became

W. E. B. Du Bois (in the very back seat of this roadster) visiting Knoxville.
Courtesy of the Beck Cultural Exchange Center.

The Rivoli Theatre, McCalla Avenue, 1928.
Courtesy of the Beck Cultural Exchange Center.

Edgewood AME. Zion Church, 1926.
Courtesy of the Beck Cultural Exchange Center.

more densely concentrated in the older wards that made up the per-1917 city. Those whites who could fled the area, abandoning deteriorating neighborhoods that rapidly were becoming black enclaves.

One observer connected with the recently created Tennessee Valley Authority (TVA) noted in the early 1930s that "although the effects are probably not yet apparent, the more rapid increase of negro population [in the old wards of the city] will undoubtedly have some bearing on problems of crime control, housing, provision of educational facilities, etc." Blacks did filter into low-paying, menial jobs, with 92.2 percent of black working females and 29.8 percent of black working males employed as "domestics" or servants. By 1925 black population density was four times that of whites in the older wards, and by 1930 property values in five of the nine old city wards had slipped badly (while only four of the city's remaining seventeen wards experienced declines in property values).[75]

As the TVA observer predicted, declining economic status, geographic segregation in deteriorating neighborhoods, and in-migrating rural blacks' problems of adjustment to their new urban environment (social and psychological problems that disturbed many who examined African American migration) had predictably created breeding grounds for social ills. By 1930 black families without a gainfully employed head of household outnumbered by over three to one families in which the head of household was employed. Over half the black families who paid rent in 1930 were behind in their payments. More serious for the future was the educational mortality rate of the city's young black population. Of those blacks who would have graduated from high school in 1934, only 14.7 percent actually did so—and only approximately one-third (34.0 percent) of the theoretical group had completed more than the fifth grade.[76]

Thus the 1920s witnessed a rapid alteration of Knoxville's traditional demographic patterns, accelerating trends observable earlier. In turn, this change created economic and social problems that would plague the troubled city for years to come. And, for blacks, the problems would be particularly severe.

It would be a mistake, however, to assume that only Knoxville's blacks failed to share in the much-ballyhooed but terribly uneven prosperity of the 1920s. Working-class whites also suffered the mixed blessings of New South industrialism. In 1930 over 46 percent of the native white male population were employed in manufacturing and mechanical industries, often for pitifully low wages; had no job security; and were struggling to move out of the older wards. Periodic unemployment characterized these industries, and in many families both husbands and wives had to work to make ends meet in the rapidly inflating economy of the 1920s.[77]

Church Street Viaduct in the 1920s, as seen when looking toward the site of the present Civic Coliseum (on right).
Courtesy of the Beck Cultural Exchange Center.

Instead of attempting to understand the larger dimensions of their problems, many whites responded by venting their frustration and rage against African Americans. In their behavior, members of Knoxville's white working class mirrored the responses of many southern whites who were blinded by color to the common economic and political interests they shared with blacks. In 1915 another Ku Klux Klan was born in Atlanta, soon became a potent force in the former Confederate states, and had even spread into northern and midwestern areas. In 1921 a klavern of the Invisible Empire was established in Knoxville, composed largely of working-class whites who lived or labored in close proximity to blacks. Membership records of the Knoxville klavern indicate that most Klansmen lived in Wards Eleven, Fourteen, Fifteen, Sixteen, Seventeen, Eighteen, and Nineteen—an area that roughly ringed the pre-1917 city. Blacks in some numbers had moved into this area, for it was close to the Southern Railway and Coster shops, where many blacks worked. A plurality (26 percent) of those Klansmen who listed their addresses as Knoxville also worked for the Southern Railway, usually at jobs that brought them into direct contact with blacks. Other Klansmen listed their jobs as being with the Louisville and Nashville Railroad, Appalachian Mills, Foreign and Domestic Veneer Company, and the Knoxville Power and Light Company. For whites who worked alongside blacks in those companies, those African Americans became the most visible symbols of their own failure to prosper in the city, of their own dilemma of merging Appalachian traditions and mores with an enforced urban lifestyle, of their own suspicions of their "betters," and of their own political impotence.[78]

By the fall of 1923, over 2,000 white men had joined the Knoxville klavern. A sprinkling of attorneys and professional men were members (joining, perhaps, to enhance their businesses), but the vast majority of Knoxville Klansmen were lower white-collar clerks and salesmen or, as noted earlier, blue-collar laborers who competed with African Americans for jobs and living space. Together Klansmen attended regular Monday night meetings in a building at the corner of King and West Fourth, traveled to nearby Sharp's Ridge for formal initiations and cross burnings, and generally tried to influence political and business leaders. In the local elections of 1923 the Klan stationed people at all polling places, presumably to influence white voters and discourage African Americans from casting ballots.[79]

But the hysteria that the Ku Klux Klan tried to whip up in Knoxville did not last. Although it expanded its attacks to include the "loose morals" of the community ("petting parties" and "wild dancing"), the Klan's membership began to decline until by 1928 the local klavern numbered but 191. The decline brought a stinging rebuke from the Imperial Palace in Atlanta, but even the lowering of the initiation fee to five dollars and then to three dollars did not halt the erosion of the KKK in Knoxville.[80]

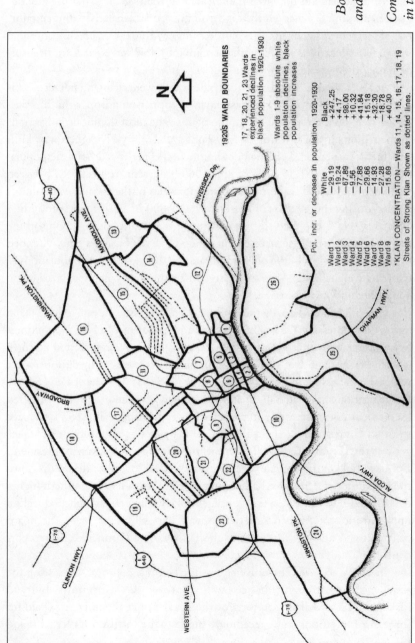

Ward Boundaries and Ku Klux Klan Concentration in the 1920s.

N

1920S WARD BOUNDARIES

17, 18, 20, 21, 23 Wards experienced declines in black population 1920-1930

Wards 1-9 absolute white population declines, black population increases

Pct. incr. or decrease in population, 1920-1930

	White	Black
Ward 1	−29.19	+247.25
Ward 2	−19.24	+4.17
Ward 3	−67.89	+98.00
Ward 4	−9.56	+10.32
Ward 5	−77.88	+41.84
Ward 6	−29.66	+15.18
Ward 7	−14.93	+32.30
Ward 8	−27.28	−18.78
Ward 9	−15.69	+40.30

*KLAN CONCENTRATION—Wards 11, 14, 15, 16, 17, 18, 19
Streets of Strong Klan Shown as dotted lines.

MAGNOLIA AVE.

WASHINGTON PK.

BROADWAY

CLINTON HWY.

WESTERN AVE.

KINGSTON PK.

CHAPMAN HWY.

ALCOA HWY.

RIVERSIDE DR.

I-40
I-75
I-640
I-75

The decline of the Klan, however, should not be taken as an indication that the white community had become more tolerant of blacks. Instead, the white exodus that accelerated during the 1920s very likely robbed the local klavern of actual and potential members. The Klan's great gathering at Chilhowee Park in 1923 marked the high point of local Klan activity but certainly not of racial hostility or unrest. On the contrary, Knoxville's blacks continued to live in a precarious world, with insecure jobs, low wages, and white suspicion only their greatest challenges.

At the same time that Knoxville's older wards were changing in racial composition and becoming lower-class enclaves, upper- and upper-middle-class whites were fleeing westward, beginning one of the most significant migrations in the region's history. Wards Twenty-Four and Twenty-Five (Sequoyah Hills and Talahi, new model-planned developments) experienced fantastic population increases of 161.55 percent and 106.69 percent, respectively, between 1920 and 1930, and real estate assessment values in the former ward almost trebled during the 1920s, going from $2,111,800 in 1920 to an astounding $6,058,950 in 1930. This decade saw one of the great building booms in the Sequoyah Hills and Cherokee neighborhoods, as the business elite, offended by the noxious odors of the older wards and by their lower-class populations—white as well as black—moved westward to the lovely new enclaves being established in West Knoxville.

One might wonder why the University of Tennessee appears to have taken no part in addressing Knoxville's confounding problems. In fact, it would not be an overstatement to say that the university seems to have exerted no force whatsoever in the life of its host community. This is especially curious, since under the leadership of university president (1887–1904) Charles W. Dabney the institution almost literally sparkled with new ideas and innovations. Hired by the board of trustees (dominated by Oliver P. Temple) in 1887 to replace the staid Humes and to "shake things up," Dabney was as ambitious and energetic as the ill-starred Louis Brownlow. In his tenure as university president, Dabney's bold and imaginative leadership did indeed "shake things up" until the University of Tennessee had become one of the leaders in southern higher education. Only when he began musing publicly about equal higher education opportunities for African Americans did Charles Dabney make the board of trustees so nervous that he and the University of Tennessee had to part company.[81]

In 1909, however, the university secured annual appropriations from the state legislature, an event that certainly improved the institution's ability to make budgets as well as plan for growth. But the price the university paid for those appropriations was exceedingly high, as the institution's leaders, and

Charles W. Dabney,
eleventh president of
the University of
Tennessee,
1887–1904.

From *The Volunteer,*
vol. 4 (1900).

View of "The Hill" at the University of Tennessee, 1902.

From *The Volunteer,* vol. 6 (1902).

especially president (1919–34) Harcourt A. Morgan seem to have believed that in return for these recently won funds, the university community had to conform to state and regional ideology and mores rather than try to change them. With a background in agriculture and extension work and as the former dean of the School of Agriculture, Morgan saw the University of Tennessee's primary role as providing technical services to the surrounding populace—certainly not as threatening relationships with the legislature or the people by standing at the forefront of economic or social change. Morgan surely would have blanched at Harvard president Abbott Lawrence Lowell's statement that "one object of a university is to counteract rather than copy the defects of the civilization of the day." Indeed, Morgan had no stomach for a fight with an elected body that controlled his purse strings.[82]

Hence Morgan stood silent when the Tennessee state legislature, awash in anti-Darwinian fundamentalism, passed an antievolution law in 1925. When the law did pass, Vanderbilt University faculty member Edwin Mims tried to unite the colleges of Tennessee in protest, but Morgan would not hear of it. Some say the rebuff exacerbated the growing hostility between the two schools. While he might have opposed the law privately, Morgan feared that retribution by the legislature and the populace would damage the university's standing in the community and hamper it in fulfilling its role. When national attention focused on nearby Dayton during the famous Scopes trial of 1925, the university, tightly controlled by Morgan, remained timorously out of the limelight.[83]

Indeed, Morgan was determined that no one at the university would embarrass the institution in the eyes of the legislature. As a result, he and Dean James Hoskins (later president of the university) in 1923–24 either dismissed or drove off thirteen faculty members (18.3 percent of the total faculty in 1923), all of them deemed by Morgan and Hoskins to be troublemakers. As civil engineering professor Nathan Dougherty recalled later, "Morgan was in a meeting with his Deans and somebody said can you fire anybody around here? He [Morgan] said yes, yes you can. . . . You got somebody you want to fire? And by gosh they just pooled their resources and each one had one almost." One member of the board of trustees joked that the "wastebasket will be filled by the process of decapitation."[84]

Undoubtedly the most well-known faculty member who was purged was law professor John R. Neal. A full-time faculty member since 1917, Neal was a well-known political figure and eccentric who, it was said, rarely bathed and often slept in his clothes. Upon meeting Neal, humorist Will Rogers commented that "I met John R. Neal, the candidate for Governor. Some say they are not going to vote for him because he is wishy-washy—well, I don't know about the wishy, but he certainly is not washy." But Neal had protested the fir-

Harcourt A. Morgan.

Courtesy of University of Tennessee Photographic Services.

ing of a faculty member who supposedly had taught evolution and become an administration gadfly, and who, according to Philip M. Hamer, led an ill-starred campaign for faculty control over appointments and dismissals and took the students' side in almost every university controversy. Finally it was determined that Neal had to go. For his part, Morgan recommended dismissal to the board of trustees, conducted a one-sided hearing into the matter, and later influenced the board to uphold his decision. Two years later, the university "announced that it would no longer give an annual John R. Neal Oratorical Award to the best debate student." Again Morgan had won, and the university remained a timid, conforming force in Knoxville's life—in essence, no force at all.[85]

In sum, then, the cultural fragmentation so typical of New South industrial towns, which was well advanced in Knoxville by 1920, rapidly accelerated in the following decade. Economically, socially, and politically, the city was divided into mutually hostile and suspicious camps of the conservative business elite, Appalachian whites, blacks, insulated and cowed university faculty, and a comparatively small middle class. From Talahi mansions to shotgun houses, from Chopin to the recently founded *Grand Ole Opry*, from opulent offices to railway shops, from illegally imported scotch whiskey to potent moonshine, the fissures in what had once been a comparatively homogeneous community by 1930 had widened until few men or women could bridge the gaps. At the onset of the Great Depression, Knoxville was a city fragmented along class and racial lines. Suspicions of change and of each other were its citizens' only common denominators.

The Great Depression

Neither elite nor workers were prepared to comprehend or deal with the Great Depression that swept over the land in the early 1930s. Symptomatic of its effect on Knoxville was the almost universal failure of the city's banking community. During the 1920s local banks had been pressed by their stockholders to pay liberal dividends, a policy that in the short run had been profitable to investors but ultimately proved shortsighted. Caught by the stock market crash with insufficient capital, with too many large loans to personal friends and stockholders, and with a too liberal dividend policy, Knoxville banks fell like dominoes before the onslaught of the national crisis. Again the city's elite, eager to take short-run profits rather than wait for long-term investments to pay off, proved hopelessly unimaginative.[86]

In 1930 the Guaranty Trust Company went into receivership, along with the largest real estate firm in the city. When the Bank of Tennessee (wholly owned by the Caldwell and Company investment house) went into receivership in November, the reverberations spread to Knoxville's major bank (in which Caldwell had invested heavily), the Holston-Union. On November 10, 1930, a run on that institution resulted in $750,000 in withdrawals, and despite a Federal Reserve loan, the Holston-Union closed its doors on Armistice Day. From there the panic spread. In an effort to merge several weakened banks into one strong one, the East Tennessee National Bank, East Tennessee Savings, and the City National Bank reformed themselves as the East Tennessee National Bank. But in spite of loans from the Federal Reserve and President Hoover's Reconstruction Finance Corporation, the new East Tennessee National collapsed in January 1932. By 1932, of the six national banks in Knoxville in 1920, three had disappeared through merger and three more had been forced into receivership. Drained by shortsighted stockholders, by poor banking practices, and ultimately by loss of public confidence, Knoxville's banks simply could not withstand the strains of the Great Depression. Some depositors escaped with their savings, but many more were wiped out by their banks' failures.[87]

As the national economy lurched downward, the city felt the full force of the Depression's fury. Construction virtually stopped, with building permits plummeting from 2,207 in 1928 to 1,246 in 1929 and on to a disastrous 757 in 1930. Telephones were disconnected, memberships in civic clubs dropped alarmingly, and bread lines and soup kitchens began to appear on once-bustling Gay Street and at the General Hospital. More serious, the city's population increase during the 1930s was a paltry 5.5 percent (from 105,797 in 1930 to 111,580 in 1940), a clear sign that many people were abandoning Knoxville, either quixotically to seek employment in other cities or to retrace their once-hopeful steps back to the hills and coves that were still seriously overpopulated, thus putting even more pressure on the tired land.[88]

As the Depression deepened, Knoxville's employment picture became exceedingly bleak. With the city dependent on low-grade manufacturing and mechanical industries, factory closings threw a high proportion of the labor force out of work. Unemployment statistics crept disturbingly upward, from 2,284 unemployed in 1930 to 7,534 in 1937. By March 1939, in spite of President Franklin Roosevelt's ambitious New Deal, over 6,000 Knox Countians were still on relief. By 1940 the picture had barely brightened, with 4,332 city residents still seeking work, 1,703 employed by Work Projects Administration (WPA) projects, and over 1,500 working for TVA.

The economic catastrophe had important effects on Knoxville. With wages of those who could find jobs badly deflated, a decline in the standard of living was almost inevitable. Nonunion wages for carpenters were 65 cents per hour, for truck drivers 40 cents per hour, for common laborers 30 cents per hour, and for textile workers (of whom there were approximately 6,000) about 35 cents per hour. Yet when the contractor hired in 1930 to build the Henley Street Bridge proposed paying his workers "New York wages," he was discouraged from doing so by local businessmen who feared that their own laborers would desert them to work on the bridge. Strikes, such as the abortive 1934 uprising at the Cherokee Spinning Company, were brutally crushed and their organizers, such as Lucille Thornburgh (1908–1998), blacklisted. Thus unemployment, frustration, and low wages took their toll on the working-class citizens, who poured out their wrath upon one another. In 1938, for the first time in the city's checkered history, homicide was among the ten leading causes of death for Knoxvillians.[89]

With banks destroyed and public revenue rapidly drying up, Knoxville's local government staggered into the Depression with an enormous bonded indebtedness. Forced to the brink of financial ruin, the municipality was obliged to pay its employees in scrip and had to refund its public debt to 1978. Since Knoxvillians were defaulting on their city taxes in droves, the harried city council had no alternative but to beg for mercy from its creditors and simultaneously to issue more bonds.[90]

The Depression also created a semitransient population in Knoxville, men and women who floated in and out of the troubled city as well as from house to house or apartment to apartment. Though homeowners appear to have been a rock of stability in the city (with but 5.4 percent of them having moved during the year 1939), lower-middle-class and lower-class renters seem to have been constantly moving about, entering the city in search of employment and leaving soon afterward, disappointed, only to be replaced by a new influx of desperate job seekers. In 1939 fully 38.4 percent of the city's renters had lived in their houses or apartments less than eleven months. Thus, below the comparatively stable middle class, Knoxville was constantly in flux, and its people were continually disoriented.[91]

Knoxville's housing had deteriorated badly before the Depression, and economic hard times made it nearly impossible to make needed improvements. A 1934 Department of Commerce real property survey ranked Knoxville "low" among sixty-four cities surveyed, with 24.3 percent of its 22,828 residential structures in "bad" condition, 28 percent "too crowded," 40 percent lacking bathtubs or showers, and 21.9 percent having three rooms or less (the famous "shotgun" house). Federal aid to a new municipal housing authority constituted an attempt to alleviate the housing problem, but it was some time before the effects of this were either felt or seen.[92]

Knoxville's blacks were hit especially hard by the national catastrophe. Whites fleeing from foreclosed farms or lost urban jobs demanded and generally received employment, as blacks were bumped off payrolls in alarming numbers.[93] Whereas in 1924 practically all the city's asphalt and paving workers had been black, a decade later only four or five African Americans had been able to maintain those politically sensitive positions. By 1934 the telephone company, which had employed blacks even to the foreman level, reported no black employees. Similar cases can be cited in other vocations and trades: the city's baking trade, formerly all black, was by 1934 all white; chefs and cooks in 1929 were all black, but by 1934 there were only two African American cooks in the city; railroads, once primary employers of blacks, during the Depression simply stopped hiring them; not only the carpentry and masonry trades, but also marble and quarry work saw declines, black employment in the latter dropping by 66 percent. And over 75 percent of black janitors and porters were replaced by whites. The economic suffering of whites was mitigated by their wholesale displacement of black workers.[94]

Nor did the vaunted New Deal cushion blacks' hardships in the reeling city. In 1934 not one black laborer was listed on the payrolls of the Civil

Works Authority (CWA), a fact that led some to protest that the CWA was consciously discriminating against Negro job seekers. The blue eagle of the National Recovery Administration (NRA) did not benefit black workers, either; in fact, because NRA codes stipulated minimum wage rates, many employers chose to fire their black workers rather than pay them the code-imposed wages. So in some cases the NRA brought reverses for African Americans, not recovery. Sensitive as they were to the political and social pulses of the region, the NRA and its parent, the New Deal, had almost no impact on Knoxville blacks, who bitterly referred to the NRA as the "Negro Run-Around."[95]

Blacks also charged that the newly created TVA was "bending over back-ward not to give any offense to the traditions of the South." It is hard to say whether the Authority's employment practices concerning blacks were due more to the New Deal's desire to accommodate itself to regional mores or to TVA director Arthur Morgan's personal racial views. Whatever the reason, blacks were excluded from the new TVA-built "model community" of Norris, were hired (when at all) only for the most menial jobs, and then were segregated into separate work crews. Clearly, the national reform movement of the New Deal, for whatever reasons, failed dismally to assist Knoxville's black population, men and women who had considerably more to fear than fear itself.[96]

In addition to bleak economic prospects, Knoxville's African Americans continued to face serious social problems. Unemployed, impotent, and angry, blacks poured out their frustration in acts of violence. Larceny, homicide, and all types of juvenile delinquency plagued the black community. In 1930, for example, the homicide rate for blacks was almost six times that for whites. Of all blacks arrested and convicted of crimes in Knoxville in 1931, almost half (48.2 percent) listed "no occupation" on their police records. Over half of black juvenile delinquents came from broken homes; desertion by frustrated males was so common that in 1934 one-third of the black families in the city listed female heads of household. School attendance among black youths decreased drastically, with only 39.3 percent remaining in school through the fifth grade. Not surprisingly, Knoxville's African American illiteracy rate was nearly three times as great as that of whites. Yet black residences were hardly ideal centers for raising children who had dropped out of school. A TVA-sponsored study showed a disturbingly low standard of living among even the most geographically stable of black families. One example will suffice: 59.2 percent of blacks surveyed by TVA used no electricity, as opposed to 15.4 percent of surveyed whites. Clearly, if the Depression was taking a heavy toll among black adults, its social byproducts augured ill for the futures of black adults-to-be in the East Tennessee city.[97]

Some Knoxville blacks chose to abandon the troubled city, as did south-ern blacks in general, either following rumors of opportunities in the North or retreating to the desperate rural regions from whence they had come. During the 1930s Knoxville witnessed a massive black out-migration, so large that the number of African Americans in the city actually declined by almost 1,000 persons, from 17,093 in 1930 to 16,106 in 1940. To the blacks of this New South city, the promise of American life seemed to lie elsewhere, and the New Deal meant only continued accommodations to old ways of white survival at the expense of black degradation.[98]

Perhaps the Depression's greatest impact on Knoxville, and one that no government agency or statistician could measure, was on the people's collec-tive mentality. Caroline Bird has called the Great Depression an "invisible scar,"[99] a psychological wound that would irrevocably separate those who lived through it from those who did not. In Knoxville the scars of deprivation were slow to heal. The optimistic booster spirit of an earlier epoch was mortally wounded, leaving a legacy of rigid conservatism and defensiveness as shrill as it was unconvincing. True, these attitudes had always been present in the city, at least since the Civil War. But the Great Depression acted to deepen these intellectual gullies and make it difficult for anything to hold out against the onrushing tide. In Knoxville the legacy included a suspicion of change and innovation; a desperate clinging to the eternal verities of family, church, pro-hibition, and making ends meet; deep lines of demarcation between economic, social, and racial groups; and a fanatical defense of the city itself against the criticisms of "outsiders," whether they represented TVA, the university, or some other group. The dreams of the New South advocates of so long ago had all come true. But for some, those dreams of industrialism and urbanization had turned to nightmares.

Lost Confidence and the
Culture of Ugliness

Knoxville in World War II and the Postwar Era

In the mid-1940s, well-known traveler and writer John Gunther briefly visited Knoxville, gathering material for his next book, planned as a sequel to the enormously popular *Inside Europe* (1936), *Inside Asia* (1939), and *Inside Latin America* (1941). The eventual result, *Inside U.S.A.* (1946), was a curious mixture of praise, criticism, and impressionistic reporting of what Gunther himself (in typical "Guntherese") called "the greatest, craziest, most dangerous, least stable, most spectacular, least grown-up, and most powerful and magnificent nation ever known."[1]

Though brief, Gunther's time in Knoxville must have been less than pleasant, for the author penned one of the most scathing attacks on the city ever printed—one so critical, in fact, that as late as the 1970s his name alone could bring forth expletives that many Knoxvillians usually reserved for Democrats or the unchurched. Gunther wrote:

> Knoxville is the ugliest city I ever saw in America, with the possible exception of some mill towns in New England. Its main street is called Gay Street; this seemed to me to be a misnomer. A recent movie, "Ziegfeld Follies of 1946," could only be shown in a cut version in Knoxville,

because one sequence shows Lena Horne. Knoxville, an extremely puri-
tanical town, serves no alcohol stronger than 3.6 percent beer, and its
most dignified taprooms close at 9:30 P.M.; Sunday movies are forbidden,
and there is no Sunday baseball. Perhaps as a result, it is one of the least
orderly cities in the South—Knoxville leads every other town in Tennessee
in homicides, automobile thefts, and larceny.[2]

Were that not enough, in his conclusion Gunther remarked that the city possessed "an intense, concentrated, degrading ugliness."[3]

The reaction of most Knoxvillians to Gunther's assault was predictable.
Years later, some remembered that the author's comments elicited more unity
(against Gunther) than almost any issue before or since. Sidewalk interviews
by the *Knoxville News-Sentinel* also revealed unanimous hostility. And for its
part, the *Knoxville Journal* refused to print one word about Gunther's remarks,
preferring instead to agonize over the communist influence in Hollywood or
to defend syndicated columnist and New Deal archenemy Westbrook Pegler.[4]

Perhaps the most interesting and perceptive reaction to Gunther's diatribe
came from Knoxville journalist Lucy Templeton, whose *News-Sentinel* column
"A Country Calendar" was a chatty, popular mixture of history, book notes,
recipes, and local color. In her column of June 1, 1946, Templeton stung fellow Knoxvillians by admitting that Gunther had been basically correct and
that the city she loved was a grimy, sooty, ugly place despite its location amidst
the natural beauty of the Smoky Mountains. Worse, she questioned whether
Knoxvillians even possessed the will to recognize their problems, face up to
them, and solve them. Readers may have seethed, but Templeton, a Bryn Mawr
alumna and a 1901 University of Tennessee graduate, charter member of the Pi
chapter of Chi Omega sorority, widow of George Mabry Templeton (a prominent Knoxvillian and local attorney), and *News-Sentinel* staffer off and on from
1904, was so impeccably connected that no one dared publicly to rebuke her.[5]

While almost no Knoxvillians at the time would have admitted it, almost
certainly Lucy Templeton was more accurate in her portrayal of the city's physical and psychological landscape than were those who blustered against the
best-selling Gunther. What even Templeton had failed to see, however, was the
true depth of Knoxville's ugliness as well as precisely why Knoxvillians in the
1940s had been unable to marshal the city's not inconsiderable assets to recover
the energy and dynamism that had given birth to the post–Civil War city in
the first place, to move the city decisively into post–World War II economic
boom, and to attack its most obvious and glaring physical and psychological
problems. Instead, as the majority fumed over Gunther's intemperate but
essentially accurate jibes while simultaneously basking complacently in modestly positive economic indicators that masked the city's deeper malaise, those

Knoxvillians who realized that all was not well seem to have been unable to rouse their neighbors from their self-imposed lethargy.

And as Knoxville's political leaders engaged in some of the most vicious and personal wars in the city's history as they joyously flogged one another almost without ceasing, they appear to have been unable to deal with—or in some cases even to recognize—the trends and forces that were buffeting the city like a cork in an angry sea: wartime economic changes and postwar readjustments; out-migration to the surrounding county or beyond; the ugliness of envy (in this case, of recently constructed Oak Ridge); the fierce opposition to any changes such as civic improvements, relaxing blue laws, legalizing alcoholic beverage sales, or improvements in public education; the specter of McCarthyism; and the harbingers of the coming Civil Rights Movement. Instead, political leaders once again acted to alter the structure of Knoxville's government without addressing the underlying reasons for its ineffectiveness.

Finally the Appalachian city began to spawn a talented coterie of artists and writers, people who could look back on the 1940s and early 1950s with perspective and sensitivity. Rather than comforting their fellow Knoxvillians, however, they drew dark pictures of the city in the postwar period, pictures filled with physical and psychological ugliness. It was as if the Appalachian city was breeding its own versions of John Gunther.

World War II and the Postwar Boomlet

The war and postwar years witnessed a dramatic rejuvenation of the American economy, a revival that eradicated all but the deepest memories of the Great Depression. Compared to the federal government's wartime spending, New Deal outlays seemed almost anemic. For example, from 1940 through 1944, the ten largest recipients of government war contracts received about the same amount of money as the *total* federal budgets from 1932 through 1939, with General Motors alone receiving wartime contracts that exceeded the total federal budget for the year 1936. Industrial output during the war years increased by a staggering 15 percent per year (the average increase between 1896 and 1939 had been but four percent) and the nation had virtual full employment, with only 1.2 percent unemployed in 1944. In addition, over six million women entered the labor force during the war, only one-third of them in clerical positions.

Nor did the end of the war see the United States sink back into depression. Continued federal expenditures (20 percent of the postwar gross national product), enforced wartime savings (estimated at approximately $140 billion), and the pent-up demand for homes and consumer goods combined to make the postwar economic climate one of the most prosperous in American history.

The gross national product continued to surge, from $283 billion in 1946 to $367 billion in 1953. Home ownership mushroomed, from 43 percent in 1940 to 62 percent by 1960, and sales of furniture, automobiles, home appliances, and newly available television sets—much of this buying spurred by the widespread availability of consumer credit—were nothing short of phenomenal. Indeed, for the new postwar middle class, which by 1956 was a majority of the American population, it appeared that government and the private economic sector had combined to solve the age-old enigma of economic booms and busts. And if everyone was not a participant in the postwar economic good times, the belief generally prevailed that those unfortunates too would be swept up eventually in the prosperous joyride.[6]

Even the South, usually the poor stepchild of the industrial era, prospered during the war and postwar years, although that prosperity was extremely spotty and much of the wartime expansion proved to be short-lived. Between 1939 and 1947, the number of manufacturing plants in the South grew from 26,516 to 42,739, and industrial capacity increased 40 percent. Southern coastal cities with shipbuilding facilities boomed, as did towns near aircraft and ammunition factories. And a happy combination of weather, low construction costs, and the seniority of southern congressmen and senators caused great numbers of training facilities to be located in the South as well. Even as the Confederate Veterans of Georgia declared war on Japan, their grandchildren and great-grandchildren were volunteering for the armed services or going to work in war plants. And if over 1.4 million white and black civilians left the South between 1940 and 1943 to work in the war plants of the North, Midwest, and West Coast and if during the war the section's farm population decreased by over three million people (approximately 20 percent), it was confidently predicted that the out-migrants would return after the war and that mechanization would take the places of the stoop labor that had abandoned small farms and croppers' cabins.[7]

On the surface Knoxville appeared to participate in national wartime and postwar trends. By 1940 roughly 40 percent of the Knoxville area's total workforce was employed in the textile industry, one of the lowest-paying sectors of the American industrial economy. Workers at Holston Mills, for example, earned an average of thirty cents per hour in 1939, a wage scale that two strikes (in 1936 and 1939) against the mill that made men's socks failed to rectify. Hence the United States' involvement in the Second World War and the concomitant labor shortages gave many people the hope that the need for more workers at plants such as the nearby Aluminum Company of America (ALCOA), Rohm and Haas (which made Plexiglas for airplanes), and Fulton Sylphon would drive wages up for everyone.[8]

And the hope was realized, as the Second World War brought prosperity to Knoxville that the Appalachian city had not experienced for decades. By March 1942, the dollar value of war contracts awarded to Knoxville-area firms had quadrupled in only ten months. ALCOA saw a 600 percent production increase, with its workforce swelling to 12,000. The Tennessee Valley Authority added hundreds of workers to finish Douglas Dam in around one year. And the new city of Oak Ridge, part of the Manhattan Project, virtually mushroomed out of the mud and clay of nearby Anderson County, with a peak wartime population of 75,000 and a workforce of nearly 90,000. Oak Ridge cost approximately $1.106 billion.[9]

The city's prosperity appears to have been fairly widespread. By 1943 Knoxvillians' annual per-capita income was $268 higher than the national average and more than twice that of Tennessee as a whole, and the city's total effective buying power was 134.68 percent higher than it was in 1938. Almost everyone was working, as employment in retail, wholesale, and service jobs doubled. By September 1943, women had entered jobs traditionally closed to them, and over 14,000 women were employed in wartime manufacturing plants (39 percent of the total workforce and over one-third of them not in textile or apparel factories). Higher wages caused women in textile mills and domestic service to abandon their jobs, and mills had to raise wages to keep their workers.[10]

And still the demand for workers continued. In her moving reminiscences, Dorie Woodruff Cope recalls her family moving to Knoxville from Sevier County in 1943 "into the first home my parents ever owned. . . . Houses sprang up like mushrooms in the fields still growing corn stalks." And if Dorie and her newly migrated neighbors from Grainger County, Union County, "and the back forty acres of Knox County" were labeled "hillbillies" and therefore "viewed with alarm," still there was work.[11]

Banking in Knoxville seemed to mirror the new prosperity. From slightly over $61 million in 1940, assets grew to nearly $210 million in 1945, with the Hamilton National Bank holding over half of the city's total assets. And while the end of the war brought a $32 million decrease in bank resources as the federal government reduced both its local bank deposits and debt obligations, the unexpected rapid shift to peacetime productivity showed the banking establishments' vitality, as loans and discounts increased by $12 million, or 59 percent. Knoxville's banks appear to have been in a good position to aid the city both in wartime and in postwar recovery.[12]

Other signs also appeared to indicate that the city would participate in the postwar recovery and continue to thrive once the fighting had ceased. The construction industry, a key employer in the region, had been artificially stimulated by the building of Oak Ridge, and in the late 1940s continued to prosper, as building permit values soared from a lackluster $2,518,728 in 1940 to over $12 million in 1946, leveling off at a still-impressive $10,290,747 in 1947. Knoxville's retail business, which in 1946 amounted to $134,253,000, by 1950 had risen to $184,487,000.[13]

The apparent postwar prosperity also seems to have infected Knoxville's civic leaders as well, for they began to make grand—and grandiose—plans for urban rejuvenation and beautification. The Knoxville Housing Authority (KHA) was organized as a tax-exempt public corporation in 1936, though it took a series of court decisions (the final one being handed down from the Tennessee Supreme Court) to uphold its status and power. Immediately, KHA undertook a survey of the city's housing stock with an eye to reform. By 1949 the survey, "a study of Knoxville's blighted areas," was completed and plans for urban redevelopment produced. This at last was a vital step in the city's development for, as one observer later noted: "Expressway construction was coordinated, to a degree, with redevelopment. The two activities together resulted in radical alterations in Knoxville's appearance, its population, and the functions of its urban systems."[14]

Further signs of modernism were seen with the opening of the Knoxville Airport in 1937, and the city's request two years later that the Knoxville Transit Lines convert trolley cars to buses on its routes. This latter request was a sure sign that civic leaders expected growth beyond the existing trolley tracks, and although the switch to buses did not actually take place until 1947, at least the plans had been made and carried out with what was, for Knoxville, uncharacteristic dispatch.[15]

Concomitantly, in 1938 the City of Knoxville took possession of its electric power system, after a six-year struggle to convert to public power. In 1939 the Electric Power and Water Board became the forerunner of the present Knoxville Utilities Board. TVA's wartime construction work on the Fontana, Cherokee, Douglas, and Fort Loudon dams stimulated the local economy. Fort Loudon Dam, built just above the point where the Little Tennessee River joins the Tennessee, was the dam closest to Knoxville on the main river system. Building it meant that TVA's nine-foot navigable channel would extend behind the locks to Knoxville, thus altering the city's riverfront considerably. This spurred the city planning commission to employ Harlan Bartholomew Associates to develop a plan for Knoxville's riverfront, potentially a beautiful area but one that in fact was badly scarred by slums and haphazard industrial siting. The riverfront plan, adopted in 1941, recommended construction of a series of riverfront parks along a projected highway from Concord Street to Riverside Drive (today's Neyland Drive). The plan, in effect, mapped out a complete facelift for a city badly in need of one.[16]

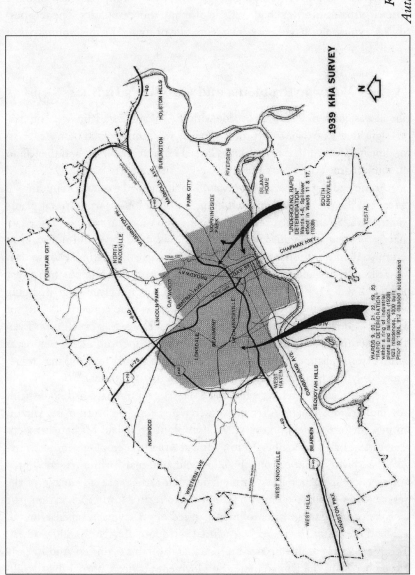

Knoxville Housing Authority Survey, 1939.

1939 KHA SURVEY

N

HOLSTON HILLS

BURLINGTON

PARK CITY

RIVERSIDE

ISLAND HOME

SOUTH KNOXVILLE

VESTAL

CHAPMAN HWY.

"UNDERGOING RAPID DETERIORATION"
Wards 1-8. Spillover
effect in Wards 11 & 17.
(1938)

MAGNOLIA AVE.

MORNINGSIDE PARK

BROADWAY AVE.

WASHINGTON PK.

NORTH KNOXVILLE

FOUNTAIN CITY

OAKWOOD

LINCOLN PARK

CENTRAL AVE.

GAY ST.

MECHANICSVILLE

LONSDALE

BEAUMONT

WEST HAVEN

CUMBERLAND AVE.

SEQUOYAH HILLS

WARDS 9, 20, 21, 22, 19, 23
"RAPID DETERIORATION"
within a mix of industrial
plants and railroads (1939)
1623 residences, 1000 built
Prior to 1904, 912 classed substandard

NORWOOD

WESTERN AVE.

BEARDEN

WEST KNOXVILLE

WEST HILLS

KINGSTON PIKE

I-40

I-75

I-75

I-40

I-40

Material improvements, organizational developments, and plans encompassing public power, public housing authority, transportation reforms, and a new airport, coupled with the economic harvest of the wartime years, appeared to have left Knoxville poised on the brink of a new era of development. Superficially, at least, there seemed every reason to believe that Knoxville had overcome the municipal financial woes of the previous era as well as the economic blows of the Depression and that the city was fully launched into the postwar urbanization so characteristic of many southern cities. The few pessimists, cynics, and naysayers were swept aside or routed by the cannonades of oratorical optimism.

Postwar Problems and Gunther's Ugliness

But all was far from well. Side by side with the favorable statistics were numerous signs that Knoxville's wartime prosperity was temporary at best. At worst, to some it appeared that Knoxvillians lacked both the resources and the will to sustain wartime economic gains.

At the end of the war, a *News-Sentinel* poll revealed that an astounding 70 percent of the women who had left homes or other jobs to work in war plants wanted to keep their current employment. Even more surprising was the fact that 57 percent of the married women who were surveyed did not want to return to their traditional prewar roles. But places had to be made for returning male veterans, and so layoffs of female war workers began more than a year before the war was over. Lack of seniority was the reason given for discharging women (a specious explanation as far as new jobs were concerned), but for women who had come to depend on those wages it was a cruel blow. Even more discriminatory was the situation of African American males, who were laid off from wartime employment in such numbers that by 1950 they represented only five percent of Knoxville's male industrial workers.[17]

Theoretically, therefore, white male veterans should have had no difficulties finding employment. After all, women were being laid off en masse (almost 60 percent of female workers at ALCOA alone were laid off between September 1943 and December 1946), African American employment in Knoxville's war plants declined roughly 62 percent, and many white veterans opted not to enter the labor force immediately but rather take advantage of the Servicemen's Readjustment Act (G.I. Bill) to secure further education (the University of Tennessee's enrollment surged after having reached a low of 1,900 in the fall of 1943). Yet by August 1946 approximately 10,800 workers, mostly males, were unemployed in Knox and Blount counties. And in early November 1946 the United States Employment Service reported that significant numbers of workers were leaving the area in hopes of finding employment elsewhere.[18]

The primary cause of Knoxville's sagging postwar economy was the decline of industries upon which the city depended. Less competitive in the evolving global economy were textile and apparel mills, which could not escape the national slump in those areas. The iron industry and railroads also experienced severe postwar troubles. Thus changing markets and transportation networks, new product development, and new technologies combined to make Knoxville's older industries less competitive. And with its traditional industrial base in decline, the city's general industrial employment growth was not robust enough to continue to absorb returning veterans, young people entering the job market, and new people from the rural hinterlands. In an article that should have awakened even the most somnolent, the *Knoxville Journal* glumly noted that between 1940 and 1950 industrial employment in Knoxville had increased a paltry 9 percent, and that Knoxville's industries, once the backbone of the city, were moribund. The city planning engineers reported sadly that the "most favorable growth opportunities are past."[19]

Not surprisingly, Knoxville's population growth in the 1940s was anemic. The Bureau of the Census reported that between 1940 and 1950 the city's population had increased a meager 11.8 percent. In fact, however, because the University of Tennessee's 5,100 students were included in the 1950 totals but not in the census of 1940, the actual rate of increase was closer to 7 percent, not even enough to equal the city's natural increase. At the same time, the population of Knox County outside the city jumped a startling 45.1 percent, the lion's share of the population outside of the city being young and solidly middle class escapees from the troubled city. As the *News-Sentinel* put it in the headline to its report on the 1950 census, "Outskirts call youngsters, but Ma, Pa, stay put."[20]

Those who remained in Knoxville after the war augured ill for the city beyond the postwar decade. In the 1940s blacks, poor whites, and the elderly constituted an increasing share of Knoxville's population. In that decade white population increased 10.6 percent while the city's black population rose by 19.3 percent. In wards with high proportions of blacks, unemployment and poverty were considerably more widespread, for blacks were traditionally closed out of jobs in the skilled construction and retail trade fields, which in the North and the South almost exclusively hired whites. Median annual income of nonwhite city dwellers, at $1,443 (1947), was nearly $1,000 less than that enjoyed by the city as a whole. In 1948 for the first time since the 1930s homicide again became a leading cause of death.[21]

In stark contrast to the inner city, Ward Twenty-Four, which contains Sequoyah Hills, was characteristic of the areas to which the prosperous industrial bourgeoisie was fleeing. Annexed in 1917 and occupying the bend in the Tennessee River west of Third Creek and above Looney's Island, this community planned for Knoxville's "better" elements had, in 1939, 858 residential structures, of which nearly 700 had been built since 1915 and about half since 1925. Two-thirds of the units in the ward had at least one bath and toilet, over half were described in 1934 as being in good condition, and over half of the households paid rent or its equivalent of more than $50 per month.[22]

In earlier decades, rich and poor, white and black had lived fairly close to one another. Even today, one can see the architectural evidence of this in the neighborhoods of Fourth and Gill (a few blocks north of downtown and east of Broadway); Happy Hollow (north of downtown and west of Broadway); the East Scott–Oklahoma Avenue area (north of downtown and east of Central); and Mechanicsville, where Welsh iron workers built imposing Victorian residences side-by-side with modest shotgun houses usually occupied by blacks. But after World War II the city increasingly became fragmented into enclaves of class and race. To be sure, this trend had begun as early as the 1880s, when more well-to-do Knoxvillians fled the city for the more exclusive neighborhood of West Knoxville (now Fort Sanders), or in the 1920s, when Sequoyah Hills and Talahi were developed. However, the dramatic acceleration of this trend after World War II confronted the city with even greater dilemmas than it had faced before.

Lack of employment opportunities after the Second World War certainly was one of Knoxville's most pressing problems, but it was not the only one. Gunther's comment about Knoxville's ugliness, however unkind, was only one of many observations about the city's physical unsightliness. In mid-1952 the business magazine *Fortune* introduced Knoxville to its readers with this description: "Gay Street, the shopping center, is old, narrow, and crowded, and the side streets fall away in further drabness; the whole is smudged with soot from locally mined coal. . . . Almost everyone thinks something should be done, but nobody does anything much."[23]

Not appreciated at the time was the fact that Knoxville was home to a small band of youngsters who decades later would grow and mature into prominent writers, craftsmen who often used Knoxville of the 1940s and 1950s as the setting for their works. They too, however, could not get the city's physical unattractiveness from their minds. In *Bijou* (1976), David Madden described the riverfront behind the Knox County Courthouse as

> where the gospel singing was coming from. Even though they reeked of
> pee-stained mustiness, stale beer, turnip greens, fried river fish, dirty

clothes, dog squat, slop, he was drawn to the old houses. . . . From one porch a pure drop down the cliff into the river . . . down here along the river Negroes and whites more thoroughly mixed than anywhere else in Cherokee [Madden's fictitious name for Knoxville].

A complex network of paths, big rocks, trees, little and scrawny, kudzu vines, made the bluffs behind the houses rugged. Lucius stood on the railroad tracks. He looked back toward the houses. The back yards were full of garbage, trash, crude rabbit hutches, beehives, chicken coops and a few pigpens. The houses looked as though they had been there since the beginning of Cherokee.[24]

And in *Suttree* (1979), Cormac McCarthy wrote of the area adjacent to the market house:

He went among vendors and beggars and wild street preachers haranguing a lost world with a vigor unknown to the sane. Suttree admired them with their hot eyes and dogeared bibles, God's barkers gone forth into the world like the prophets of old. . . .

. . . This lazaret of comestibles and flora and maimed humanity. Every other face goitered, twisted, tubered with some excrescence. Teeth black with rot, eyes rheumed. . . .[25]

Whether in journalism, observation, or writers' memories, Knoxville was physically ugly, not perhaps as ugly as John Gunther had described it, but physically unappealing nevertheless.

Little wonder that those who could do so forsook the city for better opportunities or abandoned it for life beyond the city limits in Knox County. As a 1949 report by the Tennessee Bureau of Public Administration noted, Knoxville's government was not financially sound enough to undertake physical redevelopment; land earlier set aside for parks had been virtually ignored; and, according to Edith Howard of the bureau, the whole picture was "disheartening."[26]

An earlier study by the newly established Knoxville Housing Authority only confirmed Gunther, Templeton, *Fortune,* and Howard. In the KHA inventory, over 40 percent of the city's 23,450 dwellings had been built between 1895 and 1914 and were declining rapidly. Mechanicsville and McAnnaly Flats (roughly north of the present I-40 and west of I-75), the post–Civil War working-class neighborhoods housing railroad and iron workers, were "undergoing rapid deterioration . . . within a maze of industrial plants and railroads." There were 1,623 residences in the area, 1,000 of which had been built prior to 1904, and 912 were classed as physically substandard. Throughout the entire city, 43.6 percent of the residences were said to be substandard.[27]

Among the oldest wards (Wards One through Eight), the situation was worse. These eight wards comprised the central business district (retail and wholesale trade, light manufacturing) and with few exceptions were described in 1939 as in a state of rapid deterioration. Some of the areas between Vine Street and Broadway were frankly characterized as slums, and it was noted that this blight was spreading rapidly eastward along Hill Avenue, Riverside Drive, and Mountain View along the river to the city limits. In Ward One, 25 percent of all the dwelling units had been constructed before 1885.[28]

Throughout the city, 20 percent of all houses were classed as in need of major repairs and 24.5 percent as unfit for use; 40 percent were reported to possess less than one toilet and one bath. Of course, as noted above, housing in the core was worse; in Wards Nine, Twenty, Twenty-One, and Twenty-Two, over 60 percent of the dwellings lacked one bath and one toilet. And some areas, such as the predominantly black Mountain View (site of the present Downtown Loop, Civic Coliseum, Women's Basketball Hall of Fame, and downtown Marriott Hotel), continued to slide even more into the 1960s, when President Lyndon Johnson in 1964 described residents of Mountain View as "people as poverty-ridden as I have seen in any part of the United States."[29]

Thus as other southern cities in the postwar period dreamed lavish dreams of skyscrapers (which journalist W. J. Cash quipped southern cities had as much need for as "a hog has for a mourning coat") and riches, *Fortune* magazine claimed that Knoxville's business elite was "too busy for civic projects. . . . They like it fine the way it is." Except for Lucy Templeton and a few others, most Knoxvillians thought that the best response to Gunther's charge of ugliness was to ignore it.[30]

As John Gunther had intimated, however, Knoxville's physical unattractiveness was an outward and visible sign of deep inner troubles and community malaise. And indications of this psychological ugliness could be seen nearly everywhere: in its politics, its unseemly envy over the prosperity of nearby Oak Ridge, its unbecoming battles over blue laws, its local variant of the Second Red Scare and squabbles over public education, and its response to the nascent Civil Rights Movement. In all these things and more, the Appalachian city so desperately in need of change appeared to fear and resist it the most.

Political Ugliness

Knoxville politics during the wartime and postwar years were characterized by vicious and personal warfare, not a little demagoguery, ever-shifting factional alliances, and an almost total disregard for issues of substance. Since the fall of

Louis Brownlow in 1926, the city manager form of government had never worked well in the city. Mayors and councilmen kept tight control of the purse strings and tried to force city managers into accepting their patronage "requests." To be effective, therefore, city managers often had to build alliances with some councilmen and with political "bosses" who could deliver the votes, men such as attorney W. T. "General" Kennerly, bail bondsman Ed McNew (who, it was rumored, could deliver the "floating wards"), Neil Bass, Guy Webb, or others. Though the city almost always voted predominantly Republican in national elections, national political parties meant almost nothing in the rough-and-tumble local political arena.[31]

Although Knoxville could claim to have a host of political power brokers who guarded their modest satraps and made and broke alliances, in the wartime and postwar years local politics alternately was dominated by three political figures: industrialist George R. Dempster (1887–1964), editor Guy Smith Jr. (1898–1968) and chain grocery store owner Caswell "Cas" Walker (1902–1998). Although bitter political enemies most of the time (Dempster is alleged to have said, "If I ordered a whole carload of SOB's and they just sent Cas, I'd sign for the shipment"), Dempster, Smith, and Walker embraced a political style that alternately amused and outraged Knoxville's citizenry. That they spent more time in political machinations and warfare than in working to address the city's mounting difficulties was obvious to nearly everyone. As *Fortune* magazine observed, "They [Knoxvillians] like it fine the way it is."[32]

George Dempster was a native Knoxvillian whose father had arrived in the city from Scotland in 1872 and eventually became a partner in a gristmill. During his teens, George worked as a laborer on the railroads and as a steam shovel operator on the Panama Canal. Upon his return to Knoxville, Dempster and two of his brothers founded the Dempster Construction Company, which specialized in heavy road building and grading work and later invented and pioneered an ingenious garbage pickup system known as the Dempster Dumpster.[33]

By the mid-1920s Dempster had drifted into politics, in 1929 finally gaining appointment as city manager (he had tried unsuccessfully to be named in 1927). Accused by his enemies of being hungry for power, he convinced the state legislature to amend the city's charter to combine the offices of mayor and city manager. That move probably cost him the mayoralty in 1937, when he was beaten by W. W. Mynatt who then got the Tennessee General Assembly to reverse itself on the "mayor-manager law." Dempster sought the mayoralty on three more occasions, winning only in 1951. While mayor, he attempted (unsuccessfully) to get the state legislature to allow Tennessee cities to keep two cents of the seven-cents-per-gallon state gasoline tax. Unsuccessful at that,

*George Dempster
(right).*

Photograph taken for
Fortune by Louis Schilver

Dempster then tried to raise local taxes. "They almost impeached me," he said. In the next election, he lost to Jack Dance and never held public office again.[34]

In private a tasteful and cultured individual (Cas Walker liked to characterize him as a member of the "silk-stocking crowd"), Dempster nevertheless possessed an often outrageous and dramatic political style that had its local appeal. Faced with a councilmanic revolt in which Dempster asserted that there were members of the city council who would like to kill him, Dempster strode to the dais in a public council meeting, turned his back on the council, raised his coattails, and dared them to "shoot him where the galluses crossed."[35]

When Appalachian Mills owner Roy Lotspeich (1882–1951) purchased the *Knoxville Journal* in 1936 for $450,000, he wasted little time in hiring East Tennessee journalist Guy Smith Jr. as editor. A native of Johnson City, Tennessee, Smith had started his newspaper career as a reporter for the *Knoxville Journal and Tribune* before returning to upper East Tennessee as founder and editor of a number of short-lived papers. Promised a free hand by Lotspeich (who was more interested in being accepted into Knoxville's upper social circles than he was in running a newspaper), Smith made the *Journal* a highly read-able paper that combined Republican politics, support of some civic improve-ments, and regular pummeling of his local political enemies. Of Dempster, he wrote that he deserved "to be relegated to the political ash heap and buried so deeply that one of his own Dumpsters can't dig him out. . . . This is a matter of public sanitation." In retaliation, whenever Dempster was in power, so the stories go, he used to delight in catching Smith's car double-parked (a habit of Smith's) so he could have the police tow it away. Smith then ordered *Journal* photographers that whenever a group picture was to be taken that would include Dempster he be placed on one end or the other so that his image could be cropped from the photograph before its appearance in the *Journal*. Dempster then engineered a police raid in which Lotspeich, a teetotaler, was caught with a large quantity of illegal whiskey in the trunk of his car (Christmas gifts, maintained Lotspeich, for *Journal* advertisers). As appalling as all of this was, Knoxville readers were afraid to miss one day of the newspa-per lest still another outrageous incident come to light. At his best Smith could stand above the most disgraceful aspects of the region's politics (as when he supported TVA, the *Brown v. Board of Education* decision, and *Baker v. Carr* on "one man, one vote"). At his worst, however, he could sling offal with the best of them. To a local businessman whom Smith had tried to interest in run-ning for mayor but who claimed to know nothing about municipal adminis-tration, Smith purportedly explained, "*You* run for mayor. *I'll* run the city."[36]

The person who best characterized Knoxville politics in the wartime and postwar years, however, was neither Dempster nor Smith—although both men added some substance and considerable color to the local political scene. Rather it was Caswell Orton "Cas" Walker who set the political tone for a city unable to recapture its dynamic past and afraid to go forward into an uncer-tain and frightening future. Part huckster, part spokesman for Knoxville's poor and fearful, and part demagogue, Walker served as a city councilman from 1941 until 1972, when the future finally caught up with him. In his prime, however, he was the city's most powerful political figure.

Born on English Mountain in neighboring Sevier County in 1902, Cas Walker arrived in Knoxville via the coalfields of Kentucky and in 1923 opened a small grocery, tobacco, and notions store at 1100 East Vine Avenue, in the heart of the city's red light district. The first Saturday he made twenty-seven dollars, and many people probably thought the hillbilly from Sevier County wouldn't be in business very long. As Walker himself later remembered, people viewed him as "a kinder idiotic person."[37]

But as he later would in politics, Cas Walker fooled them all. When he threw live frying chickens off the roof of his store one day, he nearly caused a riot and that day made $1,200. A greasy pig contest did nearly that well, as did an African American street entertainer "who could dance up a storm." On another occasion he advertised ice cold Coca-Cola at a ridiculously low price and then hid the Coke at the bottom of the cooler, covered it with cheap bottled soda from Kentucky called Strawberry Surprise, sold huge amounts of heavily salted peanuts and popcorn, and "locked the back door so nobody could get at the water." The hillbilly from English Mountain was well on his way.[38]

Nearly everyone who was a contemporary of Walker had his or her own favorite story about him—the time he chewed part of a man's ear off for failure to pay his grocery bill, or the free tick-and-flea dip to every dog owner who purchased over ten dollars worth of groceries, or the time on his television show when he dragged the mother of a county commissioner off the set by her hair ("She was strong as a bull"). But perhaps nearly everyone's favorite Cas Walker story is the one about his burying a man alive in the parking lot of his Chapman Highway store as a publicity stunt. An out-of-work entrepreneur, "Digger O'Dell," allowed himself to be interred in an oversize refrigerator and be fed through a long straw. Huge crowds (at 2:00 A.M. one night there were still 1,500 people in the parking lot), who Walker alleged actually came to see someone die but were too embarrassed to admit it, bought groceries in record amounts ("the register never stopped ringing"). And when Digger, who some believed had signed the contract under the influence of alcohol, repented of his premature burial and asked to be freed from his Frigidaire prison, Walker demurred, holding out for a few more days of astounding profits. The purported conclusion of the real-life thirty-day comedy-drama almost surely is apocryphal, but many insist that the crowd that showed up to witness Digger's liberation actually was larger than the one across town greeting the arrival in Knoxville of President Dwight Eisenhower.[39]

Like Dempster's, Cas Walker's move from business to politics was an almost natural one. Both men enjoyed extremely high name recognition. Both were wealthy enough (at its peak Walker's empire included twenty-seven grocery stores) to finance their own campaigns. To be sure, Dempster had better connections with the city's business elite (what Walker called the "silk-stocking crowd"), but Walker had a brand of sociopolitical populism that resonated in the black and white working-class communities.[40]

Walker's entrance into politics coincided with the 1926 rout of Louis Brownlow as Knoxville's first city manager. In fact, in one interview Walker claimed that he began his political career by supporting Lee Monday against Brownlow, although on two later occasions he publicly denied having known Monday. But Walker's real political career began in 1939 when none other than George Dempster asked him to join a "progressive" (i.e., anti-administration) city council ticket. It is said that politics makes strange bedfellows, but surely none stranger than these. It is likely that the wily Dempster not only realized Walker's potential vote-getting power in the working-class areas of the city, but also believed he could dominate what he considered to be the politically naïve grocer. For his part, Walker said he thought Dempster was attracted to him as a candidate because he had referred to one of the incumbent councilmen as being "as confused as the boy who dropped his chewing gum on the hen house floor," thus appealing to Dempster's businessman-cum-redneck tastes. In the campaign, Walker ran under the slogan that would become almost his trademark: "For lower taxes, vote for and elect Cas Walker." In his first bid for office, Walker placed a disappointing eighth, not high enough for a seat—a loss he would not repeat.[41]

And although he did not win in 1939, he had found his formula and his political voice. He appeared to speak for those working-class whites and blacks who faced ever more difficult economic prospects in the troubled wartime and postwar city. Sagaciously using newspaper and radio advertisements that combined his grocery business with his political views, Walker deftly played the card of class politics, creating the impression that he—like so many of his constituents—was the underdog battling against the rich and well born. "People like the underdog," Walker later confessed. "I played like the poor boy, like I was just gettin' along."[42]

Walker's appeal was particularly successful among African Americans, perhaps the most dispossessed in a city filled with underdogs. Buying up hundreds of poll tax receipts ("people gave 'em to me for safekeepin'"), distributing copies of already filled-in ballots that could be hidden in hats and used once inside the polls ("blacks like to think they're gettin' away with something"), hosting "chittlin and pigs' feet parties" ("the best way in the world to get people to vote for you is to feed 'em"), and making ostentatious contributions to African American churches' building or mortgage funds, he appears not to have realized that his *message* as one standing for them against the "silk-stocking crowd" probably would have been sufficient without his unethical—and on occasions illegal—electioneering tactics.[43]

Walker's combination of antiestablishment politics, outrageous self-promotion, and questionable electioneering tactics soon paid off, for in the 1941 city council balloting he led the list of vote-getters. More significant, he led in virtually every African American area of the city, as he would in nearly every election throughout the next two decades. But Walker's appeal was not just among black voters. In 1941 he opposed the installation of parking meters as well as the levying of a three-dollar local auto license tax intended to raise revenue from those who had moved outside the city limits but who still worked downtown. And in the poorer sections of Knoxville, where street conditions were abysmal, Walker would find out a day in advance from an informant at the city garage where the street repair crews were scheduled to work. At the appointed place and time, candidate Walker was there ahead of the road crew, highly visible and leaving the impression that he personally was seeing to his constituents' well-being. On one occasion, campaigning against the bootleg joints and "rough places" that flourished in the dry city, Walker arranged to have coteries of drunks loiter about his opponent's headquarters on polling day; in his own vicinity, of course, were numerous Appalachian versions of Shirley Temple, dressed in white pinafores and wearing blue ribbons emblazoned "Vote for my Uncle Cas"—proof enough that he was on the side of sobriety.[44]

Walker's election posed a dilemma for Knoxville's business elite and political veterans. Ever since the inauguration of the city manager form of government in 1923, the at-large council candidate with the greatest number of votes was chosen as mayor by his fellow councilmen. But even Walker's political allies (the antiadministration ticket, almost surely led by Dempster, E. E. Patton, Fred R. Stair, and Guy Webb) realized that he was too much of a "loose cannon" to be trusted with such power and visibility. To be sure, these men, like Walker, hoped to use their power to oust city manager W. W. Mynatt (with Kennerly, the leader of the administration faction) and find positions for their friends on the police force, fire department, and garbage collection trucks. But Walker, it was feared, would be too blatant about it, and so the antiadministration leaders passed over the neophyte grocer-politician and chose Stair (who had finished third among at-large candidates) as mayor. Realizing his days were numbered, Mynatt resigned from the city manager post before he could be fired and accepted a position with the Federal Office of Production Management. He was replaced as city manager by Guy Webb.[45]

Although technically an independent in politics, from 1939 through 1943 Walker in fact was allied with Dempster and the anti-administration forces. However, when Dempster (with Walker's help) became city manager, Dempster found it necessary to seek additional revenue sources and proposed a limited personal property tax. As Walker put it, "Dempster was a good councilman, but when he went for city manager and went for a personal property tax, I couldn't afford to be for that." Walker obviously could not, since he had spent virtually all his time flaying the rich businessmen who, he charged, had avoided paying their full taxes while the poor had paid full assessments. He claimed that the city would have plenty of operating capital if only the rich were assessed real property taxes as evenly as the poor. Walker remembered that in a stormy private meeting the city manager (referring to their mutual campaign promise of no more taxes) exclaimed, "To hell with the platform—it's only made to run on!" Walker's resulting open opposition to Dempster in a city council session and his open charge that "gambling, whiskey and prostitution have always flourished under . . . Dempster" finally blew apart the increasingly fragile alliance between these two inordinately ambitious men. And although Dempster was a man of considerable influence, he was unable to shake Walker's faithful voter base among black and white working-class voters.[46]

Indeed, by the mid-1940s Walker was virtually uncontrollable, despite the fact that the middle- and upper-class voters were beginning to find his style an embarrassment. One wrote angrily to the *Knoxville Journal* in 1943 when Walker was being considered for mayor: "Do we want a mayor who by his own admission has amassed a fortune, yet . . . tries to make the lower-income citizens believe they are being swindled and exploited by those with a little more money? Or that every man with an extra pair of socks is a predatory capitalist, who spends most of his time devising means to suck the life-blood out to the working people[?]" The civic-commercial elite grumbled that Walker was becoming less amusing and that "something would have to be done about him." For his part, Walker laughed off his growing unpopularity in the middle- and upper-class wards ("they hated to think that they was voting for some coal miner").[47]

Finally, after once again besting all the other at-large candidates in the 1945 councilmanic elections (second place went to a disappointed W. W. Mynatt, who lost to Walker by 777 votes out of 14,681 cast), the new council at last was forced to give Walker the mayoralty, a post he grandly assumed in January 1946 (the *News-Sentinel* commented dryly that the grocer-politician had taken to wearing a necktie). Realizing the humiliating fate that awaited him, Dempster (as had Mynatt before him in 1941) resigned as city manager so as to deny Walker the pleasure of sacking him.[48]

But despite the rout of his political foes, Walker's problems had just begun. Now he was mayor and no longer able to talk with impunity and conviction about being an outsider. Now he would be expected to do more than just criticize the ideas and plans of others. Instead, now Walker would be obliged to confront such thorny problems as postwar reconversion, the city's massive bonded indebtedness (the result, as we have seen, of the council's fears of voter reactions to tax increases), a bloated city pension system, the tax rate, zoning, unemployment, sewage removal and street cleaning, and Knoxville's down-at-the-heels physical image. At the same time, however, the new mayor would have to reward his political supporters, many of whom yearned for city jobs.[49]

Thus, to remain consistent with and faithful to his constituents, within a month Walker was forced to oppose the city manager whom he himself had appointed to replace the routed Dempster. The new city manager, Paul Morton, was the first professional city manager since Louis Brownlow and, like Brownlow, he came to Knoxville filled with energy, idealism, and a host of ideas to push the city forward. In an address to the League of Women Voters, Morton said that he found the city in a "state of emergency" and that strong remedies would be necessary to rouse Knoxville from its complacence and lethargy. In his first month in office, Morton set up a merit system for city employees; pushed for a full-time city planner; began to address what he called the "disgrace" of the city's filthy streets; cancelled city contracts with Dempster cronies in city repairs and fire insurance; rolled back pay raises for Dempster's favorites; and advocated enlargement of the tax assessor's office, a new general hospital, a modern sewage disposal system, new schools, and a new civic center. In an editorial supporting Morton, the *News-Sentinel* praised Nashville for regaining control of its government "from a handful of selfish professional politicians" and sounded a virtual call to arms by saying that "what Nashville is doing, Knoxville can do."[50]

Although rumblings had come from Walker almost immediately over Morton's ignoring the mayor's recommendations concerning political appointments and the city manager's opposition to spot rezoning (which, it was charged, Walker favored so that he could build a new store on East Magnolia Avenue), the battle was joined in full on January 19, when Morton presented his recommended city budget to a shocked city council. To pay for his ambitious plans, the city manager requested a budget for 1946 of $6,722,380, a whopping 8.02 percent increase over the 1945 budget. When stunned councilmen suggested that some of Morton's plans (such as the high-cost street paving) could be paid for with another bond issue, the city manager flatly refused, claiming that cowardly politicians of the past had kept taxes low by running up an enormous bonded indebtedness.[51]

In response, in mid-February the Walker-dominated council approved a budget of $5,955,330, an amount that two weeks later was trimmed even further to $5,675,777, a slashing of Morton's proposed budget by almost 16 percent. As a further slap in Morton's face, the council then cut the city's property tax rate by 10.2 percent. Walker's move was a clear signal that, while he claimed he favored progress and new ideas, in fact the mayor intended to keep things exactly as they were.[52]

Instead of bowing to his parsimonious city council and its flamboyant and exceedingly dangerous mayor, Morton challenged Walker by taking his case to the newspapers, and to the public. "Walker has been doing his best to get me fired," he charged, and added, "I guess it is time this situation got out into the open. . . . But I will not resign. Morton doesn't quit." At last the city's civic-commercial elite was sufficiently aroused by Walker's antics. In early March a roster of distinguished Knoxville businessmen formed what it called the Good Government Group, an ill-disguised sign that the elite had grown tired of Walker.[53]

But Walker would not be reined in. After all, the business elite had never been able to work together in the larger interests of the city, had not been active in the political arena since 1923, and had preferred not to descend to do battle with the likes of Dempster, Smith, or Walker, where things could get very dirty. Why, Walker probably reasoned, would they rouse themselves now when they had been so lethargic in the past?

Hence, after but eleven weeks in office, Morton was doomed. On March 19, in a wild city council session, Walker and his minions voted to dismiss the stubborn city manager. Law director W. B. Lockwood (a Morton appointee) automatically became city manager, but the remainder of Morton's staff resigned. Then, as if nothing had happened, the city council went on to discuss and vote against lifting the ban on Sunday movies.[54]

But Walker at last had overplayed his hand. Within hours of the ouster of Morton, cries for Walker's recall were heard, principally from people who apparently had been waiting for this misstep by the grocer-mayor. A Citizens Protective League, formed largely from Good Government Group members, nominated lumber company executive Edward Chavannes to oppose Walker in the December recall election and called for the removal of two Walker allies on the council as well. Ironically, the *News-Sentinel*, in comparing the ouster of Morton to the forcing out of Louis Brownlow twenty years before, failed to remember that Walker, a protégé of Lee Monday, had helped bring about that 1926 resignation.[55]

The 1946 campaign was probably the dirtiest in Knoxville's modern memory of savage political contests. Walker was opposed by virtually every elite social and business organization, from the Junior Chamber of Commerce to the Knoxville Garden Club. He was lambasted as a "champion for nobody but himself" (a slur on his image as the workingman's friend), a "political accident" of low voter turnout in city elections, a political meddler, and a mayor who in nine months had accomplished nothing except virtually bankrupting the city and reaping "a harvest of nation-wide ridicule for this community." Calling Walker "inept," the *News-Sentinel* explained that the recall effort was "an uprising against misgovernment."[56]

In such a bare-knuckled battle, Walker's political style was at its best. Claiming that the afternoon paper, a Scripps-Howard publication that Walker erroneously called "the New York Chain Newspaper," opposed him because Morton had lowered its tax assessment by $25,000, Walker held meetings throughout the city, serving familiar refreshments, providing country music, and attacking the "silk-stocking crowd." He even claimed that the principal charges against him were that he did not have a college degree and that he was not a polished, educated-sounding speaker, points designed to strike home with his constituency.[57]

Walker must have known he was in trouble, for by the end of November (the recall vote was scheduled for December 3) he had swallowed his pride and was courting his one-time archenemy George Dempster. Sensing he could apply the coup de grâce, Dempster not only refused Walker but then humiliated the mayor by announcing to the press that Walker had pled for his assistance.[58]

The end came surprisingly quickly. While Walker's own wards did not desert him, abnormally high voter turnout in other areas of the city and the last-minute opposition of George Dempster defeated Walker and his two councilman allies. Walker carried thirteen of the city's forty-one wards, principally those areas inhabited by the black and white working-class populations that had always stood by him. But Chavannes piled up such enormous majorities in what Walker referred to as the "silk-stocking" neighborhoods that he won going away.[59]

Although such a defeat would normally spell the end for a politician, for Walker it was but a temporary setback. As the civic-commercial elite naïvely withdrew once again to its offices and homes, it left the city to the grocer-politician, who was willing to work full-time and who used his own political style to great advantage. Within ten months Walker was back on the city council, finishing first among eight candidates and never dropping below fourth place in any ward. Throughout the 1940s and 1950s Cas Walker continued to win office and to oppose virtually every idea or move advocated by the elite, usually on the grounds that it would raise the workingman's taxes. And even as he later claimed that "I'm not against progress," in fact Cas Walker opposed nearly every innovation that anyone brought forth to move the city forward: annexation, Market Square Mall, a new library, a city-county building, fluoridation of the water, city-county unification, and even daylight savings time (which, one person recalled, Walker blocked because he maintained that the "extra hour of daylight would kill all the grass for the cattle"). And yet, as the economic woes of the 1950s crept across the troubled city, Cas Walker's power increased almost in direct proportion to the increases in levels of unemployment and economic suffering in black and poor white neighborhoods. So it had always been with Walker.[60]

In retrospect, Knoxville politics during the tumultuous 1940s seems to have displayed an air of unreality. Strong signs that the city's traditional industrial base was ailing and unable to keep up with job demand, the abandonment of the city by people who either moved into new suburbs beyond the city limits or left the region entirely, and the general physical deterioration were crucial issues crying out to be addressed. Yet Knoxville's political barons virtually ignored these momentous problems, preferring instead to hack ferociously at each other with ill-disguised ardor and glee. Other cities tried to overcome similar problems by annexing the suburban fringes almost as fast as people settled in them, but Knoxville (which had not annexed any territory since 1917) religiously avoided annexation for fear that required services would offset potential increase in revenue and shackle the city with even more debt. Earlier, in 1942, Knoxville business leaders were shocked and dismayed when David Lilienthal, chairman of the Tennessee Valley Authority, did not support the city's bid to become a port terminal, saying that Knoxville had become too complacent and wanted TVA to do everything. Hence, faced with the challenge of leading the city out of its postwar malaise, instead Knoxville's political leaders bowed to the fearful and dispirited voters' wishes for low taxes and limited change. The city manager system, which might have planned and executed an urban rejuvenation program, was mortally wounded in the bloody political battles of postwar years. Political life would change in Knoxville in the years ahead, but in the 1940s it appeared narrow, parochial, visionless—and ugly.

The Ugliness of Envy

As the Appalachian city seemed unable to participate in the general national economic upsurge of the 1940s, it must have galled some Knoxvillians to know that but a few miles away a new city—also to be in the new Knoxville Standard Metropolitan Area in 1950—supported by a new industry was burgeoning. Founded in 1942, Oak Ridge initially was a "city behind a fence," one site of the Manhattan Project dedicated to building the first atomic bomb. Demands for nearly all types of workers caused the new city's wartime population to reach a peak of 75,000. Though in the postwar years that population would dwindle (Oak Ridge's 1980 population was approximately 27,000), in the immediate postwar period there was no hint of the future decline. All that Knoxvillians knew was that Oak Ridgers seemed to have an almost inexhaustible supply of money and an almost insatiable demand for food, clothing, strong drink, and luxuries.[61]

Consciously and unconsciously, Knoxvillians sensed that Oak Ridge represented a future that would be denied their own city. To those few Knoxvillians who saw that Knoxville was dropping behind its southern competitors and who searched frantically for a way to reverse that trend, the coattails of

Oak Ridge seemed not only a convenience but also a godsend. A *News-Sentinel* editorial of August 7, 1945, mixing unpardonable xenophobia with furious backslapping, first publicly proffered this coattails ploy: "Detroit has only been known as the auto capital of the world; New York is the financial capital; Pittsburgh the steel center. Knoxville may well become known as the capital city of atomic energy." The editorial went on to remind Knoxvillians that they stood on the threshold of a new era: "[C]itizens of this community must realize by now that a busy and exciting future confronts us—the 'old timers,' the newcomers, and the thousands of temporary residents who may be planning to stay on here."[62]

But Oak Ridgers bridled at being associated with what many of them felt was a dying provincial city. One Oak Ridger replied to the editorial: "By what earthly right do you have the gall to suggest that Knoxville may well become known as the capital city of atomic energy?" and chided the editor for "the most flagrant case of jumping on the band wagon that I have ever witnessed." Such ill will was typical of the war years. Knoxvillians, it was alleged, had "jacked up" prices for "foreigners" and "outsiders": "We have been here since March, 1944, and not once can I say I ever got a square deal in Knoxville."

Miss W—— D—— was in a like frame of mind: "We were treated with scorn and looked upon as so many aliens to be bled dry by local merchants. . . . [W]e were charged exorbitant prices for food, rent, clothing and even at that you Knoxvillians had griped that the OPA [Office of Price Administration] had put a price ceiling on these things and you were not allowed to charge more. . . . Don't you think that after three years it's a little bit late to welcome us to Knoxville? Aren't you afraid that Knoxville might eventually be absorbed by Oak Ridge?" She then struck what was, for many Knoxvillians, a more tender spot: "Practically all of the workers of Oak Ridge came here from cosmopolitan cities, cities that extended a hearty welcome to newcomers, cities that had something to offer in the way of entertainment and recreation. But in Knoxville we saw old shows, we ran into your blue laws, we found ourselves on Sundays as strangers in an inhospitable town with nothing to do. We found your sidewalks rolled up at night the few nights we were able to leave the reservation in search of diversion."[63]

Stung by the Gunther-like attacks, startled and outraged Knoxvillians replied as best they could, heaping abuse on Oak Ridgers while defending their stagnant city. Knoxvillians were quick to respond that they, too, had suffered through the same wartime problems as others and that housing shortages, scarcities, rationing, and standing in lines were tortures not exclusively reserved for Oak Ridgers visiting Knoxville. Admitting that Knoxville was not cosmopolitan like the cities Oak Ridgers hailed from and that it was a "one-horse town," Mrs. P—— W—— of Fountain City insisted that home, in the last analysis, was what you made of it. Mrs. B. C—— of Knoxville was less apologetic: "As for entertainment and recreation on Sunday here in Knoxville, we have plenty of churches to attend. There are more religious and God-fearing people in Knoxville than most cities, and I hope we continue to have it that way." If foolish boosterism could open Knoxvillians to the barbs of Oak Ridgers over the "energy capital" syndrome, other Knoxvillians could draw upon traditional values to defend their city in the argument that ensued.[64]

The editorial-page war may have shed more heat than light. But beneath the stinging insults of those who reviled Knoxville as backward and unmodern, there was another reality, heralded by the atomic age that had recently made its debut at Hiroshima. The city was frozen in an earlier industrial era. D—— B—— of Oak Ridge was aghast that Knoxville could tout itself as the "capital city of Atomic Energy." The closest thing to atomic energy in Knoxville, he asserted, was a perfume atomizer. "You [Knoxvillians] have been floating in a castle on a cloud for a long time. The blast that Clinton Engineer Works dealt Japan ought to awaken Knoxvillians from their sweet slumber of reveries." D—— B—— suggested that Knoxvillians richly deserved for their city's title to be "The Gateway to Oak Ridge." The penultimate letter published in the ongoing debate must have rankled Knoxvillians more than any other, for its writer commented, "I am a native of Nashville and I always thought it was the most dirty, inhospitable, and corrupt city that ever was until I moved here. But Knoxville has Nashville beat a mile."[65]

The *News-Sentinel* editor remarked that the discussions of "long-suppressed feelings" by Oak Ridgers and Knoxvillians "have been revealing and interesting but prolonged discussion would not be desirable" and he cut off the debate. Prolonged discussion might well have revealed that the "long-suppressed" feelings were perhaps not long suppressed at all but were rather a fairly new recognition of the fact that in the wartime decade Knoxville at heart remained an older Appalachian industrial city.[66]

The Ugliness of Provincialism

Historians of America in the 1920s generally characterized that era as one of intellectual and cultural conflict between the forces of modernity and those attempting to hold fast to society's traditional values and morals. Hence the 1925 trial of John Thomas Scopes in Dayton, Tennessee, is viewed as a symbol of that battle between the two Americas, one emphasizing intellectual and moral freedom and individualism and the other the right of a community to enforce traditional social, cultural, and moral rules of behavior.[67]

What is less appreciated by these same historians is the extent to which that conflict did not die with William Jennings Bryan in 1925 but rather carried over with considerable strength into the succeeding decades. Especially in areas of rapid change where frightened people would cling to the rocks of cultural surety or in regions in which significant segments of the population felt themselves increasingly economically and socially dispossessed, this "culture war" was carried on with all the ferocity of a medieval crusade.

As one might expect, Knoxville was in—or near—the eye of that cultural storm. In-migrants from the rural hinterland had brought with them their traditional culture and values and looked with suspicion and hostility on anything that threatened their worldview. And as Knoxville's economic base began to erode in the postwar years, these people found themselves increasingly marginalized, scorned by their "betters," and politically impotent. Cas Walker may have spoken for these men and women, but he could not save them.

As in Dayton, Tennessee, the conflict in Knoxville centered on a law intended to protect traditional culture and values, a law opposed by a growing number of individuals, most of them affluent, who saw the ordinance as restricting the right of individual choice and embarrassing to the community. Unlike Dayton, however, the point of contention in Knoxville was an ordinance prohibiting the showing of moving pictures on Sundays. Unlike Dayton it surely was, but the battle lines and the symbolic nature of the conflict were much the same.

In 1891 a local law was enacted with the intention of prohibiting or restricting business activities on Sundays. Among the forbidden activities were "any kind of show, feat, circus, or theatrical performance, or play at any kind of game in public place for amusement, gain, or profit." And when moving pictures came to Tennessee (the first motion picture house in Knoxville opened in 1907), the state legislature passed a law banning Sunday showings.[68]

The state law, however, permitted localities to except themselves from the restriction, and a warm battle was joined in Knoxville over the issue. As the Knox County Baptist Association thundered, "We are in a great fight to save our country. . . . This mighty menace to the very existence of the day of worship must be met by militant action." Fearing for their positions, the city council quietly dropped the issue.[69]

When Memphis and Chattanooga both dropped the prohibition, however, the debate reemerged in Knoxville. Without the revenue from a seventh day of showing each week, most Knoxville theaters could not afford to rent the new releases immediately after their premieres. One might, therefore, look in a Memphis or Chattanooga or Nashville paper and see advertisements for new releases that would not arrive in Knoxville for days, or even weeks or months. One frustrated person wrote to the newspaper, "One hopes that the seven dwarves will not have grown old before they come to Knoxville." And on July 10, 1938, the vice mayor closed the Tennessee Theater and arrested the manager and cashier for showing the film *The Adventures of Robin Hood* with Errol Flynn on a Sunday.[70]

The issue was brought to the voters in a succession of referenda, none of which succeeded in repealing the Sunday restriction. In 1935 an unofficial straw poll showed voters fairly evenly divided (slightly more against the repeal). But in 1938 an official referendum was defeated by a two-to-one margin, in spite of the fact that repeal was backed by the Chamber of Commerce, the Jaycees, both Knoxville newspapers, the Knoxville Restaurant Association, and Mayor W. W. Mynatt. Hence by 1942 Knoxville was the only city in the United States with a population of 100,000 or more that still banned Sunday movies, a distinction that clearly embarrassed the city's affluent and middle class but was seen as a badge of honor by its traditionalists.[71]

In 1943 Sunday moving pictures in Knoxville again were beaten down, although the two sides were far more evenly matched than they had been in 1938. Interestingly, since the referendum was held on the same day as a municipal election, we are able to see a high correlation between opponents of Sunday movies and those voters who supported Cas Walker. Caught between a dying past and a frightening future, frustrated, frightened, and angry blacks and poor whites struck out against their so-called "betters" (Walker's "silk-stocking crowd") and against change over which they appeared to have a decreasing amount of control. It was at this point that John Gunther visited Knoxville and reported that "Sunday movies are forbidden, and there is no Sunday baseball," even though he missed the deeper meaning of what many in Knoxville viewed as a most humiliating debacle.[72]

Finally, after still another ill-starred effort at repeal in 1946, the next year the Knox County legislative delegation slipped a personal courtesy bill through the state legislature that permitted Sunday movies in the city. Expectant movie-goers lined up on the first Sunday that moving pictures were shown legally in Knoxville's theaters to see either *It's a Wonderful Life* or *The Best Years of Our Lives*. The forces of modernity had triumphed over the ugliness of provincialism, but the victory was highly questionable, certainly pyrrhic, and left a residue of bitterness as well as class and cultural suspicion for years to come.[73]

The Ugliness of McCarthyism

The University of Tennessee had shown since early in the twentieth century that it had no stomach for any tussle with the state legislature. Fearful of losing recently won annual appropriations (which had begun as recently as 1907), administrators like Harcourt Morgan and James Hoskins threatened, intimidated, and sometimes banished students and faculty who brought unwanted notoriety to the school. As noted above, in 1915 undergraduate Joseph Wood Krutch was threatened with expulsion over an article he had written in the student newspaper that was critical of the state legislature. And in the early 1920s a number of faculty who were considered troublemakers by Morgan and Hoskins had been sacked. Finally the university's board of trustees, potentially a buffer against the legislators, often were political appointees of the governor, who technically was chairman of the board but actually almost never attended board meetings. Thus the university, its highest administrators, and the governing board of trustees all were extremely sensitive to political winds blowing out of Nashville—too sensitive, as it often turned out.

It is possible that the gale force winds of the Second Red Scare were so strong in the United States that no university president, no matter how personally courageous, could have stood up to them. The collapse of the so-called Grand Alliance against Nazi Germany, Italy, and Japan actually had begun prior to the end of the war but was not fully appreciated by the American public until sometime after the end of the war, when it was revealed that several classified documents and nuclear secrets had fallen into the hands of the Soviet Union by way of espionage. In 1947 President Harry Truman established the Federal Loyalty and Security Program for federal government employees, and in that same year the House Committee on Un-American Activities conducted a series of spectacular hearings on the communist infiltration of Hollywood, with such high visibility witnesses as Walt Disney, Ronald Reagan, Jack L. Warner of Warner Brothers Studios, Louis B. Mayer of Metro Goldwyn Mayer, and others. Meanwhile, on the world scene the Berlin Blockade of 1948–49, the triumph of Mao Tse-tung in China, and the 1950 invasion of South Korea gave frightened Americans the feeling that the great sacrifices they had made during World War II were being undermined from within and without. In such an atmosphere of terror and paranoia, a potential demagogue such as Joseph McCarthy could gain power and prominence by riding the growing waves of fear.

Hence the University of Tennessee was extremely vulnerable when a combination of the American Legion, the *Knoxville Journal,* and some political figures anxious to make names for themselves began making charges of communist affiliations or sympathies against some faculty members. At the center of the storm was Samuel Haskell Baron, an instructor in Russian history who had served in the United States Army in World War II (1942–46, discharged as a captain), had arrived at the university in 1948, and was completing his doctoral dissertation at Columbia University. It was charged that Baron had been born in Russia (actually he had been born in New York City), that he taught communist propaganda in his Russian history class (his dissertation was a study of Georgy Plekhanov, one of the fathers of Russian Marxism), and that he was the faculty adviser to a film series that showed films starring Charlie Chaplin (considered at the time a notorious leftist). The *Knoxville Journal*, the American Legion, and one member of the Knox County legislative delegation called for his dismissal. And Dr. Ruth Stephens, a well-known history and political science professor since her arrival at the university in 1926, allegedly broke into Baron's office in Ayres Hall in search of communist material. In the office of a professor of Russian history whose research specialty was nineteenth- and early-twentieth-century Russian Marxism, she could not have been disappointed.[74]

In order to save Baron's career, history department head J. Wesley Hoffmann deflated the witch-hunt by announcing that Baron had completed his doctoral dissertation and therefore was moving on to greener pastures. Yet Hoffmann's diplomatic announcement, humane as it might have been, was patently untrue, since from 1953 (when he left the University of Tennessee) to 1956 (when he finally landed a tenure-track position at Grinnell College), Baron had been a sort of academic gypsy, teaching in one-year, non-tenure-track jobs at Northwestern, Missouri, and Nebraska. Ultimately he wound up at the University of North Carolina as a nationally respected teacher and author.[75]

In the midst of this incident, there is no record of anyone who lifted a finger in Baron's defense. Indeed, Baron was not the only target. Visiting economics professor George Soule (another academician driven out by Tennessee who later earned an international reputation), philosophy professor Howard Lee Parsons, and others also were accused of "communist leanings." Thus, with the faculty cowed into submission, the university could turn to more serious business: dealing with sixteen undergraduate males arrested (for disorderly conduct) in a panty raid. Dean of Students Ralph Emerson Dunford apparently failed to see the irony when, in the midst of Baron's persecution, he called the panty raid "an epidemic in the educational institutions throughout the country."[76]

To be sure, Baron himself ultimately landed on his feet. But others did not, including the university itself. University president C. H. Brehm insisted on interviewing all the applicants for Baron's position. The successful applicant, Lawrence Silverman, recalls that Brehm asked him how he would teach about Marxism, to which Silverman replied that he would teach both its strengths and weaknesses. "That wasn't good enough for Brehm," Silverman recalled. "He only wanted the weaknesses." [77]

More significant, perhaps, is the fact that the Second Red Scare widened the chasm between the university and the community. At a time when the expertise of the university was desperately needed in order to lift Knoxville out of its economic doldrums and when the community itself might have shielded its professor-neighbors from the terrors of McCarthyism, it is a tragedy that town and gown were growing farther apart instead of closer together. After all, they had so much to offer to one another.

The Ugliness of Public Miseducation

If Tennessee's institutions of higher education were vulnerable to the attacks and whims of the citizens and their elected representatives, the state's elementary and secondary schools were even more so. In the postwar years of change and insecurity, an increasing number of people came to fear that the public schools had become too independent of the communities that supported them, were indoctrinating children in strange and unwelcome ideas, and were separating young people from their families and from their traditional culture and morals. Hence while voters usually approved ambitious postwar school building programs, at the same time they combed school curricula, teachers' résumés, and school libraries for evidence of dangerous, un-American, or immoral doctrines and materials.

Knoxville and Knox County had separate school systems, one urban and suburban and the other basically rural but rapidly suburbanizing. During the Second Red Scare, both school systems fell victim to assaults by a variety of groups: red-baiters, religious fundamentalists, politically ambitious factions and individuals, etc.

In such an atmosphere, one would expect that the county schools, not a few of them still country schools (in 1946, 62.5 percent of Knox County's schools did not have indoor plumbing), would be most vulnerable to such incursions. But that was not the case, primarily because of the tough and courageous leadership of their superintendent Mildred Doyle.[78]

Mildred Doyle (1904–1989) was born and lived all her life on the same farm that was granted to her ancestor John Doyle in 1800 for service in the American Revolution. A star student and athlete, she attended nearby Maryville College but took a full-time teaching position (at Anderson School, where she taught grades one through eight) before receiving her degree. For the next twenty years, she worked on her B.S. and M.S. degrees in summer school at the University of Tennessee.

A diehard Republican (she occasionally referred to Democrats as "the rebels"), she was elected to the superintendent's position in 1946 and held it for thirty years, battling with the county court for "her children" (she never married). Many years later Tennessee governor Lamar Alexander quipped that "if Mildred wants it, she usually gets it."

On her way to building a modern school system, Mildred Doyle stood as a shield between "her" children and the school system's attackers. On three or four occasions she battled with creationists, most dramatically when it was demanded that all Tarzan books be removed from the Knox County schools' libraries because those books taught that humans descended from apes. "Whoever says that," she grumbled, "either can't read or hasn't read the books." The books stayed.

The tenure of Mildred Doyle shows that strong and courageous leadership in the postwar period not only would be successful but ultimately would be understood and supported by the people. In the paranoia of the Second Red Scare, the Knox County school system escaped virtually unscathed, unlike the University of Tennessee.

In the end Mildred Doyle gave her life to the Knox County schools but stayed too long. In 1976 she was defeated for a tenth term as superintendent by Democrat Earl Hoffmeister. Ironically, it was Doyle who had hired Hoffmeister when he applied for a teaching job. When Doyle asked him if he had any experience, Hoffmeister replied that during the war he had been a muleskinner with the Tenth Mountain Division in Italy. "You're hired," bellowed Superintendent Doyle. "If you can handle army mules, you can handle students at Central High School." At her death in 1989, Hoffmeister said of Mildred Doyle, "Everyone's goal in education is to leave it better than we found it. . . . [S]he certainly did that."[79]

Knoxville and the Emergence of the Civil Rights Movement

As it had so many times in the past, at the end of the Second World War the American South stood at still another crossroads. Economic and demographic changes during the Depression and World War II had wrought a fundamental revolution in large parts of the former Confederacy. And while many southerners looked to the future with foreboding, many others were filled with a sense of rising expectations.

As has already been shown, Knoxville too was at a crossroads. The decline of its traditional manufacturing base of textiles, apparel, iron, and railroads meant that new industries would have to be created or welcomed if the city was to survive. Out-migration to the outskirts of the county and beyond made the city demographically one of the very young, the old, and the poor. Finally, fear and anxiety about the future was reflected in a certain amount of civic ugliness that found its vents in bare-knuckle political warfare, envy of nearby Oak Ridge, local manifestations of the Second Red Scare, and squabbles in city and county over the control of public education. And yet more than a few Knoxvillians faced the postwar years with a sense of rising expectations, a heightened sense that for people who had survived the Great Depression and triumphed in World War II, the postwar world held out promises and would be better.

Almost surely those Knoxvillians with great expectations included the city's African Americans. After all, the low percentage of African Americans in Knoxville (caused in part, to be sure, by substantial out-migration since the 1919 riot) theoretically meant that whites in the Appalachian city should not have been as threatened by black strides forward as whites were in, for instance, Memphis or Nashville or even Chattanooga. Also, the African American communities in Knoxville (for there were more than one) included a full socioeconomic class structure, with wealthy blacks such as James and Ethel Beck, Artless Wheeler, Dr. James Presnell, and others; intellectuals such as Charles Cansler, Monroe Senter, Dewey Roberts, Walter Nicholson, and faculty at Knoxville College; clergymen such as Revs. William T. Crutcher, R. Waite Stennett, and others; and numerous small business owners—all of whom were capable of providing intelligent, capable, and courageous leadership of fellow African Americans in the postwar years. Finally, the white business elite traditionally had been sympathetic to Knoxville blacks, often had taken under their wings as sort of protégés African American businessmen in similar enterprises, and generally had not opposed black candidates for office.

Thus it was both extremely disappointing and frustrating when blacks' comparatively modest demands were either ignored or rebuffed. Schools, hospitals, restaurants, theaters, and public transportation remained firmly segregated; city-owned Chilhowee Park was closed to African Americans except for one day each year; the municipal golf course did not allow black golfers; the University of Tennessee resisted racial integration until a 1951 lawsuit forced the school to admit African American applicants to its graduate programs and law school, although the undergraduate colleges remained all white until 1961. For those whose postwar expectations were blunted, calls for moderation and gradualism seemed increasingly hollow. Little wonder that less than a decade later Rev. Dr. Martin Luther King Jr. told an overflowing audience at Knoxville College that Knoxville blacks were "too passive for the movement to waste valuable time on such a visit." As it turned out, he was wrong.[80]

One thing that postwar southern cities desperately wanted to avoid, however, was an uncomplimentary image on "the race question." Thus when the prestigious Southern Historical Association, composed mostly of college professors at southern institutions of higher learning, announced that it would hold its fall 1952 convention in Knoxville, there were hopes that the prestige of the organization and the respected stature of its members would cause Knoxville hotels and restaurants to reassess their discriminatory positions, for a few years earlier the Southern Historical Association had agreed to accept African American professors as members, the first being the nationally known and respected scholar-teacher John Hope Franklin. The local arrangements committee (led by University of Tennessee history professor LeRoy Graf) had planned the event meticulously and were confident that all anticipated problems had been overcome.

At the last minute, however, the Farragut Hotel, where the business meeting and banquet were scheduled to be held, announced that blacks could attend the organization's business meeting but would not be served food at the banquet. As one historian (who had not attended) later wrote, "The hotel management was unctuous in its insistence that it was not prejudiced but was only responding to the economic realities reflected by the cultural norms of eastern Tennessee." The angry delegates and the humiliated University of Tennessee faculty then walked out of the Farragut Hotel en masse, boarded a bus and automobiles, and drove to the Whittle Springs Country Club in north Knoxville, which had agreed to serve all the delegates. And perhaps even more embarrassing was the fact that Sophronia Strong Hall's cafeteria on the university campus agreed to host the association's luncheon but made the five African American members (Franklin and four others) sit apart from the other delegates.[81]

The 1952 meeting of the Southern Historical Association was a signal to black and white civil rights advocates that Knoxville, for all its supposed sympathy to African American aspirations, actually was fearful of moving forward into the new era and also, perhaps, afraid of arousing working-class whites who already were suspicious of blacks taking the diminishing number of jobs because, many felt, they accepted lower wages. Black and white leaders urged patience, but for an increasing number of younger African Americans, patience was viewed as a virtue, but an ineffectual one.

In the end, Knoxville could not shake off the memory of John Gunther. He haunted the city. As Americans generally, if not universally, basked in postwar prosperity and feared communism at home as well as abroad, Knoxville remained a city imprisoned in time, unable either to identify or cut loose from its fetters. Worse, suburbanization, core deterioration, lackluster economic growth, and political parochialism presaged even more troubled times ahead. As Knoxvillians in turn attacked or ignored their critics from Gunther to the irate Oak Ridgers, they appeared to lack the energy to do anything else.

3

The Wheels Come Off the Wagon

Knoxville in the 1950s

In 1957 the talk of the University of Tennessee's theater season was an original play by young drama professor Paul Soper. His production, *Once upon a Town,* was an ill-disguised satire on the political life of "one of them prohibition towns in Tennessee," obviously Knoxville. The idealistic city manager, played broadly by Bob Mashburn, continually struggled against an ultraconservative, parochial, and visionless city council, one of whose members proudly asserted, "Some of us is self-made." The university's Carousel Theater was packed for every performance, and the play's brief run had to be extended to accommodate all those who wanted to join in mocking the city's government. Ultimately Soper's hit outdrew *Arsenic and Old Lace, Sabrina Fair,* and *My Three Angels.*[1]

Whether Knoxvillians chose to laugh at their own government, worry over the forces that seemed to paralyze the city, hope that the modest physical improvements that did come were harbingers of better things ahead, or simply ignore the whole question, Knoxville during the 1950s was obviously a city in trouble. Never having participated fully in the nation's postwar economic recovery, Knoxville was now battered by developments over which it seemed to have little control: decline in manufacturing, rapid deterioration of its downtown core, suburbanization, and the impact of the automobile culture. While some attempted to reverse those trends, their attempts were frustrated by a badly fragmented political structure that lacked the will or power to effect profound changes. Hence, although some Knoxvillians crowded into the Carousel Theater to delight in Soper's lampoon, the city's plight clearly was no laughing matter.

American Cities in the 1950s

The Eisenhower administration inherited a national economy going at full tilt, thanks largely to postwar rejuvenation, Cold War spending, and Truman's continuation and extension of many New Deal programs. And although Eisenhower later warned Americans of what he called "the military-industrial complex," military spending remained high, including the advent in 1956 of a massive interstate highway system that was justified on the basis of national defense. Indeed, in an effort to "split the difference between Coolidge and Keynes," Eisenhower hoped to keep the economy healthy while controlling the rate of inflation and turning some fiscal and economic responsibilities back to the private sector. While Eisenhower did keep the annual inflation rate at a low 2.5 percent, the costs of his doing so included increased unemployment (peaking in the spring of 1958 at 7.6 percent) and three brief but sharp recessions, in 1953–54, 1957–58, and 1960–61.[2]

On the surface, however, it seemed the most prosperous and comfortable of decades. If the Cold War or the civil rights struggle occasionally intruded to disturb the general complacence, most Americans, especially those of the enlarged postwar middle class, were salved and comforted by their new material possessions and higher standard of living. Indeed, by 1960 the nation's per-capita income was 35 percent above that of 1945, and affluence appeared to be so widespread that some believed that the United States was moving rapidly toward the eradication of want and the creation of a truly classless society. To be sure, pockets of poverty still existed among, for example, inner-city African Americans, rural Appalachian whites, migrant workers, etc., but many exulted that a partnership between the federal government and the private sector would soon put an end to need there as well. For most Americans, the 1950s were wonderful if insecure times.[3]

Three interrelated trends highlighted the 1950s: suburbanization, the rise in installment buying, and the increasingly pervasive influence of television. Suburbs boomed as the new middle class sought to escape from the cities to the newer, cleaner, more homogeneous, and safer urban fringes. Aided by the automobile (which made suburbs possible) and by installment buying (which made those suburbs appear more affluent than they were), the new suburban communities acted as magnets, pulling a willing people toward a new style of life. For its part, television lionized suburban living with programs featuring model homes, model parents, model children, and model possessions. From *Father Knows Best* to *Leave It to Beaver,* television extolled the virtues of suburbia, where automobiles were large and problems were small. As suburbanites turned to television for enjoyment, recreation, and babysitting services, they recognized themselves and saw that all was well. If John Cameron Swayze, Douglas Edwards, or Howard K. Smith briefly disturbed their reveries, they had only to wait a few moments to be comforted once again.

Clearly, then, suburbanization was more than simply a mass migration into newer homes on the urban fringe. In fact, it was nothing less than a new attitude and way of life. The fearfulness of the Great Depression had disappeared entirely, and between 1946 and 1958 short-term consumer credit climbed from $8.4 billion to almost $45 billion. To profit from this new, credit-based affluence, retail merchants followed the mass migration into increasingly ostentatious shopping centers rapidly being thrown up in the suburbs. Some churches, too, followed their parishioners, as did YMCAs, YWCAs, Boy Scouts, and Girl Scouts. Suburbanites found fewer and fewer reasons to return to the core cities from which many of them had come. Sapped of population, energy, and tax revenue, American cities in the 1950s became troubled pockets of people, exceptions to what John Kenneth Galbraith in 1958 referred to in the title of his book *The Affluent Society.*[4]

Economic and Demographic Dislocations

Troubles, of course, were nothing new to Knoxville. From 1900 on, the city had defined its central work function as manufacturing, and, as it had in Birmingham, Alabama, and Richmond, Virginia, manufacturing had assumed increasing importance for Knoxville throughout the twentieth century. But the Great Depression and the city's failure to participate in the general postwar boom had left Knoxville in a precarious economic position, ill prepared to face the changes to come in the 1950s.

As noted earlier, Knoxville's textile industry never really recovered from the Great Depression, in spite of the enormous boost from government spending during the Second World War. And by the 1950s that part of the city's manufacturing base was almost in free fall, losing nearly 3,000 jobs (34.9 percent of the total textile workers) between 1948 and 1960. In 1954, in the midst of what Mayor George Dempster called a "general slump," the Cherokee Textile Mills and Venus Hosiery Mills announced that they were leaving Knoxville. At the same time, the city tax commission, fearful that Brookside Mills, one of the big textile employers, also might leave the city, slashed the mill's personalty assessment by over $250,000 and reduced its realty assessment by over $100,000. Yet Brookside Mills was doomed, a victim of outdated machinery, the high costs of modernization, and increased competition. Trying desperately to save itself, in 1954 Brookside announced a 5 percent wage cut, then whittled the number of employees from 1,050 to 150. All to no avail. Brookside soon was forced to close, as was Appalachian Mills, which had been operating in Knoxville for forty-five years.[5]

And textile manufacturing was not the only industry in trouble. The construction and lumber industries, after wartime expansions, both suffered, the latter losing approximately eight hundred jobs (57.1 percent) in the 1950s. Moreover, newer industries that might have been expected to take up the slack simply were unable to do so. ALCOA, for instance, had been a major employer in the region since its founding in 1928, having reached a peacetime peak in 1940 of 9,300 employees. But by 1954 that number had dropped to 7,800 and by 1960 to 5,800, a disastrous decline of 3,500 jobs (37.6 percent of the 1940 workforce). The end of the Korean War, increasingly aggressive competition from Reynolds and Kaiser, and (as the company explained) the "stretching out of the defense program" had left ALCOA with huge aluminum stockpiles and declining orders. This bulwark of the area economy survived only by slashing its workforce.[6]

Some sectors of the area economy did grow, notably the apparel industry (up 41.4 percent), the chemical industry at Oak Ridge (Atomic Energy Commission), the University of Tennessee (providing more than 1,200 jobs between 1948 and 1960), and the increasingly robust service sector. As for the apparel industry, to be sure it did grow, expanding existing facilities and adding some new factories. But most of these new jobs went to females who worked for low wages, wages often rationalized by the assertion that these women were the "second breadwinners" in their families. Given the bleak employment picture, however, it is reasonable to assume that many were not.[7]

The sickness of Knoxville's traditional industries was reflected in the city's unemployment figures. Consistently above the national average, the percentage of Knoxvillians who were unemployed rose from 5.8 percent in 1951 to a disturbing 9.7 percent in 1958 (anything over 6 percent is considered "structural unemployment"). Moreover, these percentages reflect only those unemployed persons who remained in the city. As we shall see, many did not, choosing to abandon the city in search of opportunities elsewhere. Had these men and women been included, Knoxville's unemployment statistics would have been truly staggering. Moreover, few of Knoxville's unemployed were qualified for the jobs that were available at the university, in Oak Ridge, or with TVA (which itself lost four hundred jobs between 1948 and 1960). In a characteristic understatement of the situation, one report blandly noted, "It is believed that a very high proportion of the unemployed do not have skills which are usable in today's market."[8]

With unemployment high and with many of the new jobs (in the apparel industry, for example) paying low wages, it is not surprising that real per capita income failed to grow significantly. Between 1950 and 1960 the real per capita income of the metropolitan area (comprising the counties of Knox, Anderson, and Blount) grew an anemic 16.7 percent (from $1,381 to $1,612)—4.7 percent behind Chattanooga, 5.8 percent behind Nashville, 3.8 percent behind Tennessee, and 5.7 percent behind the Southeast. Worse, the metro Knoxville figures are misleading, badly skewed by Anderson County's (Oak Ridge's) increase of 64.4 percent. Indeed, Knox County alone had a real per capita income increase of but 9.1 percent, not even enough to match the modest national inflation rate of the 1950s. Moreover, it can be supposed that Knoxville city's per capita increase (figures are not available) was even more meager, for the city contained the highest proportion of people earning under $3,000 of all metropolitan areas in Tennessee.[9]

The closings of the Brookside Mills and Appalachian Mills in 1956–57 shocked many Knoxvillians and threw the city council into a characteristic panic. To many both on and off the council, the solution seemed to be to attract new industries to offset declines in textiles and other areas. But that was easier said than done. Noting that Knoxville had been successful in attracting some small firms but had let the large ones slip through its fingers, Roy H. Bass Jr., in his freshman term on city council, proposed the establishment of an industrial commission to promote Knoxville to industries that were in the process of relocating and were looking for new sites.

Local AFL-CIO head Paul Christopher enthusiastically supported Bass's proposal, calling it "one of the best things I have seen yet." At the same time, however, Christopher warned that some interests in Knoxville would be less than enthusiastic about attracting new industries. "The reputation that has been established here," Christopher said, "is enough to disinterest any industry that might be thinking of moving here." In fact, he argued, many in Knoxville paid only the barest lip service to luring new industries that paid higher wages, "only being interested in [the] sweatshop needle trades industry that pays one dollar an hour." The actual shifts in "old line" industrial employment would seem to support Christopher's argument, since the apparel industry (the "needle trades") was the only "old line" manufacturing sector to grow in Knoxville's economy in the 1950s (by 41.4 percent).

Bass's proposal to set up an independent "industrial commission" and Christopher's support of it shows the extent to which an increasing number of people had come to believe that the Chamber of Commerce had been ineffective in attracting new industries and jobs—and might even have acted to keep new firms out. The *News-Sentinel,* however, attacked Bass's idea, asserting that the Chamber of Commerce's Committee of 100 was already trying to attract new industries, was not being subverted by the business community, and should not be "interfered with" by a proposed industrial commission backed by the city council. We are vigorously opposed," the *News-Sentinel* stated loftily, "to any deal between the city and a new industry whereby the latter receives special favors. . . . We don't think such deals are fair to already-established businesses." The extent to which the newspaper unwittingly proved Christopher's charges is a moot point. Bass's proposal ultimately was shelved.[10]

To be sure, Knoxville was not the only American city that experienced postwar economic dislocations and hard times. Unlike Knoxville, however, many of those cities had been extremely aggressive in courting new industries in hopes of altering their economic bases. Not a few cities were even directly subsidizing new industries by offering assistance in site selection, free sites, and alluring tax breaks similar to the one offered to Brookside Mills. And some cities had gone so far as to establish industrial parks with utilities, parking space, good transportation access, and pleasant atmospheres. By 1960 Birmingham had six such parks, Atlanta nine, Louisville eleven, Charlotte ten, Dallas twenty-one, and Memphis eight. Knoxville had one very small park, which was described by one report as "totally insufficient."[11]

Indeed, Paul Christopher may have been more correct than he knew. In 1960, a major industry approached Knoxville and inquired about building a large facility in the city. Predictably, site selection was a major stumbling block, and the company had been offered beneficial site arrangements elsewhere. For his part, Knoxville mayor John Duncan was anxious to lure the firm into relocating in the city. Ignoring warnings, he proposed a referendum on issuing municipal bonds that would provide funds to acquire and prepare a site for the new industry. "It may not be 100 percent right to subsidize industry," explained Duncan, a conservative Republican, "but it is 100 percent wrong to see men out of work and do nothing about it." Confident he had support from Knoxville's business elite, Duncan pushed ahead.[12]

One can hardly imagine the mayor's surprise and dismay when the Chamber of Commerce, unwilling to create "a state of affairs in which they paid taxes to subsidize a competitor for the local labor force," refused to support Duncan's proposal, as did a majority of the city's business leaders. "A man sat in that very chair," related Duncan, "and said it was good to have an unemploy-

John Duncan campaigning for mayor.
McClung Historical Collection. Knoxville–Knox County Public Library.

ment rate of 6 or 7 percent because it made people work harder." In one of the lowest voter turnouts on record (15 percent), the referendum passed, but by an insufficient majority to enact it. Interestingly, the poorer wards of the city strongly supported the bond issue, while the affluent wards opposed it.[13]

By 1961 the failure to attract new industries and the concomitant disastrous decline in jobs could no longer be ignored. Between 1956 and 1961, thirty-five separate firms had expressed interest in locating in Knoxville. Over 75 percent of those enterprises were "new line" industries (electronics, chemicals, fabricated metals), especially prized because they were clean and paid high wages. The new industrial prospects planned to employ a total of 10,300 people. Yet ultimately none of those firms chose Knoxville, preferring instead to locate their plants either in other cities or in nonurban areas along the Great Valley of East Tennessee.[14]

Over 10,000 jobs that never arrived? In desperation and near panic, the city council hired the consulting firm Hammer and Associates to find out why so many opportunities had slipped through the city's hopeful fingers. The 1962 report, however, should have surprised no one: of those firms that had rejected Knoxville between 1956 and 1961, 62 percent cited as their main reason "cost, availability, or other features of industrial sites. . . . [At] present there is an acute shortage of desirable sites for new manufacturing and related types of industry." And although some of these companies added other reasons for not locating in Knoxville, Hammer and Associates concluded that "industrial land appears to have been the main obstacle to the location of these industries in metropolitan Knoxville." And while the Washington consulting firm argued forcefully for a "major program of site acquisition and development" in order to prevent Knoxville's economic problems from becoming more "acute" in the future, at the same time Hammer and Associates feared that any such plans might be "too little too late."[15]

Some firms that decided not to locate in Knoxville also cited the lack of easy highway access as a reason for not coming. As noted earlier, Knoxville had come of age as a railroad city and had become dependent on those iron arteries to stimulate and support both commerce and industry. The precipitous decline of America's railroads after the Second World War, therefore, left a number of cities, including Knoxville, searching desperately for transportation facilities to replace the declining railroads.

For some cities, that salvation turned out to be interstate highways that after 1956 gradually formed a transportation network that could reach places where even the railroads had not gone. And on those interstate highways a new industry was born, that of long-distance trucking. Hence those cities that were able to secure access to interstate highways had a good chance of surviving and prospering.

But as a Republican enclave in a state usually dominated by Democrats, East Tennessee in general and Knoxville in particular were slow to get interstate linkages. Somewhat later, a delegation of Knoxville business leaders traveled to Nashville to plead with Democratic governor Frank G. Clement for interstate highways. "When you people learn to vote right," Clement drawled, "you'll get your roads." And not until a terrible bus-automobile accident on Highway 11W, two Republican governors, and a world's fair did Knoxville finally complete its interstate highway connections—in 1984.[16]

Knoxville's severe economic troubles of the 1950s had a nearly disastrous effect on its population. Between 1950 and 1960, the city's population actually declined, from 124,183 to 111, 800 (-9.97 percent). And if natural increase is taken into account, Knoxville's out-migration might be estimated at around 30,000. The Tennessee State Planning Commission reported that 12.2 percent of *all* the state's out-migrants came from Knoxville, and the city had the dubious distinction of being the only metropolitan area in Tennessee that lost population to all the other state metropolitan areas. But over half of Knoxville's out-migrants forsook the state entirely, emigrating to Florida, Ohio, Georgia, California, Virginia, Alabama, and North Carolina, where job opportunities were rumored to be more abundant. Akron, Ohio, might joke that it was "The Capital of West Virginia," but doubtless the tire manufacturing center became home to more than a few Knoxvillians as well. As the Hammer Report dolorously noted, "There are few metropolitan areas in the United States for which a sharper decline in population . . . has been recorded."[17]

Even more disturbing was *who* was leaving. A significant proportion of those who left Knoxville were men and women between the ages of twenty-five and forty-four, the so-called productive group that is more fully employed, upwardly mobile, consumer-oriented (purchasing homes, automobiles, furniture, clothing), and pays a comparatively high proportion of a city's taxes. Between 1950 and 1960 Knoxville lost roughly 12,000 people from that group, as its share of the city's total population dropped from 31.6 percent in 1950 to 24.4 percent in 1960. "The simple reason for this shift," observed Hammer and Associates, "was a sharp drop in the number of employment opportunities within metropolitan Knoxville during the 1950–1960 period." Indeed, throughout the 1950s unemployment in Knoxville consistently exceeded that of Chattanooga and Nashville, and far exceeded that of Chicago, Illinois, and Washington, D.C.[18]

But if the weak job market was primarily responsible for this substantial out-migration, then how many jobs would have to be added to the local economy in order to stanch the flow? This is precisely the question that some members of the civic-commercial elite began to ask themselves toward the end of the decade. The 1962 Hammer Report estimated that in order to keep Knoxville's population on a par with that of 1950, approximately 24,000 new jobs would have had to have been created. Since the city was able to add only 12,000 new jobs during the decade, one can see how critical were the roughly 10,000 jobs that did *not* come because those thirty-five firms that had investigated Knoxville as a possible relocation site ultimately went elsewhere.[19]

Hence Knoxville's people were being propelled from their homes by dual forces—the American dream of economic success and upward mobility and the American nightmare of economic failure in the face of unemployment and lost job opportunities. But whatever reasons people had for migrating out of the city proper, they left behind a population more static and disproportionately old, black, poor, unskilled, poorly housed, and badly in need of municipal, state, and federal services. Between 1950 and 1960 Knoxville's "dependent" population (those under eighteen and over sixty-five) represented an astounding 80 percent of the city's population gain, as opposed to 30 percent during the previous decade. Indeed, the city had 2,400 more people over sixty-five in

1960 (9.5 percent of Knoxville's population) than it had had a decade before. Such demographic shifts, notes urbanist Howard Chudacoff, in most cities give rise to other problems: "poverty, crime, pollution, unemployment—faced with decaying physical plants and shrinking revenue bases." Had he added "increasingly shaky retail trade," Chudacoff would have been describing Knoxville itself.[20]

Knoxville's "Crabgrass Frontier"

At the same time that the city proper was losing jobs and people, Knoxville was beginning to feel the national trend toward suburbanization, a trend that further separated Knoxvillians by class and race. Although suburbanization would not become massive until the 1960s, in the 1950s the bedroom communities just outside the city's 1917 limits grew faster than any component in the entire metropolitan area. They gained approximately 37,500 persons between 1950 and 1960, an astonishing increase of 160.3 percent. By 1960 Knoxville had 111,800 people, while the county outside the city had 138,700, mostly concentrated on the city's fringe.[21]

During the 1950s suburban growth was generally symmetrical, and developments blossomed on all sides of the city's fringe. Along Chapman Highway suburban development produced a 32-percent population increase; to the east, Burlington grew by 47 percent; along Kingston Pike to the west (the scene of the most massive suburbanization in the 1960s and 1970s) developments off Sutherland Avenue and along Kingston Pike experienced a 38 percent population increase. In the suburban development of West Hills, developers Morgan Schubert and Dean Cate had begun buying up land in the 1940s, which in the 1950s they resold to builders and prospective homeowners. By 1960 what had just a few years before been forest, crop, and pasture land held a population of around 2,500 people—most of them young, almost all of them middle class, and 2,493 of them white. And to the north, Fountain City's growth was even more impressive. A small community since the late eighteenth century, Fountain City had become something of a vacation spot for Knoxvillians and ultimately the site of impressive residential dwellings. Now people rushed to fill in the available land, and the population of the once-peaceful community soared from 5,000 in 1930 to roughly 20,000 by 1960. Planners expected Fountain City ultimately to grow to about 35,000 people.[22]

As in other cities, suburbanization in Knoxville was spurred by the city's deteriorating neighborhoods and housing stock, upward mobility, the triumph of the automobile, the increasing ease of obtaining long-term mortgages and consumer credit, and the growth in capacity of public utilities. In metropolitan Knoxville, automobile registrations increased from about 64,100 in 1948 to 74,800 in 1950 and an astounding 107,600 by 1954, statistics that kept pace with national averages. Simultaneously, by the late 1940s Veterans Administration loans and FHA mortgage insurance virtually eliminated high down payments, allowing even blue-collar workers to secure their piece of a suburban Eden. And when a Tennessee statute prohibiting the establishment of utility districts was repealed in 1956, six new districts were formed almost immediately on the city's fringes. The new suburbanites resorted to wells and septic tanks, severely taxed county law enforcement capabilities and the Knoxville Utilities Board for electricity, and relied on private companies for garbage collection and even for fire protection (supplied by a remarkably good subscription fire and ambulance company).[23]

Indeed, developers sold lots and built houses so rapidly that they far outran the ability of the city and county to plan, oversee, inspect, and regulate the new subdivisions. Streets were laid out and paved, but no curbs, sidewalks, gutters, or storm sewers existed in most of the new settlements. Many prospective homeowners were told that city water and a public sewer system would soon be available. So constructing gutters, sidewalks, etc., people were told, would be wasteful, since they would have to be removed for water and sewer connections. The cost of providing sewers alone was estimated to be in excess of $40 million. Almost no one wanted to wait, and developers and builders were only too happy to oblige. In truth, suburbanization and the suburban lifestyle was an irresistible trend that set off one of the most significant mass migrations in American history. By 1970 more Americans were living in suburbs outside of city limits than in those cities themselves, a condition that Knoxville barely sidestepped by its massive 1962 annexations of Bearden, West Hills, Norwood, Gresham, and Fountain City.[24]

To be sure, Knoxville embraced annexation only as a desperate last resort, a decision essentially made to shore up the city's eroding tax base. Nor were all of the neighborhoods scheduled for annexation happy. Fountain City residents had never felt much of a kinship with Knoxville (some still don't), and fought annexation. In 1960 a number of Fountain Citians had filed a lawsuit (later dropped) to block Knoxville's annexation efforts. They feared that Knoxville would not provide crucial urban services (including some four hundred miles of necessary water lines) but was only grasping for their tax dollars. But since 1959 the state legislature had permitted Tennessee cities to annex contiguous areas by city council action without holding a referendum. When the area ultimately was annexed in 1962, Fountain Citians held a parade and mock funeral service for their community, and one local businessman presented Knoxville mayor John Duncan with a sword of surrender.[25]

Illustrative of the new suburban way of life was Knoxville's 1954 Parade of Homes, which featured the new West Hills subdivision, mentioned earlier. That year the parade was graced by the presence of the 1954 Mrs. America, Wanda Jennings, a "prize-winning pumpkin pie baker" who dodged sunlight "because it makes me freckle." Mrs. America chortled that her husband would "be aghast when I tell him what I want after seeing your parade of homes." Her preferences were for a "pushbutton music system," floor-length windows, and a patio "shaded over in light green plastic"—the latter presumably to keep nature at a tasteful distance and preserve skin tone. The early 1950s envisioned a suburban Eden where the serpent of moral relativism had not yet intruded. Mrs. America not only knew what the happy home should look like, but how to preserve it: "Treat your family like honored guests and take your domestic problems to your family pastor."

The 1956 Parade of Homes in Fountain City's Sherwood Forest subdivision stressed the escape from urban life by advertising "a new way of living" rather than merely a house. With the verbal overkill so characteristic of mass marketing, the advertisement emphasized the three living areas of the house: family room, screened porch, and terrace for relaxation; living room for entertaining; and "playroom space in the basement for fun!" In Westhaven Village, young suburbanites were attracted to "ultramodern three bedroom, 1 1/2 baths, family room, living room, terrace" at 1,196 square feet for $700 down on the GI Bill, $89.70 per month. Obviously, the new way of life had the old in complete rout, and memories of the Great Depression dimmed in the easy-credit, television-oriented, materialistic culture of the suburbs. For the *News-Sentinel,* one word was enough to describe the lure of suburbanization: "ROMANCE." Noting the market for suburban homes, the *News-Sentinel* predicted that the "economic outlook for 1970" would be "many two-house families" with houses in the $14,000 to $30,000 range.[26]

As affluence moved to the suburbs, retail establishments, eager to capitalize on the young homeowners market, followed. In fact, they pursued this market to such a degree that placement of shopping centers in the 1950s exceeded the need. By 1960 there were ten "significant" suburban retailing operations in Knoxville with an annual sales potential of nearly $15 million each, ranging from small (23,000 square feet) to large (114,000 square feet). These were heavily concentrated to the north and west, and all had been built in the 1950s. The suburbs' massive orientation to the automobile made parking space a singular feature of the new shopping centers. The Fountain City Shopping Center on North Broadway boasted "off-street parking for 200," while Broadway Shopping Center, advertising its location ("2 1/2 miles from Knoxville, near Fountain City") and its potential market ("32,000 people reside within a one-mile radius") drawing upon Park City, Oakwood, and Lincoln Park suburbs, offered parking for 750 cars. Announcement of a shopping center near Merchants Road, to be anchored by a Winn-Dixie food store and S. S. Kresge, projected parking spaces for 1,500 cars. And nearby Norwood Shopping Center, located in the midst of a suburb created out of nursery land after World War II, boasted 2,000 parking spaces. As churches, schools, and social organizations for parents and children were founded along with these retail shopping centers, suburbanites found fewer and fewer reasons to go to downtown Knoxville at all.[27]

The City Fights Back

What greeted those suburbanites who did venture downtown was a deteriorating city with poor automobile access, limited parking, smoke and coal ash, and growing slums. Designed and developed before the impact of the automobile made itself felt, Knoxville seemed to be a city frozen in time, out of touch with the rapidly changing world. True, the coming of TVA and electric power, the conversion of coal-fired locomotives to diesel, and the removal of the Coster roundhouse to the John Sevier yards had improved the look of the city. But it was still dirty. The *News-Sentinel* exulted in 1950 that the 1949 sootfall had fallen to a record low of 143.3 tons of dust and soot per square mile, down significantly from the 1930 record high of 348.6 tons. In terms of breathing, however, it was still one of the most unhealthy cities in the country.[28]

And when compared with the new suburbs and their recently opened shopping centers, much of downtown Knoxville was unsightly, if for no other reason than its age. Vine and Jackson, Buffalo Alley, Willow Avenue, the riverfront, First Creek Valley, Morningside Heights, McAnnaly Flats, old Holston Hill, Mechanicsville, Brookside Village, to name but some neighborhoods, were remnants of an older, industrial Knoxville. In 1954 a program called Operation Facelift attempted slum improvement in a pilot block bounded by West Fifth Avenue, University Avenue, and Arthur, Douglas, and Calloway streets (Mechanicsville). The project chairman, Cliff Greenwood, stated the need for such programs in the city: "The lack of a workable program of blight prevention has resulted in 85 percent of the in-city area being blacklisted for FHA loans for new construction." Yet the pilot project was extremely modest and did not seem to encourage others to follow. To many suburbanites, Knoxville was simply unattractive.[29]

Those courageous suburbanites who tried to go downtown found the streets choked with traffic and the limited parking lots jammed to overflowing. Between 1948 and 1955, there was a 32 percent increase in the volume of traffic, while at the same time the number of passengers riding the Knoxville Transit Lines buses declined 36 percent. On the eight major arteries into the city, the peak-hour load rose to 14,000 vehicles in 1955, yet the capacity of those access routes was only 9,900 vehicles. To better understand the problem, the city commissioned six separate traffic and street plan studies between 1945 and 1959, as if successive surveys might themselves solve the problem. But each study reached basically the same conclusion. As one (1955) put it: "Knoxville and other cities face a Hobson's choice when they concentrate on moving vehicles instead of people. . . . Knoxville has come to a crossroad. It has reached a point where its major downtown traffic gateways are operated at above capacity. Its major arterial system is several years (maybe more) from completion. In the meantime mounting downtown congestion can accelerate decentralization of downtown businesses." Clogged access roads and other traffic problems discouraged the comparatively affluent suburbanites from coming downtown except to work. Small wonder that the *News-Sentinel*, urging repair of Western Avenue, the main artery into Knoxville from Oak Ridge, complained that the "condition of Western Avenue is so bad it discourages Oak Ridgers with the highest buying income in the state ($7,000 per year) from coming to Knoxville."[30]

Once the intrepid suburbanites finally reached downtown, they were dismayed to find almost no parking facilities. When the grossly insufficient number of legal parking spaces was filled, drivers blithely parked their automobiles wherever they chose. In anger and frustration, the *News-Sentinel* noted that "curb parking in no parking zones is one of the worst business deterrents in the downtown section, and is also a major cause of traffic jams." But when city safety director David Garrison, in a one-week "experiment," tried to enforce parking regulations in the downtown core strictly, businessmen were irate, complaining loudly that the overzealous Garrison was driving away shoppers. Watching another of its efforts fail, the *News-Sentinel* lamented weakly that "indiscriminate curbside parking in the retail shopping area ought to be ended; Knoxville is no crossroads village."[31]

Besides traffic flow and parking, there was another problem in the downtown core that disoriented shoppers. Recent students of shopping mall developments and downtown rejuvenation projects have come to believe that, in order to derive maximum benefits from pedestrian traffic in retail trade areas, those areas must be "anchored" by a number of very large and popular establishments such as Sears, J. C. Penney, and the like. These students see these "anchors" as both luring shoppers into these areas and, equally important, keeping them moving from one anchor to another, past smaller retail establishments in-between. These anchors, then, theoretically act to keep shoppers inside the designated trade areas; once shoppers pass beyond these anchors, they will rarely reenter the core areas to make purchases. For these reasons, shopping-center developers are extremely anxious to attract such anchoring establishments to their projects. Without these anchors, such projects are, at best, risky undertakings.

In 1950 Knoxville's downtown core was anchored by the S. H. George Department Store on the northeastern corner of Gay and Wall, and Miller's Department Store one block to the north, on the corner of Gay and Union. Across South Gay Street in this block were mainstays of downtown businesses, among them Spence's, Kimball's, Woodruff's, J. S. Hall's, and the Paul Dean Department Store. Between the two anchors on South Gay were the Strand Theater, Lerner's, Baker's, S. H. Kress, and McClellan's five-and-dime store. Behind South Gay between Wall and Union were shops fronting on Market Square and the Market House. As can be seen, the core area was very close-knit and was oriented to South Gay Street.[32]

Poor access to the core and congestion within its streets prompted some retailers to take matters into their own hands. In doing so, however, they unwittingly violated the anchor theory, with unfortunate results. In 1952 Rich's of Atlanta purchased S. H. George's, and in 1954 Rich's announced its plans to build a new store on a different site. This site, "within walking distance of the very center of the city and yet far enough away to be out of the terrible congestion of Gay Street," was on the Henley, Clinch, Locust, and Church block. Planned to incorporate a "quick service" parking garage with space for 1,500 cars, the new building replaced some familiar landmarks—the lighthouse service station on Clinch and Locust, the "whitebrick" doctors' offices on Church, and the Kincaid Apartments.[33]

The relocation of one of the principal anchors of the central business district (CBD) was disorienting: "This location had a disastrous effect on the established shopping patterns of the CBD by creating a strong attraction three blocks west and three blocks south. Land values dropped in the north end of the CBD. Specialty shops had a difficult time surviving as they searched for suitable locations without clearly defined shopper traffic." To refocus the CBD, the other anchor, Miller's, purchased the old Colonial Hotel block, which was bounded by Gay, State, Cumberland, and Main, and extended north from the Lyric Theater and Louis' Steak House. That move never took place, because Rich's soon left Knoxville. Then Miller's moved to the Rich's building on the Henley Street block, thus ultimately removing two "anchors" from the center of the city.[34]

Indeed, the problems of suburbanization, automobility, and the deterioration of the downtown, both physically and as a retail shopping core, seemed

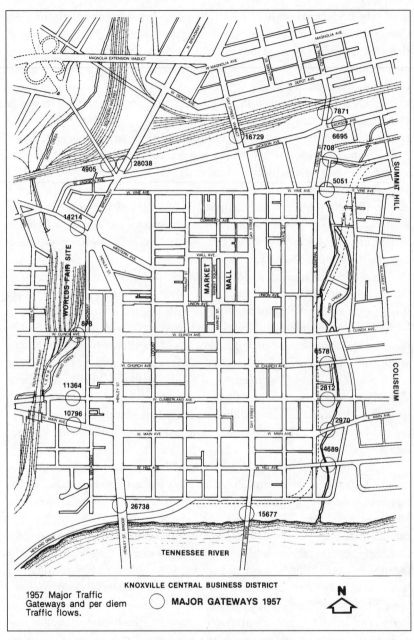

KNOXVILLE CENTRAL BUSINESS DISTRICT

1957 Major Traffic
Gateways and per diem
Traffic flows.

MAJOR GATEWAYS 1957

N

Major Traffic Gateways, 1957.

almost insurmountable. Were all that not enough, the Interstate Highway Act (1956) threatened to accelerate suburbanization and place those more affluent residential developments farther and farther from the downtown core. Downtown retailers were plainly worried; if they had not been able even to firmly situate their anchors and preserve their own core, how could they hope to prevent wholesale desertion by retailers following their more well-to-do customers into the new suburbs? Up to the mid-1950s, one study showed, Knoxville's suburbanization had been fairly symmetrical, moving out in an almost even radius from the downtown core. This fact gave many downtown merchants hope. However, interstate highway construction obviously would destroy that symmetry. Clearly, the time had come to act or die.[35]

But even in this critical time Knoxville's business and political leaders could not agree on how to deal with the desperate plight of downtown. After several unsuccessful attempts, George Dempster finally became mayor in 1952, and yet he seems not only to have had no solution for Knoxville's ills but actually discouraged others who *did* have some ideas. In 1952 Dempster was quoted in a national magazine as saying that he didn't "think anything can be done to improve cluttered Gay Street." At the same time, he opposed improved access roads to downtown ("It's a Cadillac for a Ford town"). Smarting over the voters' near-revolt when he recommended a modest tax increase, the mayor appeared to be out of options.[36]

Without strong, decisive leadership, Knoxville's business and political leaders seemed like frightened hens running in every direction. For those who believed that inadequate parking was downtown Knoxville's central problem, city engineer Robert Stuart gave them additional ammunition when in 1954 he called that dilemma "pressing and complex." And yet no one seemed to be able to think of a remedy. Mayor Dempster's scheme, to build a parking lot on top of the Market House, was so bizarre that no one took him seriously. A clause in the original 1853 deed of Mabry and Swan that forbade multiple uses for the building put an end to that outrageous idea, as did the total destruction of the Market House by fire in 1960, started accidentally by a ten-year-old boy and an illicit cigarette. Those who urged prospective shoppers to avoid automobile congestion by riding the Knoxville Transit Lines buses must have ignored the fact that bus transportation had been declining since the 1940s.[37]

Others saw poor access to the downtown core as the central issue. Dempster's successor as mayor, Jack Dance, pushed for the long-overdue formation of a Metropolitan Planning Commission (MPC) in April 1956 and the construction of what came to be called the "downtown loop." The plan, conceived by the first MPC director, Joe Whitlow, called for "a four or six lane limited access highway from Kingston Pike along the Neyland Drive lakefront

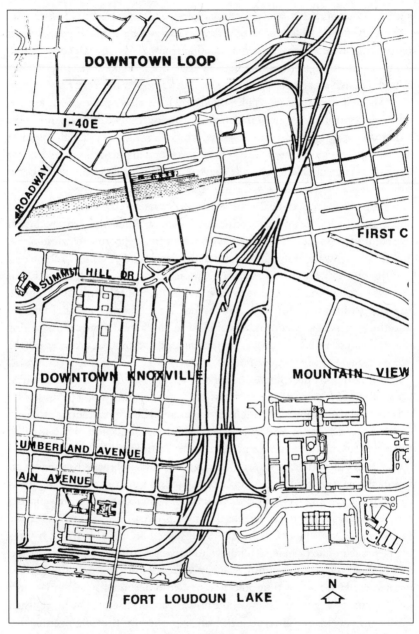

Downtown Loop.

route, up First Creek Valley, connecting with the east Knoxville interregional expressway." The goal was to improve access from West Knoxville by circumventing the congested Cumberland-Main area and linking up with the proposed interstate highway and to improve access from the east and northeast by overcoming the topographical barrier of First Creek Valley. Dempster's opposition could slow the project, but it could not stop it. Active in Knoxville politics since the 1920s, George Dempster had become a politician without a following—certain death for a political leader. He retired grumpily and died in 1964—a businessman turned populist politician who let the times catch up and pass him. The planning of the "downtown loop" was completed by 1957, although the east leg was not finished until the late 1960s and the remainder of the route not until the mid-1970s. Even so, a step toward improving access had been taken and a great incentive provided for urban renewal along the new loop and for later location of the coliseum-auditorium across First Creek Valley.[38]

Mayor Jack Dance did not live to see his dream realized. Had he done so, he might well have been frustrated by the slow pace at which his plans bore fruit. When Dance died unexpectedly in office, his term was filled by the caretaker administration of obstructionist Vice Mayor Cas Walker. Commenting on the Dance administration's urban renewal program in an editorial on May 6, 1959, the *Journal* was of the opinion that his efforts were "in line with efforts to combat suburbia" and cited "experts" who predicted that people would drift back from the suburbs "sadder but wiser," disillusioned by sewerage and garbage disposal problems and by "chauffeuring children back and forth." Indeed, the "experts" were not wrong, just several decades premature.[39]

The central question was whether downtown Knoxville would deteriorate and collapse completely before Dance's plans could take effect. Suburbanization was increasing at such a rapid rate that county mail carriers were swamped, necessitating the extension of city mail delivery beyond the city limits into the suburbs. Some downtown core retailers looked as if they were preparing to bolt for greener pastures, and others—Rich's in particular—seemed to be sinking. The anchors appeared to be drifting away, threatening to leave the downtown core anchorless and abandoned by both retailers and customers.

In an effort to unite downtown businesses that had never been able to work together, in 1956 desperate business leaders established the Downtown Knoxville Association (DKA). The DKA eventually was able to point to some successes in reinvigorating the downtown, but the problems of urban core erosion demanded bold planning, ambitious projects, and significant infusions of money—all of which were beyond the imagination and resources of the city's businessmen. With future profits precarious at best, and warily watching one

another for the first signs of desertion to the suburbs, merchants understandably were unwilling to gamble everything on the slim prospect of rapid downtown rejuvenation. Another serious defect in the DKA's ability to effect a greater
transformation was the plethora of proposals, including the imitation of the
suburbs by the creation of a downtown "super shopping center," numerous
plans to reanchor downtown in the vicinity of the new Rich's store on Henley
Street, and even the creation of "moving sidewalks and pedestrian malls."[40]

Thus most downtown businessmen realized that "something" had to be
done to revive the downtown area before it had deteriorated past the point of
salvation. But precisely what that "something" should be was hard to deter-
mine, and it was difficult for the businessmen to marshal a consensus. Having
been presented a myriad of plans and suggestions but without either unity or
necessary financial support, Knoxville's downtown businessmen opted to
undertake comparatively modest cosmetic projects while at the same time dis-
guising their lack of agreement and funds with an avalanche of press releases.

The first project undertaken by the DKA in what it called a "bold new pattern of progress" was a downtown promenade and parking plaza. Borrowing
ideas and language from suburban competitors, the Downtown Promenade
was billed as "the shopping center for East Tennessee." A privately financed
undertaking, the Promenade was an effort to refurbish the rears of the stores
on the east side of Gay Street between Union and Wall, an area one brochure
described as "old warehouses and unsightly alleys full of fire escapes and
garbage cans." One hundred and thirty-three merchants were involved in this
project, which was completed in March 1960 at a cost of $550 per linear foot,
excluding remodeling. The rundown buildings behind the Gay Street stores were
demolished and replaced with parking lots. These in turn were connected by an
escalator (oddly called a "moving sidewalk ramp") to a new promenade along the
rears of the stores, which became new store fronts with display space.[41]

The Downtown Promenade introduced Knoxville to such new ideas as the
"parking wall" concept and the "pedestrian way." DKA president J. W. Sullivan
waxed lyrical about the twenty-four-foot-wide Promenade, left roofless for one-
half of its width so that "city workers and shoppers could sun themselves." The
Promenade, said Sullivan, "would be a thing of beauty," enhancing function-
ality with graceful design by covering the rear of the stores to roof height with
aluminum mesh to hide unsightly fire escapes and other eyesores. The promenade feature, Sullivan pointed out, was, "so far as we know . . . unique among
American cities. . . . Uniform show windows at the rear of all stores" would
display East Tennessee products "because the promenade will be a community
project that will make all the people of East Tennessee want to come to Knoxville." Despite Hammer and Associates' warnings that public transit systems

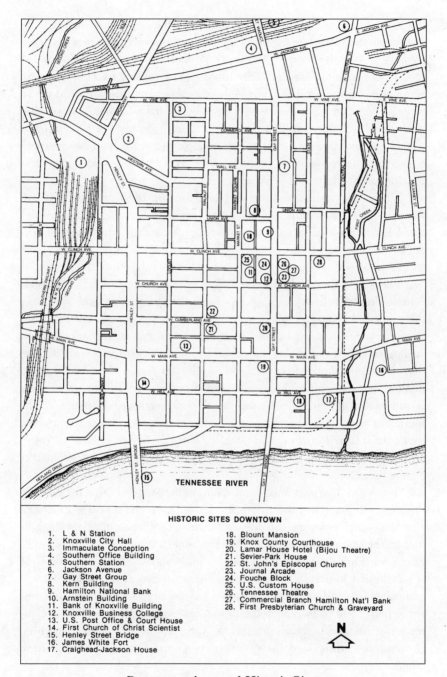

HISTORIC SITES DOWNTOWN

1. L & N Station
2. Knoxville City Hall
3. Immaculate Conception
4. Southern Office Building
5. Southern Station
6. Jackson Avenue
7. Gay Street Group
8. Kern Building
9. Hamilton National Bank
10. Arnstein Building
11. Bank of Knoxville Building
12. Knoxville Business College
13. U.S. Post Office & Court House
14. First Church of Christ Scientist
15. Henley Street Bridge
16. James White Fort
17. Craighead-Jackson House

18. Blount Mansion
19. Knox County Courthouse
20. Lamar House Hotel (Bijou Theatre)
21. Sevier-Park House
22. St. John's Episcopal Church
23. Journal Arcade
24. Fouche Block
25. U.S. Custom House
26. Tennessee Theatre
27. Commercial Branch Hamilton Nat'l Bank
28. First Presbyterian Church & Graveyard

N

Downtown Area and Historic Sites.

for people were more important than automobile movement in resolving downtown problems, the Promenade enshrined the very machines that were choking it. As both downtown and suburban business leaders would soon discover, more parking lots and wider thoroughfares only attracted even more automobiles, thus leading to even more congestion and frustration. As urban planners later admitted, there would never be streets wide enough or parking lots and garages spacious enough. In that sense, already-filled downtowns could never compete with suburban shopping centers or malls—new, antiseptic, generally leery of racial minorities or the poor with relocated anchors and acres of parking. It wasn't even a fair fight.[42]

When a fire razed the old Market House (built in 1897) in 1960, the DKA was presented with another opportunity to enhance the appearance of downtown. Located one block west of Gay Street, the Market House had been the old city's central food market, offering farmers from the hinterland and local tradesmen a venue where people could shop for their foodstuffs, flowers, etc.[43]

The destruction of the Market House prompted the DKA to talk about demolishing "all existing buildings in the Market Square Area" and converting this valuable downtown property into a genuine shoppers' mall. But a consultant hired by the DKA counseled restraint, stating that construction of new facilities would be unwise because of site limitations, the excessively high rents that would be necessary to cover costs, and the fact that in 1960 the Knoxville market area already was "overbuilt in terms of retail facilities." Moreover, according to Larry Smith and Associates, the large retail anchors that would be needed to make such a project work would not return to downtown. Finally, the consultants reported that "the local tax situation in Knoxville would present cause for concern to any potential developer undertaking the Market Square Project."[44]

Indeed, in its report Smith and Associates chided the DKA for being at once too visionary and too timid. As noted above, the report discouraged ambitious schemes for massive demolition and construction of new retail facilities on the Market House site. At the same time, it criticized downtown merchants for thinking only in the narrow terms of retail activity: "Our study of Knoxville has indicated to us that the future of downtown Knoxville will increasingly depend on the downtown's becoming . . . a true metropolitan center. Retailing will always be important, but for a city of Knoxville's size, downtown functions will increasingly give consideration to office-using activities, convention facilities and the providing of cultural services for the entire region."[45]

Yet despite Smith and Associates' emphasis on the necessity of Knoxville's becoming a "true metropolitan center" if it were to survive, the DKA continued

Old Market House.
Courtesy of the Beck Cultural Exchange Center.

Market Square Mall, early 1960s.
McClung Historical Collection. Knoxville–Knox County Public Library.

to concentrate its attention on cosmetic changes designed to entice shoppers back to the downtown core. Ignoring the consultant's advice, the Market Square Mall plan went forward—prepared by the MPC, designed as a public service by the East Tennessee chapter of the American Institute of Architects, promoted by the DKA, and participated in by 142 property owners. The total cost ran to a fairly modest $135,000, with the city paying for everything except the renovated store fronts and the canopies. Cas Walker opposed the mall, as he had opposed nearly everything else, and threatened to move his store from Market Square if the plan was carried out. It was, and he moved.[46]

Perhaps the ultimate in urban cosmetology was the "Gay Way," a 1964 project aimed at giving a facelift to Gay Street, still downtown Knoxville's major retail, banking, and office center. The unveiling of the Gay Way plan was accompanied by a virtual tsunami of press releases trumpeting the "rejuvenation" of the city's principal commercial thoroughfare. Wider sidewalks were constructed, and a modern lighting system was installed. But the most talked-about part of the Gay Way project was the erection of large, overhanging, permanent canopies to shield the hoped-for shoppers from the elements as they walked from store to store.[47]

Gay Street, however, needed much more than a facelift if shoppers were to be lured back downtown. Although the approximately three hundred merchants who participated in the Gay Way project paid around $150 a front foot, there is no evidence that the project attracted significantly more shoppers. Worse, the canopies turned out to be a disaster: critics claimed that that too little natural light was admitted through the canopies and that "at certain times because of the accumulation of automobile and bus exhaust fumes" it actually was difficult to draw a clean breath.[48]

In sum, then, although downtown businesses had begun to work together and the downtown core did appear physically more attractive, economically it was still in difficult straits. As columnist Lois Reagan Thomas remembered, "It was not much after the dedication of the new canopies . . . when the mayor [Leonard Rogers] said, 'Knoxville has great days ahead.' Shortly after this West Town [Knoxville's first shopping mall] was opened, Miller's closed its huge Gay Street store, the Riviera [movie theater] burned, and Kress and Company closed."[49]

The Politics of Parochialism and Paralysis

It would be convenient to blame the continued troubles of Knoxville's core on downtown businesspeople. After all, hadn't they ignored warnings about access and parking? Hadn't they overlooked Smith and Associates' desperate pleas to refocus their thinking? Hadn't they more than once broken ranks and fled to the more opulent suburbs? Hadn't they embraced cosmetic solutions rather than thinking boldly? Yet while each of these questions implies a kernel of truth, it would be unfair to heap the blame solely on this harried group. Hindsight allows us to see what many failed to recognize at the time—that throughout the nation demographic, economic, and technological forces were at work that were so strong that they would have overpowered even the most imaginative efforts. In the mid-1950s it was by no means clear whether these forces were to be permanent, whether there were physical and demographic limits to suburbanization, whether the massive malls (none of which had been built in East Tennessee) would become the suburbanites' "new downtowns." In sum, these downtown entrepreneurs were intelligent men and women, but their vision, obscured by their own hopes and fears, was hardly prophetic. And even if they had possessed the hindsight we now have, their financial resources were so modest that it is doubtful they could have implemented bolder plans. As will be seen later, local banks were hardly more imaginative. In short, it would be appallingly unjust to pillory downtown merchants without fully understanding both their plight and their resources.

In truth, if anything, downtown retailers merely reflected a general conservatism and fearfulness that seems to have permeated nearly the entire local populace, including its political leaders. The 1956 debate between Cas Walker and J. S. Cooper, a former political protégé of Walker and city councilman in 1954–55 and 1956–57, illustrates the level to which the city's politics had sunk. This series of verbal duels ended in a fistfight that made national and even international headlines, though more as a spectacle than as a significant event.

Initially the public argument erupted over the two men's respective tax assessments. Cooper claimed that Walker had used his markets' radio and newspaper ads to criticize Cooper. Since Cooper could not retaliate in kind, he used the city council meeting as a forum in which to defend himself. According to the *News-Sentinel* reporter, when Walker interrupted him, Cooper shouted, "Shut up until I finish."

"You make me," retorted Walker.

"Somebody will make you some day," said Cooper.

Walker's rejoinder was, "I've never run from anyone yet, and I won't run from you."

Having descended to the level of childish abuse, the two combatants seemed content to stay there while all of Knoxville looked on. Cooper accused Walker of getting preferred tax assessments; Walker countered that Cooper, his former political protégé, had had a chain-link fence erected on his property at city expense ("I did everything I could to get Cooper elected, and he traded me off for a chain link fence," said Walker). At this point Cooper resorted to what was, for the 1950s, the ultimate insult, asserting that Walker "was using his usual Hitler and Stalin tactics, telling half-truths, no truths at all, and just plain lies."[50]

A month later, on March 6, 1956, the two councilmen clashed again, this time over the peanut and popcorn concessions at Chilhowee Park. Walker and Cooper exchanged words, and Walker allegedly told Cooper, "You're going to keep on 'til I have to take you out and whip you."

Cooper replied, stooping inelegantly to the nadir of local political insult, "I'll meet you anywhere, you smart rat!"

Walker's rejoinder is unrecorded, but it was enough to make Cooper rush the grocer-councilman, daring him to take a swing at him. "I couldn't disappoint him," Walker later remembered. But Walt Martin, who worked for radio station WBIR (the station that aired live broadcasts of city council meetings) quickly stepped between the two councilmen before anything was bruised besides their egos. "Contrary to what some may say," Martin recalled, "neither councilman landed any real blows." In 1999 the Knoxville weekly *Metro Pulse* listed the fracas as one of Knoxville's ten most embarrassing moments of the twentieth century. It would be hard to disagree.[51]

This account of the unseemly uproar by Walker and Cooper (who was later dubbed by Walker "Popcorn Jim" Cooper) is not intended to suggest either that there were no political figures in Knoxville capable of rising above high school locker room antics or that there were no issues of sufficient importance for politicians to discuss. Dempster was still around, but over the years he had given and taken so many wounds that he had become politically ineffective (he died in 1964). And, as we have seen, Dance had more than his share of vision, but his untimely death in 1959 (at the age of sixty-one) robbed the city of an important leader when one was desperately needed. In addition, John T. O'Connor (1881–1968) had been especially effective during the 1930s in dealing with Knoxville's unemployment and the conversion to Tennessee Valley Authority power, but it appears that he was not very active in the 1950s, even though he held a seat on the city council. Finally, Max Friedman (1888–1967) was an extraordinary example of integrity and decency in local politics, but he probably was too liberal for his fellow councilmen (where he served, except for one term, from 1948 until his death) and invariably voted in the minority. "The older most people get," Friedman once said, "the more conservative they become. . . . [T]he older I get the more liberal I become." And unquestionably there were crucial issues that urgently needed to be addressed. Yet in Knoxville good civic leaders never seemed to come to grips with crucial issues, and the city seemed regularly to be sidetracked by antics like the

*Cas Walker (left) and Jim Cooper fistfight at city
council meeting, March 1956.*

Knoxville Journal.

Walker-Cooper joust. Many of the voters who earlier might have demanded
action had moved beyond the city limits into the more affluent suburbs. With
a few exceptions, the UT and TVA newcomers tended to stay well behind the
walls of their respective citadels. Those voters who remained in the city tended
to reinforce the area's traditional conservatism. Against this potent combination, the forces of change fared poorly.[52]

The conservatism of Knoxville's voters can be seen in a series of referenda
held in the city during the 1950s and early 1960s. Perhaps the most interesting of these was the vote on the consolidation of city and county government.
In an effort to give Tennessee's cities a weapon to deal with rapid suburban
growth beyond the city limits, the Ninetieth General Assembly enacted a
measure that authorized popular votes on city-county government consolidation. The act mandated that a proposed charter be drawn up by a charter commission on which both city and county were represented and that the charter
had to be approved by voters in both the city and county in order to go into
effect.

In 1957 a charter commission was established in Knoxville/Knox County and, after nineteen months of work, produced a draft charter. Both major newspapers and a majority of workers in both governments supported consolidation. The referendum was scheduled for April 9, 1959. Interest was extremely high, and Lee S. Greene, University of Tennessee political scientist and executive secretary of the charter commission, reported, "I'm having to fight off requests for copies of the charter proposal now." Public talks and debates were sponsored by, among others, the League of Women Voters, the Technical Society of Knoxville, the Chamber of Commerce, the Jaycees, the Knoxville Ministerial Association, the local AFL-CIO, and the Knox County Council of Community Clubs. Several individuals claimed that government consolidation would attract industries that, as attorney Harley Fowler put it, had "generally shunned the area because of its Byzantine politics." It was high time, said Fowler and others, "to wipe the slate clean."[53]

Consolidation, however, never had a chance. George Dempster, a longtime spokesman for city teachers, opposed consolidation on the grounds that it would dilute Knoxville teachers' pension fund by "taking in the teachers from the county's hills and valleys." The City Teachers' League was an enormously powerful and influential body in city politics and its opposition alone might have doomed consolidation of the city and county. Dempster explained, "I don't think Knoxville should be a guinea pig for this kind of thing."[54]

Long Dempster's political nemesis, Cas Walker temporarily sided with his foe and also opposed consolidation. Hinting darkly that metropolitan government was a communist plot to destroy democracy, Walker distributed an article by Jo Hindman in the *American Mercury* titled "Terrible 1313" that purported to prove precisely that. Once Walker, known for his savage in-fighting, came out in opposition, many people and groups backed away. As the chairman of Knox County Republicans put it, "We had expected that the civic groups, the Chamber of Commerce, civic clubs and groups like that would lead the fight for metro. Cas Walker was using his television programs and newspaper ads to claim that metro was Communistic."[55]

Meanwhile both city and county officeholders, fearful that their jobs might be eliminated in a combined government, surreptitiously worked against consolidation. Other voters feared that extending fire protection, city water, sanitation sewers, street lighting, street cleaning, garbage collection, and more police protection to the county would necessitate a massive tax increase. For Cas Walker, any tax increase was too much. During this debate, he responded to a person who criticized him for hurting schools by cutting two cents from the tax rate by offering to throw his critic (Oak Ridge engineer A. P. Fraas) off the platform. Finally, in these early years of the civil rights era, some county voters were afraid that consolidation would mean the forced racial integration of the county schools.[56]

The vote was not even close. Both city and county voters rejected the charter. In the city, only 21 percent of those who voted supported consolidation, while in the county that figure was a miniscule 13.8 percent. Given the turnout in the city (44 percent of the registered voters), it is possible that many voters who might have supported the referendum stayed away from the polls because of the controversial nature of the issue.[57]

At the same time that Knoxville voters rejected government consolidation, they also turned out at voting booths to oppose fluoridation of the water, legalized liquor sales (twice, in 1955 and 1957), and school consolidation. Years later, students of Knoxville politics wondered why political figures tended to avoid plebiscites on any issues. What had developed was a static system of mutual distrust, in which the leaders distrusted the people and the people distrusted them. All too often, fear carried they day. While audiences might chuckle knowingly at Paul Soper's satire, the city lurched toward the postindustrial age, an age that it might be prohibited from entering.[58]

Knoxville and the Civil Rights Movements

Although Knoxvillians long had prided themselves on the fact that their city had remained comparatively free of racial tensions, issues regarding race, as in the past, lay not far from the surface. What was not immediately perceived was that important trends and forces such as suburbanization, economic difficulties, and downtown decay would act to push those racial issues and tensions to center stage. As upwardly mobile whites and African Americans moved to the suburbs, urban populations increasingly were composed of poor whites and blacks and the elderly of both races. With job opportunities declining relative to population, with housing stock deteriorating daily, with television constantly beaming out messages of abundance and good times, and with national attention since the *Brown v. Board of Education* decision in 1954 increasingly focused on the denial of civil rights to blacks, it was almost natural that blacks and sympathetic whites would begin to press for a more just society.[59]

But while white Knoxvillians might have congratulated one another on what they believed were the city's good race relations, they did not necessarily support increasingly insistent cries for racial integration of schools, public facilities, and private establishments that claimed to cater to the "general public." A 1958 poll of white Knoxvillians revealed that 90 percent "strongly disapproved" of school desegregation, 85 percent did not believe that the *Brown v. Board of Education* decision was "the law of the land," and 100 percent opposed enrolling "one or two white children" in a previously all-black school. Clearly Knoxville whites liked peace and quiet, but they also preferred racial separation. One of the more outlandish examples of this resistance to change occurred in 1956 when singer Chuck Berry came to Knoxville to perform in a local club but was turned away by the proprietor, who insisted that "he had no idea that 'Maybellene' was recorded by a niggra man." Berry claimed that he spent the evening in a rental car outside the club listening to a white band play his songs.[60]

As the reader may have noticed, the author has referred above to the civil rights *movements.* One of those movements, supported by the NAACP, advocated using the courts to chip away little by little at the walls of racial separation. Many whites supported these gradualist efforts, this particularly moderate civil rights movement. In addition, however, a growing cadre of younger African Americans, in part in a generational conflict with the moderate leaders of the NAACP, called for direct confrontation with the system of segregation. In early 1960, college students at primarily black North Carolina Agricultural and Technical College in Greensboro, North Carolina, initiated the first "sit-in," in which they entered previously all-white eating establishments, demanded service, and refused to leave when they were denied. Clearly this was a different "movement"—more immediate, more confrontational, to some whites more threatening.

On December 11, 1959, Josephine Goss and sixteen other young African Americans filed a suit in federal court, asking the court to order the desegregation of the Knoxville schools. The plaintiffs were more than confident of success: when the Supreme Court issued the *Brown* decision, both Knoxville newspapers agreed with the decision, albeit cautiously. Normally very conservative, *Journal* editor Guy Smith wrote: "No citizen fitted by character and intelligence to sit as a Justice of the Supreme Court, and sworn to uphold the Constitution of the United States, could have decided this question other than they way it was decided. . . . [N]o person who understood the meaning of the language could read the Fourteenth Amendment and conclude that school segregation was other than in direct violation of what it means."

As expected, the *News-Sentinel* also supported the *Brown* decision, albeit timidly, opining that "given time, our southern states will find a way to live with the Supreme Court decision." Two years after Brown, both major newspapers denounced Arkansas governor Orval Faubus for his attempt to block the desegregation of Central High School in Little Rock, a move that resulted in violence and President Eisenhower's calling out of the Arkansas National Guard and U.S. Army paratroops to protect the nine African American schoolchildren. Finally, when the *Goss* suit was filed, most local business and political leaders had anticipated such a move and gave it their cautious support.[61]

The Knoxville school board responded to *Goss* by adopting a desegregation strategy known as the "Nashville Plan." In that plan, desegregation would begin in the first grade and proceed forward in a stairstep method at the speed of one grade per year. In 1960 federal judge Robert Taylor approved the Knoxville proposal but the Sixth Circuit Court of Appeals overruled Taylor on the grounds that the plan was too slow, forcing the school board to regroup and start again. A revised plan was filed in 1964 and approved by Judge Taylor in 1967. The plaintiffs continued to win modifications until 1973, when the United States Supreme Court refused to hear an appeal by the plaintiffs of the circuit court decision that Knoxville had achieved a "unitary" school system.[62]

For the most part, African American plaintiffs won their lawsuits and gradually the walls of racial segregation began to be dismantled, albeit brick by brick. Not so patient were African American young people, especially students at Knoxville College. Less than a month after black students in Greensboro started the sit-in movement, Knoxville College students began to plan their own strategy of confrontation and demonstrations. The college's administration tried to dissuade the students, claiming that the gradualist strategy of negotiations and, as a last resort, lawsuits were more effective than sit-ins. But the students threatened to expose the administration as "Uncle Toms" and on March 7 staged a "file-through," in which the African American students walked through downtown stores en masse but did not actually sit down. As a clear warning, however, Knoxville College student body president Robert Booker stated, "We do not intend to wait placidly for those rights which are already legally and morally ours to be meted out to us one at a time."[63]

Meanwhile Mayor John Duncan was working hard behind the scenes to achieve the desegregation of downtown eating establishments and theaters without demonstrations or violence. He quietly lined up support among the Chamber of Commerce, the Downtown Knoxville Association, the Association of Women's Clubs, the Central Labor Council, and the Knoxville Ministerial Association. He then took two Knoxville College students and two officers of the Chamber of Commerce with him to New York City in an attempt to convince the corporate executives of the four chains that operated lunch counters in downtown Knoxville to desegregate voluntarily. But the chain store owners stalled, perhaps reasoning that after spring final examinations at Knoxville College and the dispersion of students the situation would be defused. When Duncan and his party returned home, they learned that their requests had been turned down. The Knoxville sit-ins began on June 9, 1960. Nervously, Knoxvillians braced for trouble.[64]

On the whole the demonstrations were orderly, and the violence many feared failed to materialize. Duncan ordered police to protect the demonstrators, and generally they did. Already viewed by many as a pack of liberals from outside, TVA put pressure on its employees not to participate, as did the University of Tennessee (although from behind the scenes). Some ugly incidents did occur, much of it directed at the handful of white demonstrators. But the fear of violence—and the urging of Knoxville College students to "stay away from downtown"—caused downtown shopping sales to almost collapse. By July 19 the merchants' ranks were broken, and resistance caved in. It would take more demonstrations, court orders, and threats by the Justice Department (as in the 1965 case of threatening the University of Tennessee Hospital with the loss of federal funds if it did not desegregate its facilities) to consolidate and move forward the gains won by the young people of Knoxville College, but by 1967 the Urban League said that Knoxville had the "appearance of an open city."[65]

Yet while many African Americans understandably took pride in their ability to force the white community to open its doors to them, at the same time even the hottest heads among the young people understood that substantial victories in the future would require the cooperation of white business and political leaders as well as the white middle class. "We didn't want to push the issue," recalled civil rights activist and Knoxville Area Urban League cofounder Avon Rollins in a 2001 interview, "not to flood the eating establishments." Rollins helped distribute a flier that read in part, "If you should go to a restaurant and see other Negroes seated and being served, . . . go to another."[66]

More serious, of course, was the fact that Knoxville's sit-in demonstrations failed to alter the basic economic and social fabric of the city. Indeed, the victories, while important symbolically, were really quite modest in addressing the real problems of Knoxville's black—and white—communities. For in the troubled city of the 1950s, the real problems touched nearly everyone—white as well as black, old resident as well as recent arrival, rich as well as poor. Caught in the lag of the postindustrial age, the city seemed to lack the financial resources, the leadership, the unity, or the will to confront the trends and dilemmas of the 1950s. As some concerned citizens began to talk of Knoxville's need to "catch up" with the times, Paul Soper's *Once upon a Town* gave them an outlet, an opportunity to laugh at themselves and their agonies and frustrations.

4

New Energy for an Old City

Knoxville in the 1960s–1980s

In his 1972 inaugural address, new Knoxville mayor Kyle Testerman predicted, "I firmly believe future historians will record this period as our finest hour." Not one to hide his light under a bushel, Testerman was a man of boundless energy, great ambition, and even greater dreams for himself and his city. When the thirty-seven-year-old attorney-developer became mayor after a bitter election campaign against incumbent Leonard Rogers, Knoxvillians had the distinct feeling that things would be different.[1]

For years Testerman had heard booster-type promises that were never kept and had seen countless plans that never went beyond the drawing boards or the closed-door committees. "I'd seen so much money spent on plans," he later recalled. "Why, you could have *rebuilt* Knoxville with the money they'd spent on plans." Instead of more plan-making, the new mayor proposed to attack Knoxville's problems on all fronts, rewarding those who shared his vision and publicly mocking those he considered too timid. "My goal was to drag Knoxville kicking and screaming into the twentieth century," he stated, even his language bristling with verbs of force and action. A modern version of Henry Grady and the New South boosters, to Kyle Testerman no obstacle was too large, no opponent too powerful, no vision too grand.[2]

Testerman was not, however, so much the *cause* of Knoxville's change of direction as he was the *product* of it. The city's 1962 annexation of Fountain City and the Bearden area brought into Knoxville's political mix a sizable and rapidly growing number of suburban voters, many of whom had come to the city from elsewhere and in general were more progressive in their political thinking. Those additions to the city's voter registration rolls sharply eroded the power of Cas Walker and the black and white working-class wards of the old city. At the same time, traditionally conservative business owners once again were roused from their lethargy and were anxious to reawaken their city as they themselves had been reawakened. Finally, an even younger and more aggressive group of developers, bankers, and new businessmen and business-women (a business-developer bloc, represented in part by Testerman, Pilot Oil Corporation president Jim Haslam, and others) appeared on the political land-scape in the 1960s, complete with vision, a less doctrinaire and more prag-matic approach to Knoxville's difficulties, and the money to provide the necessary loaves and fishes to make themselves heard and felt on the political scene. Hence Kyle Testerman was the beneficiary of new elements as well as new thinking in Knoxville during the 1960s.

"We were more suspect in the more staid business community," recalls Testerman, "principally because we were too impatient to wait for things to

James Haslam II.
Reprinted by permission of the Knoxville News-Sentinel Company.

happen by themselves." More recently risen to wealth than the leaders of the reawakened business group, this business-developer bloc was composed of young mavericks who had little sympathy for older ideas and methods and little patience with the slow wheels of Knoxville's traditional government. They longed for rapid change in a region notably resistant to either rapidity or change.[3]

Yet forces opposing change still were extremely powerful, joining the traditional Appalachian and the old elite brands of conservatism with newer strains that opposed the most blatant forms of boosterism or (as in the newly annexed suburbs) significant tax increases necessary to bring new ideas to fruition. In part victims of their own impatience, excesses, and style, the business-developers by the mid-1980s had yet to prove that they could change a city that was so resistant to change. For Knoxville, then, like the New South of Henry Grady's generation, the Appalachian city's golden age remained just over the next horizon.

The American City in the Postindustrial Age

In general, the 1960s and 1970s were troubled times for America's cities. Those dependent on heavy durable-goods manufacturing faced economic difficulties in almost direct proportion to the extent of the ill-health of their particular industries. Blacks, Puerto Ricans, and southern whites fleeing rural poverty continued to add to these troubled cities' economic and social strains. Moreover, as these people poured into the cities in search of opportunities, lower-middle-class and middle-class whites fled in more than equal numbers, in some cases causing absolute declines in urban populations (the most dramatic being that of St. Louis, which suffered a 44 percent drop in population during the 1960s and 1970s, a virtual hemorrhage of lower-middle-class and middle-class white taxpayers). Strange neighbors and their even stranger ways, disturbingly rising crime rates, and increasing tax burdens drove whites out of cities they felt were no longer theirs. Their departures meant that an important source of revenue for cities was drying up. With those who fled went many of the retail merchants, who followed neighbors and dollars into burgeoning suburban shopping malls. They left behind them cities increasingly populated by the black, the poor, the aged—those whom modernization had left behind.

On June 11, 1971, the mayors of twelve major cities, representatives of the Legislative Action Committee of the U.S. Conference of Mayors, appeared before the House Ways and Means Committee to plead for more federal dollars for America's troubled cities. The mayors' stories were indeed depressing ones: as city government expenditures skyrocketed (up 141.8 percent since

1960 in cities—like Knoxville—with populations between 100,000 and 199,999), the very taxpayers who would be called on to pay those bills were deserting cities in favor of new suburbs, which increased from 18 percent of the nation's population in 1930 to 37.6 percent in 1970. Faced with declining tax collections, city governments were forced to borrow money, and interest on debts had risen by 245.6 percent since 1960, the second greatest percentage increase of all city functions in cities with populations of 100,000 to 199,999 (public housing was first, up 581.2 percent). In sum, the picture was appalling.[4]

Perhaps it was New York Mayor John Lindsay who addressed America's urban problems most directly: "Over the last couple of decades, our cities have become the guardians of the country's unwanted stepchildren. We have inherited the Nation's problems of poverty, race, and class conflict, physical deterioration, drug addiction, archaic public education systems, pollution. Over the last two decades, the chief problems of the country have grown and festered in these cities, and we are the ones who have been asked to find the solutions." To the mayors, *the* solution was federal money.[5]

To be sure, some cities *were* able to halt economic and demographic erosions. Most were able to do so by offsetting the declines in durable-goods manufacturing with the attraction of "new line" industries (electronics, fabricated metals, synthetics, and chemicals) to their rims and beltways; these industries drew high-salaried employees who gave boosts both to construction trades and retail establishments. In turn, those newcomers created a demand for goods, services, educational institutions, and cultural attractions that further stimulated those fortunate cities. Of course, "fortune" in fact had little to do with the successes of those cities, for those that had been able to lure new line industries (thereby becoming successful in the postindustrial age while "old line" industries declined) had done so through aggressive sales campaigns, favorable land acquisition policies, good interstate highway connections, and friendly political leaders. From the 1960s on, those cities (Seattle, Washington; San Francisco–Palo Alto–Berkeley, California; and others) became the models for all of urban America.[6]

For its part, however, by the early 1960s Knoxville was a city in trouble. As noted earlier, the city's industrial base (durable-goods manufacturing, with a heavy emphasis on textiles and apparel) had experienced mounting difficulties, so much so that between 1948 and 1960 approximately 4,200 manufacturing jobs had evaporated. Jobs in construction also had declined, and the service sector, which on the national level had taken up much of the decade's employment slack, in Knoxville grew only slowly. The service industries' failure to fill the city's employment vacuum was due to the area's exceedingly low wage scale. With 46 percent of Knoxville's and Knox County's industrial employees earning under $5,000 per year and with apparel workers averaging $3,100 per year, it would be surprising if the service sector had been healthy. At those wages, men and women simply lacked the discretionary income to spend for services. Add to that a Standard Metropolitan Statistical Area unemployment rate of 7.7 percent in 1961, and one has the disturbing picture of a city still in the grips of a real economic dilemma. While these problems were hardly new to Knoxville, since they were part of a pattern that went back at least fifty years, by the early 1960s they had become so serious that they threatened Knoxville's very existence.[7]

Especially crucial were forces that seemed to make the attraction of new line industries and their many benefits exceedingly difficult. As shown earlier, cities that had been successful in attracting—or founding—such industries had established favorable terms (including industrial parks) for land acquisition, had been linked into the developing interstate highway system (which fit new line needs better than did the declining railroads), had maintained a politically friendly climate for development, and had avoided social tensions and racial problems that tended to scare newcomers away. But in Knoxville all of these factors appeared to be obstacles to the city's changing direction in the postindustrial age.

To begin with, much of the city's traditional business elite (which had shown tendencies toward economic, social, and political conservatism since the turn of the century) seems to have preferred Knoxville as it was. This group was unfriendly to new enterprises that might either compete for the skilled labor pool or be more receptive to unionization. Thus they opposed industrial parks that might lure these new enterprises, opposed bond issues for industrial recruitment (on the grounds that public money should not be used to assist private businesses), and made sure that local banks (which they controlled) did not make loans to such new people or new ventures.[8]

Commenting on the local banking community, Kyle Testerman opined, "When you have an executive of a major local bank earning around $16,000 a year, it's hard for him to *conceive* of someone wanting to borrow a couple of million dollars for a new business venture." Testerman's opinion of local bankers as people who lacked vision and imagination dated back to his initial attempts to seek local financing for his ambitious Northshore office buildings: "The whole bank board sat around and wrung their hands when I presented my idea. Finally one of them said, 'Well, Mr. Testerman, what will happen if you fail?' I told them, 'Well then you'll have the biggest damn bank building in West Knoxville.' [Laughs] That just scared the hell out of them." Knoxville's bankers, like the traditional elite to which they belonged, seem to have feared change, whether it came from "outsiders" (potential new line industries) or from Knoxvillians like Testerman who challenged both their views and their power.[9]

Clearly a sizable portion of Knoxville's old elite families opposed any changes in the city. Deriving a significant part of their income from the ownership of downtown real estate as well as local banks and industries, this group of old elite families opposed any plans to rejuvenate the central downtown area on the grounds that they would increase property values and, with them, property taxes. Hence this group more often than not sided with political figures like Cas Walker (whom they personally ridiculed and abhorred), whose constituency almost universally opposed change, albeit for other reasons. At the same time, downtown merchants appear to have been interested in little but schemes to improve downtown retail trade and therefore did not support the 1959 metropolitan government referendum or Duncan's idea of an industrial bond referendum. Indeed, even as they disliked and distrusted one another, the city's old elite and working classes together held Knoxville in a grip of hostility to newcomers, and to change. Proposals for tax increases were almost always rejected, even in the face of pressing needs to maintain services and schools, to attract more visitors (who in 1961 accounted for only 9 percent of all Knoxville's retail business) by building a civic coliseum-auditorium, and to extend services (the most pressing of which was sewers) to recently annexed areas. In 1966 those who supported a scheme to raise the city's tax ceiling were routed by the voters (approximately 65,000 opposing it and only about 34,000 voting for it), with those areas most in need of increased services (especially Beaumont) most firmly against the increases. Through all of this, Cas Walker spoke for those who feared that change would be achieved only at terrible financial and psychological costs. Truly, though Walker was an embarrassment to some, for many (even for some of those who would not admit him to their fashionable circles) he was the most consistent defender of Knoxville as they wanted it to remain.[10]

Hence Knoxville's political climate lacked both the stability and the spirit of friendliness to innovation and newcomers that were so necessary in order to attract or grow from local seedlings those new line enterprises that promised to invigorate the troubled city. Viciously personal, often corrupt, and almost universally masters of a political style that Louis Brownlow earlier had called "East Tennessee screamology," Knoxville's political chieftains had waged brutal warfare almost solely to protect their modest baronies or to extend their influence. That the stakes appear to have been small mattered little; that local politics was so unstable that it might have frightened away potential new businesses and investors mattered not at all. Dempster had vision (especially concerning public education) but was willing to wink at the questionable dealings of others to achieve his goals. Walker himself was honest, but he spoke for a populace fearful of change and engaged in the most blatant forms of influence-peddling and cronyism. Guy Smith of the *Knoxville Journal* was a newspaperman in the best and worst sense of the word: independent, articulate, and willing to call dishonesty by its true name, he preferred instead to stoke up petty controversy and use the *Journal* to befriend his allies and castigate his enemies. For his part, Friedman cried for honesty and a businesslike approach to government, principles that had governed this remarkable man's business and life, but his integrity, honesty, and liberalism on social issues caused him to be regarded by other politicos as some species of village idiot. His secure place on city council, where he invariably voted in the minority, was an embarrassing reminder to Knoxvillians of what their local politics ought to have been—and was not.

Several local observers believe that the city's unstable political situation was the principal discouragement to new business. "The savage infighting between men like Cas Walker and George Dempster often turned city council meetings into three-ring circuses," one recalls. One councilman was rumored to have been connected with the bootleg liquor traffic, while another had been suspended from the certified public accountants' association for "failure to meet minimal professional standards in conducting the post-audit of the county's books." Probably equally worrisome to potential new businesses was the high turnover of mayors and councilmen, which gave the distinct impression that the city was politically unstable. Clearly, Knoxville's political climate in the years from the end of World War II to the early 1960s was another factor that prevented the city from moving in new directions in the postindustrial age.[11]

To the lack of a stable and functional political system must be added the inability to secure interstate highways, the paucity of a skilled labor pool, and increased racial friction. By 1960 the city's African American population for the most part was employed in domestic service (56 percent of the black working males and 73 percent of the black working females) and unskilled jobs. Predictably, wages were almost uniformly low, the African American family's median income in 1960 being only $2,237. Over half of Knoxville's blacks lived in slum conditions, one slum (Mountain View) so bad that in 1960 it was rated 20,875th of 20,915 urban census tracts in the entire nation in terms of housing stock. Illegitimacy, crime, and health problems all were disturbingly high.[12]

The sit-in demonstrations of 1960 and 1962 and the *Goss* decision struck down racial segregation in eating establishments, theaters, and public schools. Employment opportunities, however, remained severely limited, as did African American representation in the city's so-called power circles. "We cannot get jobs as city bus drivers," complained one group of African Americans, "even on routes which carry predominantly Negro passengers." As for health care, the group claimed, "We cannot get service at East Tennessee Baptist Hospital, at [Fort Sanders] Presbyterian Hospital, or at St. Mary's Catholic Hospital." No African Americans sat on the city council, the board of education, the Knoxville Housing Authority, the Knoxville Utilities Board, the board of directors of the city auditorium, or the Library Board. Of the 168 African Americans employed by the Tennessee Valley Authority, not one held a position above grade eight, and 71 percent (119 of 168) were maintenance workers, elevator operators, and clerical helpers. Although most Knoxville whites continued to believe that the city's race relations were "fine," racial tension lay just beneath the surface, a most unwelcome situation for those who hoped to attract outside industries. As one writer observed many years later, "Privileged people don't march and protest; their world is safe and clean and governed by laws designed to keep them happy." Others, however, did.[13]

To be sure, few of these problems were unique to Knoxville—on the contrary, they were dilemmas facing nearly every American city at the beginning of the 1960s. What made Knoxville distinctive was its citizens' apparent failure of will. Its politicians were locked in savage but essentially meaningless battles; its bankers were cautious and timid to a fault; its working-age population was fleeing the city to the county or beyond; it was excessively defensive about its image, as if it felt John Gunther would return. Knoxville entered the 1960s poorly equipped to confront its problems, problems faced by most American cities in the postindustrial age.

The Search for the New City

And yet, despite the city's many difficulties, those who wrote epitaphs for Knoxville wrote prematurely. Beginning in the mid-1960s, a fortuitous combination of national trends, new political configurations, and good luck acted to arrest the decline, turn it around, and set the city on a new course. To be sure, serious problems persisted, and some people felt that the new directions were only short-term flurries rather than long-term trends. But by the mid-1970s few could deny that Knoxville was a vastly changed city from the one it had been but a decade before.

One could hardly have missed the changes. The downtown area, once richly deserving of Gunther's barbs, began to see important alterations. Face-lifting the retail establishments along South Gay Street was mere cosmetology, but the new Market Square Mall (on the site of the old Market House), the TVA twin towers (on the north end of the Market Square Mall), a new city-county government building, the Summit Hill project, the new United American Bank building (at 27 floors, Knoxville's first "skyscraper"), and plans for an east-west pedestrian mall (designed as a link between Gay and Locust streets behind the "Customs House") were not. Nor were efforts to clean up the riverfront area (previously known as "Shantytown") and undertake a major downtown slum clearance and urban renewal project in Mountain View, an African American neighborhood that, as noted previously, President Lyndon Johnson had described in 1964 as containing the worst poverty he had ever seen. In addition to new housing, Mountain View also became the site for the city's new Safety Building and the new Hyatt Regency Hotel, completed in 1972. In the 1960s, White's Fort, the original 1786 settlement, which had been dismantled and moved from its original site to private property on Woodlawn Pike in 1906, was restored on a bluff overlooking the reawakening city. Thus, while one could not quite boast that downtown Knoxville by the mid-1970s had become a beautiful urban showplace, one could say that the city had overcome some of the worst features of its unattractiveness.[14]

And as the downtown was undergoing what many hoped would be a major revival, Knoxville's suburbs were booming, especially westward along the Kingston Pike–Interstate 40 axis. Land that as late as the 1950s lay in bucolic pastures by 1970 was rapidly filling with suburban developments. West Hills, Bearden, and even the Concord-Farragut area (over twenty miles from downtown) mushroomed. Interestingly, almost none of these suburbanites were native Knoxvillians, or even native Tennesseans. The story may be apocryphal, but in the early 1970s it was said that there were more children in the Cedar Bluff Middle School who had been born in India than in Knox County. Generally affluent, well educated, and more liberal in their social and political views than the general Knoxville community, these new suburbanites tended their lawns, grilled outside on barbecues, raised their children according to Dr. Benjamin Spock's *Baby and Child Care* (1946), and demanded services and educational facilities like those in the places from whence they had come.[15]

Several factors were responsible for Knoxville's reawakening. To begin with, as the nation's largest cities had become, as New York Mayor John Lindsay had remarked in 1971, the scenes of "poverty, race, and class conflict, physical deterioration, drug addiction, archaic public education systems, [and] pollution," midsize cities suddenly became far more attractive to industries as well as to mobile Americans. Indeed, one might even say that Knoxville became more attractive to "outsiders" simply because it had *not* changed: family values, religion, and "manners" still seemed to be important; streets were comparatively safe; drug abuse, juvenile delinquency, crime and gangs still were under control—albeit growing. For many newcomers, Knoxville was a city that had retained those things that so many of America's large cities had lost. Added to the residents of Fountain City who had been annexed to the city in 1962, these newcomers comprised a potentially powerful political coalition that, if they could vote together as a bloc, would be a force to be reckoned with in Knoxville politics. Even as they threw themselves into PTAs, church groups, social and professional organizations, and civic clubs, so also might they act to change the city's archaic political culture.[16]

Knoxville certainly benefited from the sudden attractiveness of the nation's midsize cities. From 1965 through 1968, new industries located in the city and county, adding approximately 1,500 new jobs and roughly $7.5 million in capital investment. And, as might be expected, construction, retail trade, and services all showed robust increases as well. From 1964 through 1967, 1,559 building permits were granted in the city and 4,779 in the county, adding over $70 million to the area's economy. Employees in wholesale and retail trades had reached 30,800 by 1968, while employees in service industries increased 43.6 percent between 1960 and 1967. Even durable-goods manufacturing experienced some increase, though it was not significant and was mostly at the lower wage levels. Hence unemployment, which had been 7.7 percent in 1961, shrank to 2.8 percent in 1965 and was still under 4.0 percent in 1970.[17]

Despite the increases in manufacturing, trade, construction, and services, perhaps the most significant change in Knoxville's employment picture was the growth of government jobs. By 1967 there were over 16,000 federal and state employees in the metropolitan Knoxville area, an astounding increase of almost 65 percent over 1960. By 1970, almost one in four (23 percent) of the wage earners residing in the city worked for government at some level. Moreover, government money—especially federal money—provided a tremendous boost to the city's economy. Between 1972 and 1976, Kyle Testerman's mayoral administration received approximately $84 million in federal revenue sharing and grants. And that was only a fraction of the federal money pouring into the city in the form of food programs, loans, grants, salaries, pensions, and contracts. Indeed, according to one report, in 1979 the federal government spent roughly $1 billion in Knoxville.[18]

At the same time that Knoxville was receiving impressive injections of federal money, the University of Tennessee was expanding in an equally dramatic fashion, thereby also pumping startlingly large quantities of money into the local economy. Indeed, the comparatively modest campus of around 5,000 students in the early 1950s by the early 1970s had become a megauniversity with around 30,000 students. By 1967 it was estimated that the university annually added over $70 million to the community (exclusive of new construction)— $36 million in payroll (up from an estimated $10 million in 1959) and the remainder spent in Knoxville by students as well as contracts to local jobbers for furniture, equipment, and materials. Construction contracts awarded by the expanding university (approximately $73 million in the decade from 1957 to 1967) further enriched the area. Although not everyone was delighted by the university's expansion (west of Volunteer Boulevard, the Yale Avenue neighborhood had not greeted warmly its virtual annexation to the university and the wholesale tearing down of homes, churches, and businesses to make way for UT's West Campus), clearly another important new economic force had been added to the community.[19]

Considerably more dramatic than Knoxville's economic or physical changes, however, was a new spirit evident in portions of the community. Less defensive, more able to admit the city's shortcomings, less willing to fall back on the "that's a good idea but it would never work in Knoxville" mentality, this new attitude was strengthened by the economic and physical progress that had been accomplished and made further changes possible, if not certain. John Gunther's earlier comments more often drew laughter than apoplectic anger. Indeed, by the mid-1970s some Knoxvillians thought in grand terms of hosting a world's fair. To be sure, this new spirit was considerably less than universal, but its appearance promised more changes—and conflicts—in the future.

Nor was that new spirit confined to the newcomers of west Knoxville. In the 1920s and again in the 1940s, the newcomers who arrived in Knoxville had come from the surrounding rural Appalachian hinterland and had found jobs in the city's low-wage textile, apparel, and other non-durable-goods industries. Suspicious of the city's elite and loathing the African Americans who were all-too-near them on the socioeconomic ladder, they consistently supported political demagogues like Cas Walker and opposed nearly every proposed innovation that might have benefited the people of the city—including themselves. By the late 1960s, however, many of the children (or grandchildren) of these men and women had adjusted successfully to the demands of the urban environment and the industrial and postindustrial ages. Education, vocational training, decades of urban living, and the communications revolution had made them all aware of the values and expectations of middle-class urban society. In many cases two generations had been sufficient for these people to absorb the entire immense urban revolution.[20]

Studies of two Knoxville city wards attest to this generally successful adjustment by some in-migrants to urban life and demands. Wards Thirty-Six (Gresham) and Forty (Norwood) in the northern part of the city are settled, middle-class areas that experienced considerable in-migration from the Appalachian hinterland in the waves of both the 1920s and the 1940s. A 1977 study showed that only 42.1 percent and 42.9 percent, respectively, of a sample of the wards' 1976 registered voters had been born in Knox County. Most adults in the sample were members of skilled labor groups, and an impressive proportion (64 percent) either owned their own homes or lived with relatives who did so. Most interesting, out of twenty-one Knoxville city planning units in 1970, Gresham and Norwood ranked thirteenth and seventeenth, respectively, in cumulative severity of school dropouts, venereal disease, adult arrests, juvenile delinquency, and number of families receiving public assistance. Clearly, in these neighborhoods, the children and grandchildren of the in-migrants had adjusted successfully to the rigors of urban life. Better-paying jobs produced higher incomes (by 1977 Norwood's mean income was $15,496, compared with the entire city's average of $11,190), bringing a measure of financial security and an opportunity to participate more fully in the consumer culture of the 1960s and 1970s. More to the point, economic mobility made these men and women more receptive to new ideas, more inclined to support political figures who possessed visions of a new Knoxville. More confident and less fearful than their in-migratory parents and/or grandparents had been, they hoped to ride the crest of the new wave, send their own children into the business and professional class (through the avenue of college educations), and adopt a lifestyle that their parents and/or grandparents had both ridiculed and envied.[21]

Annexation, newcomers from outside the region, and the upward mobility of many rural-to-urban migrants from Appalachia virtually spelled the end of Cas Walker as a major political force. To be sure, Walker was able to retain his traditional power bases among lower-middle-class and poor whites and blacks (especially in Wards Seven-N, Seven-S, Nine-N, Nine-S, Twelve, Thirteen, Fourteen, Sixteen, Nineteen, Twenty, Twenty-Two, and Twenty-Four-N). But in the 1960s these groups steadily declined as a proportion of the total voting population, as a continued exodus from the center city met the mushrooming neighborhoods (especially Fountain City and West Knoxville) annexed to the city in 1962. To the legions of newcomers—upper-middle-class business and professional people from outside the region—Walker was a laughable but dangerous retrograde, a political Neanderthal who (as Henry Adams once said of President Grant) should have been extinct for ages, or lived in a cave and worn skins. They failed to appreciate that Walker was more than a caricature of a regressive political style; that as much as anything else he was the representative of an Appalachian constituency; that he shared their distrust of change, of newcomers, of outsiders; and that he was the last political hope for citizens caught in the cogs of modernization. But now the savage warrior, who made no money personally from his years in local government but who had been generous with jobs and other favors to political friends, saw the political handwriting on the wall. In the eyes of the newcomers, he simply had to be eliminiated.[22]

In the November 1963 city council runoff among eight candidates, Walker placed a dismal eighth in three of the newly annexed wards, seventh in one, sixth in two, fifth in three, and nowhere higher than fourth. He did little better in 1967. "They was embarrassed to be seen votin' for an ole coal miner like me," Walker mused in 1977. Thus, though Cas Walker continued to win a place on the city council, with each election his margin of victory eroded and with it his power in that body. Finally, in 1971, faced with stern opposition and with the demographic cards stacked against him, he withdrew before the city council election, later maintaining that his wife had begged him not to run again. Thus ended an era in Knoxville politics that had lasted for nearly five decades. While Walker was far from silent, what influence he retained in the latter 1970s came from different and surprising new constituencies.[23]

Thus by the mid-1960s the stars appeared to be in their proper alignment for Knoxville to move in decidedly new directions. The physical revival of the downtown, the mushrooming suburbs of newcomers, the 1962 annexation of Fountain City and Bearden, the increase in nearly all economic sectors (especially that of "government"), the mobility and increased maturity of the children of rural-to-urban migrants, and the concomitant decline of Cas Walker together seemed to herald the rise of a new spirit in the city, a spirit more eager to change and less willing to continue with "business as usual." Although these forces did not always move in the same direction in a unified, harmonious fashion, and new directions were not universally endorsed or logically conceived, clearly these forces together tended to produce a climate more receptive to change than any other in Knoxville in the twentieth century.

Rogers, Testerman, and the Politics of Change

To those who historically had sought to move the city onto new paths, it appeared that the two greatest stumbling blocks had been a complacent and highly provincial business elite that preferred things as they were and was suspicious of new ideas and new people and a political system that displayed the most retrogressive aspects of populism in which voters howled down nearly every figure whose ideas meant tax increases while at the same time winking at the most blatant forms of corruption that promised city jobs for relatives or themselves, filling in potholes in streets, or some other political favor or two. Since the demise of the city manager form of government in the 1940s, political power in Knoxville had been so evenly balanced among personal factions that bold policies had been avoided and turnover in office had been high.

Voters had been fickle, tending to cast their ballots for those who promised to keep taxes low, even at the risk of hurting essential services.

By the mid-1960s, however, an increasing number of businessmen within the elite-controlled Chamber of Commerce had had enough. For years they had been ashamed of the vicious, often corrupt, and highly flamboyant political scene, but had become involved in the fray only sporadically. Probably no less conservative then their fathers and grandfathers had been, these businessmen understood better than their elite predecessors that Knoxville's future depended on attracting new industries to replace the sagging textile, apparel, and other non-durable-goods enterprises. Embarrassed by the civil rights demonstrations of 1960 and 1962 but relieved that they had remained peaceful, they appreciated the fact that a city's public image was of immense importance and therefore were determined to refurbish Knoxville's image and clean up its politics. Encouraged by the large number of comparatively progressive newcomer and annexed voters, this elite business group was eager to test its strength in the local political arena.

Thus, when Mayor John Duncan won election to the U.S. House of Representatives in late 1964, the way was open for these businessmen to replace him with one of their own. The man selected for support was Leonard Rogers. Rogers had come to Knoxville from Shelby County in 1932 to attend the University of Tennessee on a 4-H Club scholarship. Majoring in agriculture and graduating in 1937, he took a job with Security Mills, a large feed-manufacturing concern. There he remained for eighteen years, finally holding the position of regional sales manager for East Tennessee.[24]

Rogers first came to the attention of the business elite in the mid-1950s when he became secretary-manager of the Tennessee Valley Fair. "Agribusiness was still very important in Knoxville at that time," recalls Pilot Oil Corporation's Jim Haslam, "and Leonard Rogers was part of that business group. . . . And the fair was still a big deal," Haslam adds, "and whoever ran the fair was a very prominent and visible person." Elected president of the Chamber of Commerce in the late 1950s, Rogers earned the trust and confidence of the business elite. When city councilman Ernest J. "Ernie" O'Connor died in office in 1964, the business group persuaded Mayor Duncan to appoint Rogers to fill the vacancy on the city council. And in the 1965 special election to fill Duncan's unexpired term, Rogers surprised political cynics by winning the mayoral election handily and carrying a number of more progressive candidates onto the city council with him. Councilman Max Friedman told Rogers that the two years after Rogers's victory had been "the two happiest years of my life," since at last he was voting with the majority.[25]

Although he owed his victory to powerful support by the Chamber of Commerce–oriented business elite and the votes of newcomers and from the

Leonard Rogers (third from left).
Courtesy of University Tennessee Photographic Services

Kyle Testerman.
Reprinted by permission of
the Knoxville News-
Sentinel Company.

annexed areas, perhaps Rogers's greatest appeal came from the fact that he was no politician at all. After decades of savage political in-fighting, issueless campaigns, and bitter personal attacks and ripostes, voters seem to have wanted an end to politics as usual and a political breath of fresh air. "Leonard was a good person," remembers Haslam, and Testerman once admitted that Rogers was "cleaner and fresher" than many of his own associates. Described by nearly all who knew him as "an honest, decent, Christian man," Rogers was especially popular with church groups smarting from their recent loss on the issue of liquor sales by the bottle, and with business people and others who believed Knoxville desperately needed to take advantage of the "window of opportunity" that appeared to open in the 1960s. With a comfortable majority on the city council (despite Walker, who had supported Rogers during the mayoral race but had tried to barter that support for political appointments), Rogers possessed an almost unmatched opportunity to move Knoxville in new directions. With continued backing from a so-called Citizens' Group (actually an organization of elite businessmen), Rogers won election to a full mayoral term in 1967.[26]

Observers of Knoxville politics were surprised at the apparent ease with which the old political system had been overturned. And yet, as has been shown, the demographic, economic, and ideological changes in the city all played into Rogers's hand. Not only had the balance of power shifted toward the middle-class and upper-middle-class fringes of the city, but the old "floating wards" (principally Wards One, Two, Three, Five, and Seven-S in the center city, where vote buying was notorious) made up a steadily shrinking proportion of Knoxville's total voters—especially after the Vine Street–Morningside Heights federal urban renewal project had removed much of the residential housing and population from the city's core. Therefore, what many people believed was a political revolution in 1965 and 1967 actually was the product of demographic and economic revolutions.[27]

Given the constraints imposed by a charter-mandated property tax ceiling (which Rogers initially thought politically unwise to challenge), the new mayor's list of accomplishments was impressive. In an attempt to improve the city's bond rating, he employed Wainwright and Ramsey, a professional bond consulting firm from New York, to put together a printed bond prospectus. It was the first time Knoxville had ever done so, and bidders for the important sewer bonds were encouraged. Then, to ease the load on the newly annexed homeowners, he worked out a plan whereby the bonds could be paid off through slight increases in the water bills. Understanding that tax increases had been the undoing of several previous mayors and city managers, Rogers preferred to use further bond issues and increased federal monies to achieve his goals. Three new high schools (Bearden, Central, South-Young) were built in this way, as were the Safety Building, traffic improvements, and the eastern leg of the Downtown Loop. And other ambitious projects were begun, including the new McGhee Tyson Airport terminal and the Morningside and Mountain View urban renewal projects. If Rogers did not move as boldly as some would have liked, he had acted more energetically than had most of his predecessors.[28]

Anyone who expected Rogers to be bold, however, simply did not know the man. Having made his reputation as a cautious and judicious (even a trifle conservative, as a result of his rural upbringing) businessman, he was not about to abandon the instincts that had carried him so far. Identifying the principal needs as constructing schools, providing services (especially sewers) for the areas annexed in 1962, and attracting new industries, Rogers moved in a businesslike manner to address these challenges with the limitations imposed by the city charter as well as by his own personality. "Leonard Rogers," explained Jim Haslam, "was a *very* conservative person."[29]

Rogers's tenure was the longest of any Knoxville mayor to that time since the Civil War. Even so, by the late 1960s his political position had deteriorated badly. For one thing, the Chamber of Commerce–oriented business elite that had chosen Rogers and, in one sense, actually had created him as a visible personage and mayor once again proved itself temperamentally unsuited to the daily demands of politics, preferring instead to select one of its own and then, assured that all was well, retreat to the safety and comfort of their boardrooms and the Cherokee Country Club (Rogers never belonged) as it had so many times in the past. Hence, as Rogers's political problems mounted, he looked around for those who had urged him to become mayor in the first place. But they had deserted him, leaving him exposed before the screaming political winds.

As a leader with a diminishing number of followers, Rogers was vulnerable both to old and new forces in Knoxville politics. Almost from the day of his reelection in 1967, the mayor had fallen out with the still-dangerous Cas Walker, at first because Rogers had rejected Walker's patronage demands and later over the issue of sewer financing for the annexed areas. Walker hammered at Rogers almost incessantly, hinting darkly of conflicts of interest and undue political pressure on city employees. This pressure was alleged to emanate mostly from the office of Toby Julian, a Rogers appointee whose official duties concerned the city garage but whose primary value to Rogers was as political consultant and wheelhorse. "They beat me to death with Toby Julian," Rogers remembers, "but he was the only man I had who had any political savvy."[30]

Certainly Rogers had little himself. As Walker and his allies attacked Rogers at every opportunity, the new political force of the business-developer bloc had grown impatient with what they considered to have been the mayor's judicious, gradualist approach to the city's problems and were making plans to oust him. Forming a strange and impermanent alliance with Cas Walker to overthrow Rogers, the business-developer bloc called for an even newer vision, newer ideas, and newer leaders. Kyle Testerman, the titular head of the business-developer bloc, grew increasingly critical of Rogers from his seat on the city council, while at the same time planning his own campaign for mayor. Popular and influential attorney Claude Robertson, the state chairman of the Republican Party and Richard Nixon's Tennessee campaign manager in 1968, had been a valuable aide to Rogers in his 1965 victory. But Robertson was planning a run for the governorship in 1970 and could ill afford to be tied to Rogers (who was a Democrat) and what appeared to be the mayor's sinking ship. Newcomers who had been annexed in 1962 either had grown impatient with the mayor or had become hopelessly lost in their adopted city's Byzantine political intrigues.[31]

Rogers, then, had become a leader without followers. His attempts to overhaul the city police department, which he claimed had been riddled with graft and corruption when he took office (Rogers said later that gambling and prostitution had enriched some police officers), led to charges of a political purge and earned the embattled mayor a host of enemies. His inability to stave off a comparatively modest city property-tax increase was met with howls of rage and anguish and charges of waste. Similar protests met Rogers's scheme to bring in an outside assessor, who would be impervious to local political pressure, to reassess property for revenue purposes. In the face of these attacks, Rogers seemed strangely paralyzed. "Some of my friends came to me," he remembers, "and told me I ought to go out and campaign in the country clubs. But what would I say to them? I'm a stranger out there."[32]

The end for Rogers came quickly but painfully. Facing Testerman in 1971 in a typically savage Knoxville political campaign, Rogers discovered how untenable his position had become. Testerman's campaign was energetic, well coordinated, and well financed, its major theme being that Rogers lacked the vision and energy to get Knoxville moving. Rogers was portrayed (though never by Testerman personally) as a redneck bumpkin, a political naïf whose job was simply over his head. Rogers countered that his opponent was a wheeler-dealer, a candidate of the country club group, who would abandon the interests of the majority of the citizens in favor of those of the developers and the "silk-stocking crowd."[33]

Testerman's support of liquor by the drink, his biggest political gamble in 1971, also appeared to influence voters' behavior. Antiliquor religious groups began leaning toward Rogers, who often mixed religion and politics by campaigning from the pulpits of various local churches. But Testerman made inroads among Knoxville's business and professional newcomers, most of whom believed that the city's drinking ordinances were archaic. As we shall see, for some liquor by the drink had become both symbol and metaphor for Knoxville's modernization.[34]

University faculty members supported Testerman, although without much enthusiasm. Many of them had been outraged by Rogers's waffling behavior during the 1970 Billy Graham Crusade, which was held in Neyland Stadium on the university campus and featured an appearance by President Richard Nixon. The president recently had ordered the bombing of Cambodia and, as a result, was greeted by a small but vocal group of anti–Vietnam War students and faculty. When Nixon rose to speak, approximately 200 protesters unleashed their vocal—and occasionally obscene—criticisms, which in turn were almost immediately overwhelmed by the more than 75,000 attendees. Occasionally the shouting back and forth resembled some kind of 1960s-era guerilla theater,

Dr. Billy Graham and President Richard Nixon at the Knoxville Crusade, May 1970.

Reprinted by permission of the Knoxville News-Sentinel Company.

as when Nixon stated, "Even if we *are* on the twenty-yard line, we are going to be *over that goal line* before we are through," to which the protesters replied, "Push 'em back, Push 'em back, Wa-a-ay back!"[35]

Nine of the protesters were arrested on the spot, and later fifty-seven other arrest warrants were sworn out, the charge being the unlawful disruption of a religious service (Tennessee Code Annotated 39-1204). Mayor Rogers refused to stop the arrests, even ignoring a magnanimous request by the Nixon White House that the protesters not be arrested. Although the penalties were small, the Knoxville police had been energetic, and Rogers suffered the brunt of faculty attacks for his failure to rein them in. And while many faculty members viewed Testerman as a cultural barbarian (some faculty saw *all* Knoxville political figures in this light), they clearly preferred him to the conservative and low-key Rogers.[36]

In reality, Rogers never had a chance. Although he carried the affluent "old money" areas like Sequoyah Hills (where Testerman was seen as a young, arrogant upstart) and some of the older neighborhoods of North Knoxville, he had been badly outmaneuvered by his opponent. Testerman had won Cas Walker's endorsement and, while that was not the political prize it once had been, that support probably helped him among the black and working-class white voters. More important, Testerman carried the populous newer West Knoxville suburbs, the "floating wards" of Mechanicsville, and a large share of the business community. Testerman carried a whopping 63.1 percent of the vote (garnering 27,260 votes to Rogers's 15,918), giving him the most decisive mandate that any new mayor had had in decades.[37]

An embarrassed and embittered Leonard Rogers vacated the mayor's office, taking a position with the University of Tennessee Institute for Public Service. And even by the time of his early retirement ten years later (in 1981), the bitterness had not totally evaporated. Lampooned by his political foes and deserted by his allies, he felt that the city had failed to appreciate the progress he had made. And perhaps it had. For the Rogers years (1965–71) were important ones in redirecting Knoxville away from its troubled past and into new channels. If Rogers did not create all the forces responsible for this redirection, at least he knew how to use them judiciously. Indeed, if anyone can be credited for laying the groundwork for what was to come, Rogers clearly can. Ironically, although he was elected in 1965 principally because he was not a politician, ultimately that fact proved his undoing.[38]

In many ways Kyle Testerman was the opposite of Leonard Rogers. Born to a well-to-do Knoxville family, early in life he struggled with infantile paralysis, and some physicians said he would never walk again. But by sheer self-discipline and force of will, Testerman did walk, then ran, then became a champion tennis player, then played on the University of Tennessee basketball team. By the time he became mayor at the age of thirty-six, Kyle Testerman fairly bristled with physical energy and "presence," whereas Leonard Rogers might well have been mistaken for a small-town bank president who preferred a quiet game of horseshoes. The new mayor favored well-tailored, expensive clothes and the latest fashions (including body jewelry), whereas Rogers dressed modestly. Testerman was bold in personality and vocabulary, whereas Rogers was almost shy. Indeed, no better symbols of the aggressive business-developer and the more conservative and cautious business-progressive could be found than Kyle Testerman and Leonard Rogers.[39]

But the differences between the two men went far beyond surface impressions. Rogers lacked political acumen, whereas Testerman was more sagacious. In a comparatively short time, the new mayor had accumulated a massive amount of local political knowledge. He knew who had real power and who did not, who held the strings and where they led ("On the school board, Sarah Moore Greene wouldn't go to the bathroom until she'd checked with Cas Walker"),[40] who could deliver the votes and who could not, who knew where the political bodies were buried and who had buried them. By the time he came to be head of the business-developer bloc and unseated Rogers in 1971, Testerman was one of the most knowledgeable political figures in the city's modern history.

Nor did Testerman lack well-thought-out goals or bold dreams. To him the time for planning and debate was over. He realized, as a developer would, that downtown Knoxville would never again become the region's retail shopping center. "It's a national trend," he mused, "and even Rich's couldn't fight it." Following Knoxville's "1990 Plan," a development plan created while he was on the Metropolitan Planning Commission in 1970, Testerman envisioned the Gay Street area as the business-financial district. West of that would be a major north-south outdoor mall development, bounded by the TVA towers on the north and a new city-county building on the south. An east-west mall, mixing exclusive new townhouses, pedestrian walkways, and specialty shops would intersect the Market Street Mall.[41]

If Knoxville were to achieve those ambitious plans, the new mayor believed, two things had to happen. First, federal funds from revenue-sharing and community-development grants had to be attracted, and attracted in a magnitude that Knoxville had never seen before. Second, new private money had to be lured downtown. "One of the things that held Knoxville back," the developer-mayor explained, "was that a high proportion of downtown property was controlled by a small number of old-money families. For downtown development to take place, those old estates had to be broken up. Private money could do a lot of that, but I'd use the power of eminent domain if necessary."[42]

Indeed, the new mayor seemed almost daily to explode with new ideas. The youthful Testerman brought into city hall with him an aggressive and innovative group of young people, some barely out of college. There were a few, such as Guy Smith IV (Testerman's press secretary and grandson of the powerful former editor of the *Knoxville Journal*), who had political ties to some of the old power groups, but most were a new breed of apolitical managers whose brainstorming sessions went on well into the night and whose days were spent trying to implement their schemes. Men like Darcy Sullivan, Steve Blackwell, Jim Easton, Robert Booker, Graham Hunter, Mike Hill, Buddy Palmore, Louis Hofferbert, and others may have had little political clout themselves, but they had something more valuable in the awakening city: access to Testerman, whose political savvy and flamboyance both stimulated and publicized their dreams.[43]

Fortunately, the money was there. A combination of aggressive and imaginative grant-proposal writing and wily political horse-trading with the Nixon administration secured about $84 million in revenue-sharing and community-development money. Money was acquired for the TVA twin towers, the city-county building, the Bicentennial Park, and the double mall. In a major downtown cleanup effort (dubbed "Bury City Hall"), tons of garbage were collected from streets and alleys by private citizens and dumped on the steps of City Hall. In truth, it seems as if Testerman could make good his boast that he was going to "bulldoze downtown and start all over again."[44]

In his campaign against Rogers, Testerman had vowed to liberalize the city's liquor laws. Though few could vouch for their veracity, there were oft-told stories of convention business that Knoxville had lost because it did not allow the sale of liquor by the drink. But referenda on that issue (the most recent in 1966) had failed before, killed (it was rumored) by a strange combination of church groups and liquor dealer interests, and by the apathy of those who belonged to private clubs where they could evade the spirit of the law while drinking as they pleased. Finally in 1961 (on the third try in seven years) a liquor-by-the-bottle referendum had passed, largely because private clubs were being raided and bootlegger sources drying up. But in the meantime other southern cities had passed liquor-by-the-drink referenda and, presumably because of that, had seen an upswing in their convention business.

Testerman threw his full weight on the side of change. First, he secured a separate city referendum (previously, county and city had voted together on this issue, and the county vote had been strongly anti-liberalization). Then the mayor visited every private club in the city, vowing to close all of them down the day after the vote if the referendum failed. Hoping for convention dollars as well as potential new hotel construction, much of the business community went along. The result was a triumph for Testerman: the 1972 liquor-by-the-drink referendum passed by more than two to one. Fittingly, the first legal drink was mixed for and consumed by the ebullient mayor at Ireland's Restaurant on Cumberland Avenue. Trivia buffs may note that it was a gin and tonic, which Testerman, never famous as a teetotaler, consumed with ill-disguised satisfaction.[45]

The event was thoroughly symbolic. For the first time since the World War I era, when Mayor John E. McMillan had stood against overt racism and the Ku Klux Klan, a Knoxville mayor had broken with traditional local mores and had cast his political lot with the progressive and demographic future. In response to a 1972 invitation to a ribbon cutting for a retail establishment, Testerman sent his aide Robert Booker, an African American who had been one of the principal leaders of the 1960 sit-in demonstrations. An angry store manager complained to the mayor, "If you can't do anything better than that, we're just going to cancel the whole thing." Testerman refused to budge, and the store opened without ceremony. And in that same year, the mayor willingly proclaimed Halloween "Trick or Treat for UNICEF Eve," ignoring the fact that but a few years earlier Knoxvillians had argued over whether or not the United Nations was a communist organization (mayors Duncan and Rogers both had called such a proclamation "political dynamite"). Testerman proposed the trial consolidation of city and county schools, despite warnings that the always-dangerous issue of racial integration lurked not far below the surface. He openly castigated the elected school board as timid, interest-ridden, and shortsighted. His occasionally colorful speech, reminiscent of Harry Truman's on his saltier days, drew both gasps and sympathetic laughter in just about equal doses. His immediate embrace of the world's fair concept earned him both praise and condemnation. Indeed, it was as if the mayor's office was too staid and confining, almost suffocating, for this young, athletic man. His ideas and energy seemed almost boundless, and he appeared to want to offer new and innovative ideas even before his older ones had been brought to fruition.[46]

As Rogers before him had been, Testerman was aided by a number of fortuitous circumstances. The University of Tennessee, which had expanded to approximately 26,000 students, now had an enormous payroll and almost inexhaustible construction money. By the mid-1970s the Blount Mansion Historic Area was completed, and the restoration of the famous Lamar House–Bijou Theater was under way. The Hyatt Regency Hotel was about to see the light at the end of its profit-and-loss tunnel. The Summit Hill Project was well underway, opening up the northern section of downtown and providing a future connector into the Fort Sanders–University of Tennessee area. Federal money continued to flow, and the entertainment and liquor taxes were providing needed revenue, even generating the luxury of a budget surplus and property tax decreases from time to time. Indeed, it seemed as if all was well and Knoxville finally had reawakened from decades of slumber.

But for Testerman all was not well. His impatience with the normally languid processes of government, his open contempt for those who disagreed with him, his reputation as a wheeler-dealer developer, and his willingness to take positions on even the most controversial issues overwhelmed him in the end. Perhaps he wanted Knoxville to change too rapidly; he wanted the city, after decades of inertia, to be remade overnight. In 1975, in a reelection bid, he failed to secure a majority on the first ballot and was forced into a runoff with the popular Randy Tyree. Testerman was stunned, bewildered, hurt, and angry. In an ill-advised election eve outburst that was widely covered by television reporters, he lashed out at the voters who he believed had betrayed him. Tyree won the runoff, principally by carrying North and South Knoxville, where voters were largely white middle-class and blue-collar workers. While Testerman won in East Knoxville (mostly black voters) and West Knoxville (upper-middle-class business professionals and prosperous newcomers), the heavy turnout in the older and more populous northern and southern areas of the city overwhelmed him.[47]

Looking back on his defeat, Testerman believed himself to have been a victim of the Watergate backlash that had turned out incumbents throughout the nation. And he may have been more correct than he himself realized. Both Richard Nixon and Kyle Testerman had shown impatience with the often cumbersome and inefficient democratic process. Both were peevish and even arrogant in the face of opposition or harsh criticism. And Testerman's youthful and ambitious staff seemed too much like local versions of Haldeman, Erlichman, Ziegler, and Dean—men of the new, nonideological, apolitical, and often antidemocratic managerial class. In some ways, they probably were.[48]

But to see Testerman simply as a victim of the backlash against Richard Nixon is both inaccurate and unfair to the defeated mayor. Testerman's successful push for liquor-by-the-drink had alienated large portions of the city. Many felt he had been too favorable to developers, substantial business interests, and the newcomers who poured into the affluent suburbs of West Knoxville. His favorable comments regarding city-county school consolidation frightened those who worried that a unified school system would fail to meet federal court standards on racial desegregation. On the more partisan political front, Testerman's early falling-out with Cas Walker (who seemed to fall out with every candidate soon after he had backed him or her) gave him an enemy who as late as 1975 could not be underrated. Also, supporters of Leonard Rogers's 1971 reelection bid were only too eager to get revenge. Finally, Testerman's effective but comparatively brutal breaking of a 1974 strike by municipal garbage collectors (later he was to brag about how he had so frightened a union organizer that the man immediately had left the city) shocked unions and liberals, especially around the university. In sum, Kyle Testerman had made too many political enemies, had given and taken too many political wounds, had shown himself too contemptuous of the average voters for them to support him any longer.[49]

One must not, however, overlook the fact that Testerman's principal opponent in his 1975 reelection bid was an attractive and popular candidate. Indeed, in many ways Randy Tyree was everything Testerman was not. Born in 1940 in Smith County, Tyree was the son of a sharecropper and had known poverty from the beginning. Fiercely ambitious and determined to rise from his humble origins, he joined the FBI after graduating from high school, starting in the records section and working his way up to field investigator. Realizing that his lack of a college education prevented him from rising further, Tyree enrolled at Middle Tennessee State University in 1962, graduated in three years, and then entered the University of Tennessee Law School, from which he was graduated in 1967. His love of police work, his FBI experience, and his recently acquired education made him an asset to the Knoxville Police Department, where he specialized in undercover operations aimed at reversing the city's growing narcotics traffic. In 1969 he first came to the public's attention with Operation Aquarius, a massive roundup of drug pushers principally in the university area. In 1971 he became Leonard Rogers's safety director, resigning when Testerman asked him to do so in January 1972. On that date, according to his critics, he began his four-year campaign for mayor. Unsullied by the city's often fetid political trenches, Tyree radiated modesty, decency, a self-deprecating humor, and sincerity (one of his critics said, "He can look at you with those sincere blue eyes and lie to you and you come out *believing* him").[50]

Blue-collar workers in North and South Knoxville saw Tyree as one of their own. Even though many had sons and daughters attending the university, at the same time they often saw that place as a haven for radicals, drugs, and unwholesome sexual activity. Thus Tyree's role in Operation Aquarius gained him numerous supporters, as did the backing of local gospel music promoter J. Bazzel Mull. Tyree's initial support for a referendum on the proposed world's fair led critics of that project to believe they had a friend in him. Finally, those North and South Knoxvillians who believed Testerman was "giving too much" to West Knoxville and had placed the city's government in the hands of greedy developers supported Tyree.[51]

In all, however, probably Testerman's greatest foe was himself. In a city that had just awakened from decades of virtual slumber, he pushed too hard,

Randy Tyree.
Reprinted by permission
of the Knoxville News-
Sentinel Company.

moved too fast, advocated too many changes at once for a populace used to
more judicious and conservative political leadership. In the end it was his
undoing.

So the political days of Rogers and Testerman, who both had done so
much to rejuvenate and redirect the ailing city, ended similarly in defeat and
bitterness. Rogers had been a casualty of his own cautiousness and political
innocence, Testerman of his own reckless courage and political style. Interestingly, both saw the solutions to Knoxville's problems as coming from outside the city, from new private money, from newly arrived residents, from
Washington agencies. Both seemed to believe that Knoxville itself lacked the
resources and the will to effect major changes in its character. Rogers sought to
deal with political reactionaries by demonstrating how sound, conservative
business techniques could effect great wonders, whereas Testerman tried simply to kick his political opposition to death. In the end both suffered the same
fate, one as a result of local factionalism and the other as a victim of a genuine
political uprising.

And despite some of the most dramatic changes the city had ever seen, one is forced to wonder whether in truth anything had changed at all. More properly put, had either Rogers or Testerman been able to harness the forces that in the 1960s and 1970s had buffeted nearly every American city? Rogers, the older of the two men, had tried to use the methods that had succeeded for him in business, without fully appreciating the magnitude of the forces he faced. For his part, Testerman understood those forces better and was less beholden to traditional solutions. But the forces of demography and history appear to have been too powerful for either man to conquer or even to withstand.

Mall Fever, Downtown, and the "Quantum Jump"

For one thing, the continuing waves of affluent newcomers, mostly business and professional people, tended to settle in the new developments along the western axis. By the early 1970s the population center of Knox County had shifted westward to approximately the area of the new Bearden High School, roughly ten miles from the center city. In the Rocky Hill–Bluegrass area alone, population jumped an astounding 69 percent between 1960 and 1968. A large proportion of these newcomers settled west of the city limits, depriving the city of needed tax revenues. More important, these newcomers tended to form attitudinal enclaves of their own, hence deepening the chasm between them and the older residents of the city. Generally younger, better educated, and more liberal in their social views (dramatized by the liquor issue, for example), less tied to traditional ideas, more accustomed to demanding educational and social services, and more inclined to organize themselves into homeowners' and issues-oriented groups, these men and women made the story of Knoxville truly a tale of two cities.[52]

As we have seen, the downtown area had received a much-needed facelift in the late 1960s. But affluent newcomers rarely came downtown to shop, preferring instead the accessibility and spacious free parking of the shopping malls that had sprung up all along Kingston Pike in the 1970s. The Chrysler Corporation had started this boom in 1965 when it announced plans for constructing West Town Mall in the Bearden area. Chrysler sold the almost-completed project to other interests, but the mall boom had begun. West Town opened on August 2, 1972, with 600,000 square feet of retail space and seventy-five stores, anchored by Miller's, J. C. Penney, Proffitt's, and Sears. Almost immediately retail trade downtown plummeted. By 1978, every motion picture theater in downtown Knoxville was closed, while over ten had opened in the western suburbs. Restaurants, except for the well-established and twice-renovated Regas, generally suffered, and specialty shops on Gay Street and the Market Square began pulling out. As Testerman and the Center City Task Force recognized, if downtown Knoxville was to be revitalized as a retail trade area (and Testerman was dubious on that score), then major residential projects would have to be undertaken to lure affluent newcomers to the center city.[53]

But no major residential development took place in the downtown area. Instead, city consumers and taxpayers in the 1960s and 1970s increasingly tended to be elderly, black, and poor or living on fixed incomes severely threatened by the national inflation of the Vietnam and post-Vietnam eras. By 1970 over 11 percent of Knoxville's population was sixty-five or over, and approximately 30,000 people (17 percent) lived on fixed incomes. In spite of some rather massive urban renewal projects, the city's blacks continued to live in depressed conditions, which became breeding grounds for social problems. A 1973 study by the Knoxville–Knox County Community Action Committee (of which Testerman was the vice-chairman) showed that city planning units with high proportions of black residents led the city in school dropouts, infant mortality, tuberculosis, venereal disease, adult arrests, juvenile delinquency, and reliance on public assistance.[54]

For the city government the problem was clear. The center city, largely inhabited by the poor, the black, and the elderly, continued to demand services that took more money to provide than the city collected in tax revenues from this area. At the same time, an increasing number of affluent newcomers were settling west of the city limits (the areas from Cedar Bluff to Farragut was rapidly becoming one enormous suburban development), were not returning downtown to shop, and were luring retail businesses away from the city and into the malls. Should the city government continue to chase and envelop these people and businesses on the western rimland? If so, was continued annexation or a countywide metropolitan government (similar to Nashville's) the easiest and most efficient method? In short, if the people that Knoxville wanted would not come to the city, then should the city go to them? And how would these people react to this blatant but understandable urban imperialism?

For some people, the answer was a countywide referendum on metropolitan government, to be held on November 7, 1978. An earlier attempt, in 1959, had ended with the proposal's resounding defeat in both the city and county. But enormous changes had taken place since 1959, and backers such as businessmen E. B. Copeland, James Dempster, and Jim Haslam; University of Tennessee president Edward Boling; public officials like county school superintendent Mildred Doyle, county judge Howard Bozeman, county trustee Bob Broome, and Mayor Randy Tyree; and the Greater Knoxville Chamber of Commerce believed that this time a referendum on metropolitan government would pass. These people formed the nucleus of Citizens for

Knoxville–Knox County Government, the titular head of which was former University of Tennessee professor and popular civic leader Dr. Earl Ramer. "Given the opposition to annexation and the growing city problems," Ramer recalled later, "the idea made sense to me, and I allowed them to make me president."[55]

Assuming that county voters would oppose metropolitan government (although it was hoped that suburban newcomers would make the county vote close), campaign strategists planned to sell the concept hard in both areas, in the city promising lower taxes and in the county raising the fears of annexation if metro government were not approved. Large community meetings were scheduled, as were talks before civic clubs, a door-to-door campaign, and heavy advertising using supporters with high name recognition.

But metro backers underestimated their opposition, the traditional intransigence of the voters, and many newcomers' fears that metropolitan government would mean that county property owners would see their tax dollars used to aid the struggling city to which they had no loyalty. Predictably, Cas Walker immediately raised howls of protest, once telling the mild-mannered and courtly Ramer, "I don't want to *talk* about it—I want to fight it." Walker and others turned the public meetings into loud anti-metro harangues. As opponents became more vocal, some corporate contributors to the pro-metro war chest got nervous and pulled out, leaving the Citizens for Knoxville–Knox County Government perpetually short of funds. In the end, the referendum on metropolitan government carried in the city (25,408 to 20,137), but failed to secure the necessary majority in Knox County.[56]

Without the hoped-for bailout of metropolitan government, the city became even more dependent on continued injections of federal and state dollars, an approach to urban problems that was both naïve and foolish. Testerman had presided over Knoxville in the days when federal grants had been large and readily available. But in the mid-1970s, toward the end of Testerman's administration, it was already becoming clear that the flow of federal-, state-, and university-induced money could not go on forever. The university had expanded to the limits of its classroom and dormitory space, and any future growth would take massive capital outlays—funds the state simply did not have. Federal and state money continued, but inflation diminished its buying power. The burgeoning suburbs and growing tendency to shop in the new malls put even more strain on city services, and an increasing dependence on automobiles meant streets simply were inadequate to handle the traffic flow. Harried public school officials looked for programs to cut and were even forced to consider slicing academic as well as extracurricular programs. Parents' groups campaigning for new programs, such as regular physical education or foreign

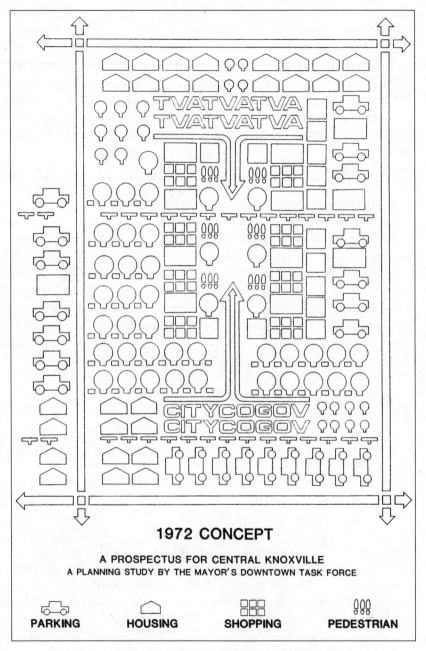

1972 CONCEPT

A PROSPECTUS FOR CENTRAL KNOXVILLE
A PLANNING STUDY BY THE MAYOR'S DOWNTOWN TASK FORCE

PARKING　　**HOUSING**　　**SHOPPING**　　**PEDESTRIAN**

Downtown Concept Map, 1972.

languages at the elementary school level, found themselves swimming against the tide.

But if the problem was clear, the solution was less so. Concerned business people and developers increasingly talked of a "quantum jump" needed to revitalize downtown, get construction rolling again, continue to attract massive amounts of public money, lure tourist dollars (one city official jokingly proposed inventing a machine to "stop tourists going to the Smoky Mountains at the city limits, turn them upside down and shake some money out of them"), and increase city revenues. Before long, the term "quantum jump" was on the lips of many merchants and government officials.

They knew what they wanted to do. In the early 1970s the Boeing Corporation had sent planners to the region for the purpose of building a new city, to be named Timberlake, near the Tellico Dam (which was under construction). From the beginning, the TVA Tellico Dam project had been surrounded by controversy, and although the Knoxville city council under Leonard Rogers had endorsed the project, many Knoxvillians opposed the dam as unnecessary, wasteful, an exercise in self-justification by TVA, and harmful to the environment. Lawsuits by environmentalists, including a famous suit to preserve a small fish called the snail darter by placing it on the endangered species list, blocked the development of Timberlake. Finding the Boeing planners in Knoxville with nothing to do, Mayor Testerman convinced the giant corporation to lend the planners to the city at no cost. The result was a General Redevelopment Plan, adopted by the city council in 1972. The plan was a bold one. It proposed opening up downtown to massive mall-like developments and residences, overcoming the topographical features that separated the university from the central business district, and incorporating massive amounts of accessible parking space. But developers, business people, and political figures still bemoaned the lack of the "quantum jump" necessary to translate the plan into reality. Testerman could get grants, start public buildings, cajole downtown property owners, and use the powers of eminent domain. However, even that would not be enough.[57]

On a trip to Tulsa in 1974, W. Stewart Evans, a retired military officer and president of the Downtown Knoxville Association, happened to meet King Cole, the man who had developed an international exposition in Spokane, Washington, in 1974. Returning to Knoxville aflame like a person saved at a revival meeting, Evans jubilantly announced, "I've found our quantum jump—a world's fair in Knoxville!" Never one to think small, Mayor Testerman was immediately excited, understanding the "concept of utilizing an International Exposition as a catalyst to achieve [downtown] development goals." In other words, Testerman saw the advantages of using massive outlays of public and private money to buy a large tract of downtown real estate that could be developed after the exposition closed. King Cole was hired as a consultant, and Testerman appointed banker and ambitious political figure Jake Butcher to head a committee charged with doing a feasibility study. No one doubted what the recommendation of such a study would be. Thus strode to center stage one of the most interesting figures in the city's entire history.[58]

Jacob Franklin Butcher was born in Dotson's Creek in Union County (approximately seven miles from Maynardville) in 1936. The son of Cecil H. Butcher, who had risen from a "rolling store" operator to general store owner, founding partner (in 1929) of the Southern Industrial Banking Corporation (which made loans to farmers for farm equipment and automobiles) and the Union County Bank (1950), Jake served a long apprenticeship under his father, one associate recalling that "he started in banking by sweeping the floors and then counting pennies." After attending the University of Tennessee, serving in the Marine Corps, spending a year at Hiwassee College, and then two more years at UT (he never graduated), Jake Butcher was ready to enter the business world.[59]

Although he founded and ran the Bull Run Oil Company (an Amoco distributorship) and dabbled in commercial farming, Jake Butcher's real interests were banking and politics. In 1986 Jake and his younger brother Cecil H. Butcher Jr. purchased their first bank, the First National Bank of Lake City. Immediately the Butchers started making enormous internal loans to themselves, a practice that earned them a warning from the United States Treasury Department. With the borrowed money, they began purchasing other banks, only to repeat the process. In 1974, with capital borrowed from his other banks, Jake Butcher began purchasing stock in the Hamilton National Bank, at the time Knoxville's largest banking institution, with 39.2 percent of the city's total banking resources. In early 1975, after a brief fight, Butcher won complete control of the bank and changed its name to United American.[60]

The Butcher victory represented more than just one man's personal triumph. As has been noted above, up to the time of the Butcher takeover Knoxville's bankers had been a closely knit, cautious fraternity, generally suspicious of new people (like the business-developer bloc) and radically new ideas. But Butcher's inclinations and thinking closely dovetailed with those of the business-developer bloc. Moreover, few at the time appreciated how fragile and vulnerable Butcher's banking empire was. His imagination, boldness, and willingness to take risks obliged other local banks to become more venturesome. Though Butcher's attention was often absorbed by two unsuccessful bids, in 1974 and 1978, to become Tennessee's governor, his willingness to gamble on redevelopment and new industries made him—and the business-developer bloc—a major force in Knoxville's economic and political life. By 1982 the United American bank accounted for over half the business loans made in the city, and together the Butcher brothers owned twenty-eight banks throughout Tennessee and Kentucky. As Jake Butcher once joked, "the only way you can lose money when you have a bank is to shovel it out the back door." No one knew at the time how close to the truth that was.[61]

Butcher's banking practices and his extravagant lifestyle (he owned a forty-room mansion with thirteen bathrooms, a $2 million private jet, a $600,000 helicopter, and a $500,000 yacht) needed more and more infusions of money in order to stay afloat (the Butchers' associate Jesse Barr later said that "Jake's spending was out of control"). Doubtless he saw a world's fair as an opportunity to siphon millions of dollars out of the enterprise to save his huge but rickety banking empire. After an unsuccessful campaign for the governorship in 1978 (in which he was defeated by Republican Lamar Alexander), Butcher turned his full attention to Knoxville's world's fair.[62]

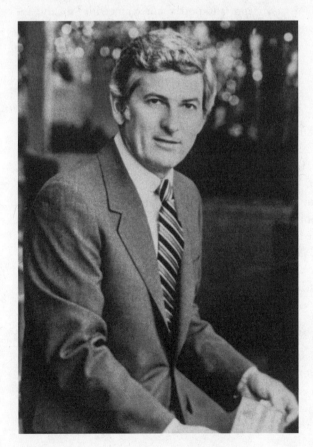

Jake Butcher.
Reprinted by permission of the Knoxville News-Sentinel Company

The Knoxville International Energy Exposition, Incorporated, a private nonprofit organization, was formed in early 1976. The Bureau of International Expositions (BIE) in Paris was contacted, and Evans (with the combined power of Testerman and Butcher behind him) began drumming up public support.

Although it was claimed that a number of sites for the exposition were considered, in reality only one site fit both the Boeing plan and Testerman's dreams of downtown redevelopment: the lower Second Creek area, a parcel of roughly seventy acres running south from Western Avenue to the Tennessee River, in the corridor between the university and downtown. Once called Scuffletown, for years the valley had been the scene of slum dwellings around the Southern Railway yard that bisected the valley. By 1972 most of the houses had been torn down, although over sixty businesses still inhabited the area. Since the university moved to its present campus in the early 1800s, Second Creek had effectively separated the campus from downtown. In the Boeing plan, this area was immensely important, both for "reconnecting" the university with downtown and for establishing residential housing and parking near the center city.

Needing a theme to present to the BIE, planners settled on "Energy Turns the World," hoping that UT and Oak Ridge connections might attract "new, high-tech" energy-related industries to Knoxville after the 184-day exposition. Later, George Siler, the exposition's executive vice president, admitted that the "energy theme was a fluke that just fell in our laps." But the *real* theme was the redevelopment of Knoxville, the "quantum jump" many felt was so necessary.[63]

Essentially, then, the project was a private enterprise clothed in the garb of a public institution. Through the Knoxville Community Development Corporation (KCDC), the city acquired the land and prepared the site, using an $11.6 million city bond issue for money. The administration of President Jimmy Carter delivered $20 million for the United States Pavilion, the federal government appropriated an additional $12.45 million for site development, and forty-three banks wrote over $30 million in loans to complete preparations for the World's Fair, scheduled for the summer and autumn of 1982. It didn't hurt that Jake Butcher entertained President and Mrs. Carter at his fabulous mansion "Whirlwind." As S. H. "Bo" Roberts, president of the Knoxville International Energy Exposition, commented, "The world's fair would not have taken place without Jake."[64]

The Spokane World's Fair had been held in spite of the fact that a majority of voters in a special referendum had voted against the project. Evans, Testerman, and Butcher—who probably feared that innate conservative feelings, combined with suspicion of outsiders and aversion to any tax increases, would stop the expo in its tracks—had no intention of holding such a referendum. Instead, they tried to woo the citizens with artists' renderings of highway improvements and visions of tourist dollars, while staving off calls for a vote on whether or not to hold the exposition. As KCDC executive director John Ulmer put it, the "average beer-swillin' Knoxville citizen" would not take the time to study the issues and would simply vote "no" as a knee-jerk reaction to any proposal for change. For his part, during the 1975 mayoralty race, Randy Tyree had favored a referendum. Once in office, however, the new mayor swung into line, in April 1977 breaking a four-to-four tie in the city council on a referendum and in May 1977 crushing council voices for a referendum by virtually ignoring *Robert's Rules of Order* and maintaining that a referendum was not necessary, since there would be no city money in the exposition (the $11.6 million bond issue had been approved by council the previous January). The BIE gave its final approval and the KCDC began acquiring property. An embittered Richard Marius, a University of Tennessee history professor, urged defeated opponents to gather and join "in singing that sweet invitational hymn":

> Softly and Tenderly
> Expo is calling,
> Calling for you and [for] me,
> See in the papers
> The benefits falling,
> Manna from Randy Tyree.[65]

Every single poll taken—and there were several—showed that healthy majorities of Knoxville voters favored a referendum on the world's fair. Interestingly, those same polls showed that opponents of Expo 82 (as it was coming to be called) were a curious mixture of old and new Knoxville. Cas Walker initially was adamantly opposed, singing his old song to his old constituency about higher taxes and huge profits for the "silk-stocking crowd." But many professional people and affluent newcomers were opposed also, fearing that their "peaceful little city" would be the scene of massive traffic congestion and cheap carnival atmosphere. University political science professor Joe Dodd, a leader of the movement to block the expo, hinted darkly of poor planning, underfinancing, and probable financial failure. But the city council and the mayor's office were too strong for the opponents and had too many resources for the anti-expo forces. Walker gradually lessened his opposition, and Dodd lost ground as the pro-expo coalition wore him down.[66]

Indeed, if anything, many Knoxvillians came to see the World's Fair and its aftereffects (dubbed "residuals" by fair promoters and supporters) as the answer to all the city's problems. In this, the World's Fair officials were in part culpable. While they always added the caveat that the ambitious project could not do all things for all people, their responses to attacks and criticisms tended to emphasize the notion that the 1982 World's Fair would turn the city around.

The Knoxville International Energy Exposition opened with much fanfare on May 1, 1982. President Ronald Reagan did the official honors, while popular singer and native Tennessean Dinah Shore was the mistress of ceremonies. By noon, around 87,000 people had passed through the gates to see exhibits by 22 nations (those by the People's Republic of China, Egypt, and the Philippines were the most popular), 90 private corporations, and 6 states. The impressive and jovial crowd consumed funnel cakes, Danish waffles, gyros, and Australian beer while listening to music, watching parades, and participating in the general excitement and good times. On May 16, the World's Fair greeted its one millionth visitor, and by May 30 it had passed the two million mark. For a brief moment, Knoxville's inferiority complex was forgotten.[67]

By the time the fair closed on October 31, 1982, 11,127,786 visits had been made to the fair—close to the 12,970,000 predicted in 1976 by consultants Haworth and Anderson. As the organizers basked in the fair's success, a billboard near the fair site took an ill-disguised shot at the *Wall Street Journal,* which earlier had looked down its nose at the world's fair that would be held in such a "scruffy little city." The billboard simply announced, "The 'scruffy little city' DID IT!"[68]

In some sense, however, the Knoxville International Energy Exposition *already* was a success by opening day. Approximately $80 million in public money had been pumped into the fair site and surrounding area. The city now owned almost seventy acres just west of the central business district that could be used for downtown redevelopment. To handle the anticipated visitors, Interstates 40 and 75 were widened to six lanes, their junction (nicknamed "Malfunction Junction") was rebuilt, and the I-640 beltway was constructed to divert through traffic away from the center city. Taking advantage of Knoxville's new visibility, the Knoxville Sports Corporation was formed, which eventually brought to the city the Women's Basketball Hall of Fame, the 1994 National Track and Field Championship, the 1996 United States Gymnastic Trials, and two visits by the United States Junior Olympics. In all, then, the World's Fair had opened up almost limitless possibilities for the city.[69]

This is not to say that everyone benefited from the World's Fair. People who owned rental housing near the fair site evicted approximately 1,000 monthly tenants in order to cash in on inflated nightly rentals. But many of those expensive nightly rentals remained vacant. At the same time, a group of

*World's Fair site as it looked in the 1920s. Photograph taken from
the hill at the University of Tennessee in the 1920s, when the
area was known as "Scuffletown."*

Courtesy of University of Tennessee Photographic Services.

*The World's Fair site, with the University of Tennessee
campus in the background, 1982.*

Printed with permission of Knoxville International Energy Exposition.

investors (including Tom Jensen, a state representative from Knoxville and house minority leader) had purchased several modular housing units, trucked them to Knoxville, hooked them together, named them the "Notell Motel," and advertised rooms for $60.00 per night. The cheap-looking rentals for the most part remained empty, and the Notell Motel ended up around $12 million in debt. And off-site attractions such as the Knoxville Dinner Theater, the Knoxville Zoo, entertainment events at the civic coliseum, and an original musical at the downtown Tennessee Theater titled *The Murder of Buster Drumright* actually lost money (*Buster Drumright* lost around $750,000). Finally, while the World's Fair itself broke even, the city of Knoxville was left with a massive short-term debt of $50 million, which forced the city to refinance its debt, initiate a tax increase in 1985, cut the number of city employees, and turn garbage collection over to a private company in order to save money.[70]

Most individuals who lost money, however, did so because their greed overwhelmed their common sense. Most visitors had so much fun and so many things to see and do on the fair site that they remained there and ignored the lures of off-site attractions. In addition, many visitors were "day trippers" who did not require local lodging. And those who did stayed at the more than 14,000 quality hotel and motel accommodations in the area, or at the approximately 4,700 campsites.[71]

The major question, however, is *not* whether the Knoxville International Energy Exposition or individual speculators made or lost money. More important (indeed, it was *always* more important) is whether Knoxville would be able to use the recently acquired Lower Second Creek acreage intelligently to effect what Stuart Evans had called a "quantum jump" in downtown redevelopment. Of prime importance to fair supporters had been the revival of the center city, a truly formidable task. For almost a half-century, the old Knoxville (the pre-1962 city) had declined by almost every statistical indicator. While average family income in Knoxville in 1977 was $11,190 (and for the exclusive Sequoyah Hills $34,562), the central city's census tracts of Beaumont ($5,660), Mountain View ($6,486), and Broadway ($7,542) were well below the city's average. Could the redevelopment following the World's Fair reverse that trend?[72]

And, as one would expect, severe social problems accompanied the center city's low income. Of Knoxville's twenty-three planning units in 1975, the eight center city planning units that ranked lowest in family incomes were also the areas that ranked highest in social disorders (venereal disease, infant mortality, tuberculosis, school dropouts, adult arrests, and aid to dependent children). Nor were these areas simply poor African American enclaves: one of

Beaumont's three census tracts contained the highest percentage (53.2 percent) of poor in the city, yet it was but 7.9 percent black. These were the remnants of yesterday's people in today's city. Could post-fair redevelopment solve their problems as well?[73]

Many urban planners had come to believe that the revival of downtown Knoxville depended on the ability to attract young, affluent, childless couples ("DINKs," an acronym for "Double Income, No Kids") to *live* in the center city. Indeed, the 1977 Regional Urban Design Assistance Team (RUDAT) reported that stimulating a "gentrification" movement in the center city was critical to the success of post-fair redevelopment (RUDAT's recommendation was for 1,200 residential units—town houses, apartments, single-family homes—on the fair site). This, however, would be no easy task. Up to 1980, the very people the city would hope to attract to live in the center city did not appear to show much interest in being pioneers on this new urban frontier. In August 1981, the Metropolitan Planning Commission's study *Knoxville's Center City* reported that "a significant middle-upper class 'back-to-the-city' movement has yet to develop." To be sure, the Fourth and Gill neighborhood and Kristopher Kendrick's Masonic Square were interesting efforts at "gentrification," but it was too early to tell whether they would be pioneers or lone outposts. Could post-fair development in Lower Second Creek spur a genuine gentrification movement?[74]

Of course, the Downtown Knoxville Association always hoped that a world's fair and a post-fair gentrification movement would spur the revival of the downtown as a major retail center. For those worried property owners and retailers, such a stimulus could come none too soon. By 1977 (with the Knoxville International Energy Exposition already on the drawing board), the center city's share of the metropolitan area's retail sales was *less than half* of what it had been in 1967. Downtown boosters hoped that "mall fever" had spent itself, and yet a new shopping mall (initially named East Towne) was already under construction, and West Town Mall was adding on. Would one of the World's Fair's residual benefits be a revival of downtown Knoxville's retail business?[75]

Still others pinned their hopes for a center city resurgence on the dramatic increase in downtown office space. As Knoxville's economy shifted from industry to the government and service sectors, office space was in greater demand, and offices became the fastest growing land use in the central business district. Between 1974 and 1981, nearly $140 million was invested in new and renovated office buildings, for a total of almost three million square feet of downtown office space. By 1981, the TVA towers, the United American Bank Plaza, Park National Bank, Summit Hill Towers, and the Summer Place garage

(TVA) accounted for *over half* of the property tax yield in the center city. Could post-fair optimism maintain this encouraging growth in downtown office space?[76]

In October 1982, not a few Knoxvillians joked that their World's Fair should never close, but continue to lure tourists to the city. Three major hotels had been built in anticipation of World's Fair crowds (the Radisson, the Hilton, and a Holiday Inn). The Holiday Inn abutted the fair site and was connected to a medium-sized exhibition hall. Could convention business be lured to Knoxville? What would be the "destination attraction" that would bring tourists and conventioneers to the city? Would the nearby Smoky Mountains, Gatlinburg, and Pigeon Forge be attractive enough, or would those two cities in adjoining Sevier County want to keep all the tourists and conventioneers to themselves? After the World's Fair closed, could Knoxville sustain four major downtown hotels, whereas before the fair there was but one (the Hyatt Regency)?

In all, Knoxville basked in the limelight of a wonderful World's Fair. As noted above, however, the fair was but a means to an end, which was the revival of the center city. Whether it be gentrification, office space, retail revival, tourism and convention business, or a combination thereof, many Knoxvillians hoped that the 1982 World's Fair would give the city the "quantum jump" that many people felt it so desperately needed.[77]

In 1981 David Stockman, President Reagan's director of the Office of Management and Budget, remarked that when "you have powerful underlying demographic and economic forces at work, federal intervention efforts designed to reverse the tide turn out to have rather anemic effects." In the 1980s, virtually every city in the United States sought to "reinvent" itself, to attract DINKs, increase office space for the service sector, reverse the loss of retail trade to the malls, and create and/or publicize a destination point for tourists and conventioneers. For his part, Stockman was doubtful that long-term demographic and economic trends could be reversed by massive infusions of government spending. Was he right?[78]

No longer a sleepy little town on a new railroad, Knoxville had become a modern city, sharing the opportunities and problems of all modern cities. But could it overcome its past and move in new directions? On October 31, 1982, the Knoxville International Energy Exposition came to an end. The slate, many believed, had been wiped clean, and a dazzling future awaited the post-fair city.

The next day, November 1, 1982, it all began to come unraveled.

5

---~~~---

Perils and Promises
of a New South City

Knoxville in the Modern Age

On November 1, 1982, the day after the World's Fair closed, 180 bank examiners from the Federal Deposit Insurance Corporation (10 percent of the entire FDIC audit force) swooped into the city and appeared simultaneously at all the Butcher banks. A November 1981 audit of Jake Butcher's United American Bank (UAB) had raised suspicions at the FDIC, in part because of the large number of "insider" loans and in part because the bank's reserve funds were too small to cover the number of risky loans. Begging pressing World's Fair business, Butcher was able to put off a full audit and a meeting of the FDIC and UAB officials. Then, once the fair began, the FDIC could not secure enough hotel rooms in Knoxville for its staff. Even later, a bank failure in Oklahoma diverted the FDIC's attention. But on November 1 it was ready. "When the auditors came in," recalled one former UAB official, "it was almost like a death smell."[1]

What the FDIC auditors found shocked even them. Clearly the bank was close to insolvency, with approximately $90 million in uncollectible loans and reserves of only around $40 million, causing one FDIC examiner to claim, "I'm not used to seeing this much wrong." And the deeper the auditors dug, the more

167

seamy and fraudulent practices they found, until the entire $3 billion empire of Jake and C. H. Butcher Jr. teetered on the brink of a collapse that could not be far away. And as United States Attorney John Gill began to suspect that Jake Butcher was "the biggest thief in the history of the state of Tennessee," G. W. Harrell of Tazewell predicted, "Once he's down, his friends'll drop like fleas off a dead dog."[2]

On January 25, 1983, FDIC officials informed the UAB board of directors that the bank was insolvent and that a buyer for the bank would have to be found. On January 29 Jake Butcher stepped down as president of UAB, causing a run on the bank—on one day alone, February 11, 1983, roughly $25 million was withdrawn by frightened depositors. Finally, on February 14, state banking commissioner Billy Adams padlocked UAB, a move that Jake Butcher claimed was politically motivated by Governor Lamar Alexander. The next day, February 15, the bank reopened as the First Tennessee Bank (the purchase had been approved the night before by the FDIC). Finally, on March 10, 1983 C. H. Butcher's Southern Industrial Banking Corporation (SIBC) closed and filed for Chapter 11 bankruptcy protection, leaving 6,300 depositors, whose accounts were uninsured, out in the cold. The Butcher house of cards had collapsed, and indictments for bank fraud and other offenses would follow.[3]

To be sure, the Butchers had been gigantic freebooters and pirates—buying or creating companies and then plundering their cash while loading them with bad debt; writing up phony loans to individuals and companies (often forging the borrowers' signatures) and then keeping the money; making real loans to individuals and firms in exchange for kickbacks; making insider loans to themselves, family, and friends from their banks; and swapping loans and assets *between* their banks, then finally trying to escape by loading all the bad loans onto SIBC. And they had lived like the robber barons they were, the most dramatic example of which is the oft-told story of a party in the Butcher brothers' suite in the UAB Tower in which well-lubricated hosts and guests brought $750,000 in cash up from the vault to toss back and forth like footballs.[4]

And yet, how much had Knoxville *really* been hurt by the fall of the Butchers? True, dozens of businesses failed, but more than a few of them were paper empires of the Butchers and their cohorts (over sixty separate companies listed Suite 2136 of the UAB Tower as their address) or enterprises that were created to try to make financial killings from the World's Fair. All the depositors in Butcher banks had accounts that were insured by the FDIC, the one glaring exception being those with funds in C. H. Butcher's SIBC, which technically was not a bank, and even then almost two-thirds of all those depositors eventually got their money back. Finally, the city owned the World's Fair site (approximately seventy acres just a few blocks west of the central business district), which could be used for downtown redevelopment. To be sure, the *psychological* blow resulting from the collapse of the Butchers was severe, but the financial wreckage was nowhere near as bad as many had feared. And while many of the old elite openly gloated over the fall of the nouveau riche brothers (even to the point of hosting Butcher bankruptcy parties in the enclaves of fashionable Sequoyah Hills), most Knoxvillians understood that the Butchers' boldness had carried the city into a new era. Those Knoxvillians had no intention of returning to the past, the past of a city hostile to change, with an incredibly conservative banking community, and closed to "outsiders" and to new ideas.[5]

Several questions still remained unanswered for post-fair Knoxvillians. Could Knoxville maintain the new self-confidence and momentum of the World's Fair to address its numerous problems—and in doing so overcome the psychological shock of the Butcher collapse? Could the city's leaders come up with a plan to develop the World's Fair property in order to reinvigorate the sagging downtown? Could the city's government maintain necessary services in the face of ongoing suburbanization of residents, businesses, and shoppers? Could Knoxville employ what assets it possessed to lure more businesses to the city? Could the post–civil rights era's racial chasms be narrowed? Could more problems having to do with the environment, with homelessness, with AIDS be brought out into the open and confronted? And perhaps most important, could Knoxville put its defeatist self-image behind it as it approached its own bicentennial and the twenty-first century? As the Butcher brothers and some of their cronies headed for federal prisons, many wondered if the city could free itself and no longer be a prisoner of its past.[6]

The Reemergence of Testerman and the Politics of Downtown Redevelopment

After his defeat by Randy Tyree in the 1975 mayoral runoff election (by a whisker-thin margin of 396 votes), an embittered Kyle Testerman told the *News-Sentinel,* "Even if I had a chance, I wouldn't run for mayor again." And yet Tyree's rout by Lamar Alexander in the 1982 gubernatorial race and revelations of his closeness to the Butcher brothers effectively removed him as a candidate for reelection in 1983, thereby leaving the door open for Testerman to make a political comeback.[7]

In April 1983 a "Draft Testerman" committee had been formed, headed by respected physician and "friend of Testerman" Dr. Robert Overholt. For his part, Testerman claimed that the committee was not his idea, even though it was no secret that he had been calling on influential people and in other ways behaving like a candidate. By summer 1983, Testerman was a candidate in everything but name.[8]

As noted earlier, the real purpose of the 1982 World's Fair had been to put just under seventy acres in Second Creek in the city's hands to be used for downtown redevelopment. In that vein, soon after the fair the Tyree administration had signed a preliminary agreement with Fairfield Communities, a well-known and respected development corporation that was in the process of developing, among other projects, Fairfield Glade near Crossville, Tennessee. In harmony with the earlier fair site redevelopment plan by the Regional Urban Design Assistance Team, the Fairfield plan called for around 1,200 residential units as well as "festive retailing" on the fair site.

Even before he formally announced his candidacy, however, Testerman began making noises that the Fairfield Communities plan was unacceptable. "In my opinion," Testerman was quoted as having said almost two weeks prior to his formal announcement, "the last thing we need is 1,200 condominiums on the fair site." Then, after his announcement (on September 7), he asserted that the Fairfield plan was "not remotely feasible," claimed that the market would not support residential development on the fair site (on this Testerman said there was "no room for compromise"), and "ridiculed the concept of festive retailing." Faced with the near inevitability of a Testerman victory, the city council withdrew its initial endorsement of the Fairfield plan and the development corporation understood that its days in Knoxville were numbered and quietly prepared to seek more hospitable climes.[9]

Testerman's victory was resounding. Against six weak opponents, he received 62.8 percent of the votes cast in the late September primary, thus making a runoff election unnecessary. Indeed, within ninety minutes of the closing of the polls, all six of Testerman's foes had conceded his triumph.[10]

And yet, in spite of his landslide electoral victory, Testerman's second mayoral term would be anything but smooth. In November 1983, the few voters who went to the polls in the city council election (14 percent of the registered voters) chose candidates who together would be a strong council. Commenting on that election, the *Journal* was prescient when it interpreted the council vote as a check on "any runaway policy on the part of the new administration." As a result, the next four years would be a period of standoff between the dynamic and impatient mayor and an increasingly recalcitrant city council. After only one year in office, the frustrated mayor lamented, "If I say it's daylight outside, they are going to say it's night." By the end of his term, Testerman and some council members were barely speaking to one another, and the mayor openly mourned that "they lack vision and insight." In something of an understatement, H. T. Hackney CEO and Testerman supporter William Sansom said of Testerman, "I think his style was a problem, he offended some people."[11]

Why anyone was surprised by Testerman's political style is something of a mystery, for it was that same style that had been the hallmark of his first mayoral term (1972–76). A strong man with equally strong opinions, Kyle Testerman was impatient to effect changes in Knoxville, or as he once put it, "drag it kicking and screaming into the twentieth century." During his first term, however, a young and talented staff and general good times (symbolized in part by the steady flow of federal grants) for the most part had kept the voters mollified. Even so, in 1975 the electorate had discarded him in favor of the less combative Randy Tyree.

Symptomatic of that political style, the morning after his September 1983 electoral victory (and long before he was to be formally inaugurated), Testerman met with outgoing mayor Randy Tyree and officials from Fairfield Communities, and on that same day "requested" that city council not vote on the Fairfield plan. Not surprisingly, Fairfield pulled up stakes and headed for greener pastures. As for what *ought to* happen on the fair site, one year later Testerman announced that nearly all of the site should become a public park, to be paid for by a federal grant.[12]

During his first term as mayor, Testerman had unveiled a comprehensive downtown redevelopment plan, the central features of which were a revived Gay Street and renovation of the area from the Market Square Mall to the Tennessee River. Much had happened since that plan was made public in 1974 (the TVA Towers had been built, just north of Market Square, in 1976, as had the City-County Building, south of Market Square near the river, in 1980; the United American Plaza in 1979; two downtown hotels, the Hilton and the Quality Inn, in 1981 and 1982; the Convention and Exhibition Center, on the fair site, in 1983; and the Riverview Towers, in 1985), and Testerman realized that his 1974 plan would no longer be appropriate. But, committed to comprehensive planning, the mayor appointed a Downtown Task Force to create a new, updated comprehensive downtown redevelopment plan. Testerman tapped Chris Whittle to chair the task force.

Chris Whittle is one of the most interesting people in Knoxville's recent history. The son of an Etowah, Tennessee, physician, Whittle came to the University of Tennessee, where he became president of the Student Government Association in the late 1960s and led the fight against the timorous university administration's campus speakers' policy, which required the administration's approval of all speakers invited to the campus (Whittle won). After graduation, Whittle and four other former University of Tennessee students (Phillip Moffitt,

Bryant Mayfield, Ed Smith, and David White) founded Collegiate Marketing and Management, Inc., devoted to publishing customized magazines for college towns—*Knoxville in a Nutshell* was the first such effort, appearing in 1969. Approximately $1.5 million in debt by 1973 and never having turned a profit, in that year the five young men (by now incorporated as 13-30 Corporation, designing magazines for readers between 13 and 30 years old) came up with the concept of a single-advertiser magazine. Companies eager to reach the "13 to 30 market" quickly signed up, and the company showed its first profit in 1974. By 1981 the 13-30 Corporation was publishing fifteen separate magazines and grossing a total of around $52 million. In 1986 Chris Whittle announced plans to build the new $43 million headquarters for the company (now renamed Whittle Communications) on two square blocks at the corner of Gay and Main streets. An aggressive and imaginative dreamer (like Testerman), Chris Whittle was the perfect individual to head the Downtown Task Force.[13]

Chris Whittle.

McClung Historical
Collection.
Knoxville–Knox County
Public Library.

And while the Testerman administration could point to a number of accomplishments (including stabilization of the city's finances after a $57 million fair-related debt caused a decline in the city's bond rating; the merger of city and county schools; $7 million in road improvements; a new 911 emergency system; new fire station facilities; an improvement in city services; renewal projects in the Mechanicsville–Five Points area; new airport facilities; and the beginning of downtown restoration), unquestionably his most lasting achievement was the 1987 Downtown Plan, anchored by the Whittle Communications Building (nicknamed "the campus"), the City-County Building, and the TVA Twin Towers, and featuring a renovated Market Square, and the beautification of part of Gay Street. "They love to crucify me," Testerman boasted. "But after it's over, I bet you can walk up and down Gay Street, . . . and they'll say, 'We really did a good job.'"[14]

At the same time, however, Testerman's style proved his undoing. Even as plans for the revival of the central business district gave hope to downtown merchants, the failure to develop the fair site meant that downtown redevelopment was incomplete. Also, almost continuous battles with an increasingly pugnacious city council caused the mayor to meddle in council races in order to stack the body with more amenable council members, an ill-considered effort that resulted in a backlash and an even more stubborn council. In retaliation, the council hired an internal auditor and began an investigation of the mayor's frequent and expensive out-of-town trips (Testerman repaid some of the expenses). Finally, in January 1986 Testerman filed for divorce from his wife of twenty-two years. She in turn accused her husband of using city funds to carry on an extramarital affair with one of his staff members. After a bitter—and public—squabble over Kyle Testerman's net worth, the divorce was granted early in 1987.[15]

It is inconceivable that city council was not aware of the mayor's dalliances when it called for an investigation of Testerman's junkets. Thus one might be tempted to surmise that in the midst of the mayor's personal difficulties (complete with a private detective "who followed the mayor and the city official [on one out-of-town trip] in August 1985"), the council saw the opportunity to flog the mayor while he was down. In a town that lived and breathed Volunteer football, one might even accuse the council of "piling on."[16]

Even amid these difficulties, however, Testerman was determined to run for reelection in 1987. Yet with the mayor in a weakened position, other potentially strong candidates were not wanting. Former mayor Randy Tyree was still a popular figure, in spite of his ties to the discredited and jailed Butchers and his ill-considered 1982 gubernatorial race against incumbent Lamar Alexander. Jean Teague, Bill Pavlis, and Casey Jones each had some supporters—probably not enough to win a mayoral election but surely enough to prevent Testerman (or whoever was the top vote getter) from winning without a runoff.

Testerman's most interesting—and dangerous—challenger, however, was former state representative and senator Victor Ashe. Ashe was a native Knoxvillian from an impeccably elite family that had made a considerable fortune in the textile and communications industries. A graduate of Yale University (where he had been a classmate of George W. Bush), Victor Ashe had proved himself to be a tireless campaigner who on numerous occasions had shown a wide streak of political independence and flexibility. As a result, although Republican Party and state government officials (from governors to house speakers to legislative colleagues) often found him impossible to control, at the same time he was immensely popular with his West Knoxville voter base, even winning election to the state senate at age twenty-nine, one year before he would be constitutionally eligible to take office (Knox County Republicans tapped his mother to serve until Victor reached the required age of thirty). Only once had Ashe politically stumbled, in 1984 in an ill-considered United States Senate race against Albert Gore Jr. Thus, even though Victor Ashe had accumulated a growing list of political figures who fervently loathed him, nevertheless he was a potential challenger who could not be taken lightly.[17]

Throughout the summer of 1987, Mayor Testerman toyed with the voters as to whether or not he would seek reelection. As late as July 22, he hinted in a speech to the West Knoxville Sertoma Club that he would not seek another term. "I've been nailed to the cross and talked about and everything," the mayor complained. At the same time, however, he was lining up potential support and commissioning secret polls in efforts to find out whether he could beat Tyree and Ashe (Tyree, it was discovered, would not be a problem).[18]

On August 17, Testerman filed the necessary qualifying petitions, announcing his intentions to seek another term. But he had waited so long, while at the same time Ashe appeared to be gaining strength, that voters and the press alike were skeptical as to whether he actually would *stay* in the race. To quiet the restlessness, two days after he had filed his qualifying petition Testerman insisted that he would remain in the contest. Interviewed by the *News-Sentinel,* this author stated, "My personal opinion is that he cannot win. . . . He's going to test the water. If he finds it's not there, he will withdraw." Eight days later, just after the publication of a *Journal* poll showing Testerman trailing Ashe, the mayor did just that, in an emotional and tearful announcement. As anticipated, none of the six remaining candidates was able to win a majority in the September primary (Ashe was the leading vote getter, but with only 37.4 percent of the votes cast). Tyree, who finished second to Ashe, desperately tried to line up support among the eliminated candidates, but to no avail. In the November runoff, Ashe defeated Tyree by 18,888 to 15,842.[19]

Although almost no one appreciated it a the time, University of Tennessee political science professor and part-time political pollster and commentator William Lyons was correct when, on the night of Ashe's mayoral victory, he described that election as the beginning of "a new political era." It surely must have been so, for Victor Ashe won reelection races in 1991, 1995, and 1999, thus making him the longest-serving mayor in the city's history. Indeed, he might have won even more races were he not prevented from doing so by term limits.[20]

Near the end of Ashe's fourth mayoral term, Lyons (who occasionally engaged in polling for the mayor and, as a result, was fairly close to Ashe's campaigns) elaborated on his election night statement by saying that in 1987 Victor Ashe had "set the tone for how to win in local politics." Before Ashe even announced his candidacy, he did a considerable amount of polling (to identify "hot button" issues as well as to assess his voting strength in various parts of the city), raised a great deal of money, and secured important endorsements. "Victor wanted to go in early with a knockout blow," explained Lyons,

Victor Ashe.
Gift of Victor Ashe.

and thereby "create a sense of inevitability." Such tactics also might discourage potential opponents from entering the race.[21]

Victor Ashe also was one of the first to recognize and exploit new political configurations among Knoxville voters. Increasingly more potent than party affiliations or progressive versus conservative gulfs was the growing division between business interests (which tended to support development, change, and downtown economic renewal) and homeowner, or neighborhood, interests (which often opposed development and change and were more focused on the delivery of basic services). Neighborhood or property owners' associations had been formed in the suburbs for some time and were growing in power, as were grassroots groups like the Knoxville–Knox County Community Action Committee, which attempted to identify, train, and empower neighborhood leaders, especially in the more economically modest areas. Although this comparatively recent political reorientation could be seen in conflicts over the 1982 World's Fair, rezoning, and unified government (which in 1983 again had failed to win voters' approval), it was Victor Ashe who was able to use this political shift to his advantage, principally by assuaging the progressive business elite while at the same time paying attention to the growing concerns of the neighborhoods and homeowners.[22]

Nowhere can Ashe's political philosophy and tactics be better seen than in his first mayoral contest in 1987. In that year, progressive business leaders (not infrequently referred to as "the twelve white guys" by neighborhood leaders and others)[23] had come to believe that Testerman had been so badly weakened by his running battle with city council and his much-publicized personal difficulties that he could not win reelection. As they were casting about for someone to support, Victor Ashe came to them to solicit their endorsements and financial backing. Conventional wisdom among the progressive business group, however, was that Ashe, while perhaps desirable, was not electable. But when Ashe commissioned a secret poll that showed that he could beat both Testerman and Tyree, the "twelve white guys" were won over and gave him their fealty.[24]

With progressive business backing in 1987, Ashe outspent his most serious opponent, Randy Tyree, by better than two-to-one ($150,000 to $61,000). And with his affluent West Knoxville voter base secure (once Testerman dropped out), Ashe campaigned almost ceaselessly in the neighborhoods, even in Tyree's supposedly strong areas in East Knoxville and North Knoxville. In the November 1987 runoff election, it was assumed by many political observers that Tyree's only chance to defeat Ashe was to garner two-thirds or more of the African American vote (mainly from East Knoxville) and at the same time carry North Knoxville (including Fountain City, middle class and substantial blue collar) by comfortable margins. Thus when Tyree was able to win only 54 percent of the African American vote and just a shade over half of the North Knoxville ballots, it was evident that he had been outmaneuvered, and beaten. Still a comparatively young man at 47, Tyree would remain on the political scene for several years, but an increasing number of observers came to believe that his political career was over.[25]

The Ashe Years: Triumphs and Troubles

On the same day that the *News-Sentinel* reported Victor Ashe's 1987 electoral victory, the paper also reported that Fowler's Furniture Store, a mainstay on Gay Street since 1904, was closing its downtown store. The announcement was symptomatic of the many problems the new mayor faced as he took office in January 1988. To begin with, although the Testerman administration had created an imaginative plan for downtown renewal, not a great deal had been accomplished and too many retail spaces on Gay Street and the Market Square remained empty. At the same time, people still were leaving the city (almost 10,000 during the 1980's), some to burgeoning Knox County but many to other locations farther away. The gap between the affluent western suburbs and the center city wards continued to widen, with African American neighbor-hoods especially troubled (having almost triple the poverty rate of white neigh-borhoods, less than half of whites' per-capita income, and more than double white unemployment). The Rev. Harold Middlebrook, a strong spokesman for Knoxville blacks, warned that in "the African-American community [which in 1990 was approximately 16 percent of Knoxville's population], government is viewed as an instrument for the white community." Finally, federal govern-ment budget deficits led to the irresponsible approval of unfunded mandates that were passed onto the states which, caught between their own budget squeezes and rebellious taxpayers, in turn passed them onto the cites and coun-ties. Indeed, the new mayor had more than a full plate before he even sat down at the table.[26]

Faced with these and other dilemmas, Knoxville and cities like it had a number of unpalatable options. For one thing, cities could cut back on services, thus forcing people to expect less from their local government. On the other hand, cities could maintain services and institute tax increases to pay for them. Needless to say, either choice might well prove to be politically hazardous.

Other alternatives, however, were potentially even more fearsome. If tax-payers continued to abandon the city to live in the county, then a policy of selected annexations would allow the city to recapture its much-needed tax dollars. Failing that, center city gentrification held out the promise of luring affluent young professionals ("yuppies" or DINKs) back inside the city limits. Finally, if all else failed, the city could push hard for a city-county unified government, whereby the city in effect simply went out of business.

In his 1987 campaign, however, Ashe had not vowed to *decrease* services but rather to *increase* them. In order to even out the delivery of city services throughout the city, the new mayor established six equally equipped service zones (for garbage, leaf and brush removal, etc.), divided road paving funds equally among all council districts, and undertook a program of parks construction that ultimately resulted in Haley Heritage Square, major improvements at Chilhowee Park, and what ultimately will be an urban showcase at Caswell Park. Over time, the city began to look better—and *work* better.[27]

In some ways Knoxville's African Americans benefited more than others from the mayor's largess. In 1987 Ashe had come close to carrying a number of African American precincts, and he was determined to add those neighborhoods to his power base. In addition to the enhanced services for all neighborhoods noted above, in his first seven years in office Ashe was able to increase the number of black police officers from eleven to thirty and complained (through his press secretary George Korda) that even those results were "discouraging." More than a few of the new public parks were those that served African American neighborhoods. On a more symbolic note, Ashe approved the naming of Martin Luther King Jr. Avenue and declared Martin Luther King Jr. Day a city holiday. Finally, Sam Anderson and Thomas "Tank" Strickland were only two of the most visible African American appointees, Anderson serving as the powerful director of parks and recreation and Strickland as director of community relations.[28]

To finance his plans and promises, Ashe resorted to a combination of a sales tax increase and selective ("finger") annexations. Warned by some advisers that a tax increase in his first year in office would be political suicide, the mayor forged ahead, securing the increase in spite of some voter grumbling and the opposition of some powerful local politicians, including County Executive Dwight Kessel and Superintendent of Knox County Schools Earl Hoffmeister. Yet Ashe understood better than these politicos (thanks in part to sagacious polling) that voters would not oppose paying more taxes if they actually *received something* in return. In exchange for their taxes, they got improved services and streets, more parks and a physically more attractive city, more consumer-oriented executive departments, the expansion of regulatory boards to include consumer representatives (places often filled by appointed blacks and women), more police officers (increased from 280 to 400 during Ashe's tenure) and firefighters, a virtually scandal-free and financially sound city

"We've Been Annexed!" cartoon by Charlie Daniel, December 12, 2000.
Reprinted by permission of the Knoxville News-Sentinel Company.

government, and a more accessible chief executive who was famous for his "Mayor's Night In" and "Mayor's Night Out" sessions.[29]

The mayor knew that a sales tax increase would not be sufficient to straighten out the city's finances and pay for his pet projects. Temperamentally opposed to unified government and recognizing that any benefits derived from gentrification would be years—and possibly decades—away, he turned to annexations of selected areas of Knox County, especially commercial areas that generated sales tax revenues. According to Tennessee state law, property owners in unincorporated areas had no voice in whether or not they would be annexed by an incorporated municipality. Thus, the only way they could stave off annexation was by incorporating themselves, as the opulent bedroom community of Farragut (in far west Knox County) had done in order to prevent being gobbled up by Knoxville. Such antiannexation municipalities often were derided as "toy towns," for they provided virtually no services except tax protection.[30]

Through his pliable city council, Ashe began his policy of "finger" annexations. Predictably, annexations raised howls of protest from the affected property-owners. But that was nothing compared to the bellows of outrage from County Executive Dwight Kessel (who claimed that he had exercised enormous restraint when, on a whitewater trip with Ashe, "I didn't hit him in the head with my paddle") and county commissioners, especially the eleven (of nineteen) commissioners who represented non-city districts. County Finance Director Kathy Hamilton claimed that in 1990–91 Ashe's annexations had cost Knox County $3.8 million in lost sales tax revenues and an additional $3 million in 1992–95. And yet, even as Knoxville's mayor continued his annexation of county businesses and homeowners, the city's percentage of Knox County's total population continued to slip, from around 54 percent in 1980 to 46 percent by 1998.[31]

With the city and county close to open warfare, the progressive business elite saw an opportunity to push for metropolitan government. In 1983 county voters had rejected unified government, with only 31 percent voting in favor of metropolitan government and a whopping 69 percent voting against. But Knox County voters might think differently, the elite reasoned, if their only other option was to be swallowed up by the city. But in spite of yeoman efforts by elite members Sam Furrow and Bill Baxter, the opposition of County Sheriff Tim Hutchinson (who was in the process of building a powerful political machine), Knoxville firefighters, city employees, and secretly (although he continues to deny it) Mayor Victor Ashe proved too strong. An unholy alliance of county voters (who rejected metro government by 62 to 38 percent) and inner-city voters (who feared a diminution of their power in a countywide metro government) rejected consolidation and left the city and county essentially in the same place they had been.[32]

In an effort to bring a modicum of order out of a plethora of chaos, in 1998 the Tennessee state legislature approved an act requiring Tennessee cities and their surrounding counties to create twenty-year growth plans that would set mutually agreed-upon limits to urban annexations and create comprehensive plans for long-term county development. On the surface, both Ashe and new county executive Tommy Schumpert (who had defeated incumbent county executive Dwight Kessel by claiming that he could work more harmoniously and productively with Knoxville's mayor than Kessel had been able to do) supported the legislation. But Ashe's determination to annex more county land and Schumpert's opposition to further Knoxville imperialism meant that the chances that the city and county would be able to agree on a single growth plan were, in the words of county commissioner Frank Leuthold, a bitter foe of annexation, "somewhere between nil and none." The feisty commissioner, who had built his political base as the chairman of the West Knox Homeowners' Association, warned, "If any county commissioners who represent a non-city district vote for an urban growth plan [that contains provisions for

Samuel J. and Ann Furrow.
Courtesy of Ann Furrow.

further annexation], they won't finish their term of office. They will be run out of town." And when Leuthold was told that Ashe had no plans for further annexation, he was quoted as saying, "That's a bunch of bullshit." By this time Ashe was so unpopular in some areas of the county that in a contest sponsored by the alternative newspaper *Metro Pulse,* the mayor was chosen by readers as "The Knoxvillian You Would Most Like to See Abducted by an Alien."[33]

As the twelve-person planning committee that had been appointed to hammer out an agreement plowed forward, Ashe continued to annex county parcels, 112 in 1999 and 201 by August 2000. Indeed, the pace of annexations actually increased, in part because the state had set July 1, 2001, as the date by which annexation boundaries for the next twenty years would have to be set. "I intend to accelerate the pace between now and next July 1," the mayor was quoted as having said in early August 2000. Just a few days before Ashe's promise, the city council declared that an impasse had been reached on a growth plan. This presented both the city council and the county commission with a real dilemma: according to the law, if no agreement could be reached, a three-judge panel would draw up a growth plan that both the city and county would have to live with. Faced with an alternative that neither side wanted, one representative each from the city and county finally reached a compromise that in general would allow the city to annex "between the fingers" but little more. Although the compromise favored the city, the county commission went along with the agreement because it feared that the three-judge panel would favor the city even more than the compromise had done.[34]

Given Knoxville's demographic and fiscal problems, Ashe had almost no clear options *except* annexation (taxes already had been increased). And yet the way in which the mayor accomplished his goals, annexing almost twenty-five square miles during his time in office, revealed a political style that even his most steadfast supporters found difficult to defend. Tending to see all political opposition as being against him *personally*, Victor Ashe often practiced what some observers described as a "take no prisoners" political style, which was most clearly seen in his need to control and to completely triumph in every contest. Although some elements of this political style could be seen as early as his days as a state representative (1969–75), these characteristics grew increasingly evident in his latter terms as Knoxville's mayor.

Nowhere can these more distressing elements of Ashe's political style be seen more clearly than in the federal lawsuit brought by five Knoxville firefighters and in the issue of how to fill the city council seat of the popular Danny Mayfield, who died in 2001 at the age of thirty-two after waging a valiant battle against bone cancer.

In early 2000, five city firefighters sued the mayor in federal district court for having violated their civil rights because they had opposed his reelection in 1995 and 1999. In retaliation for this political apostasy, Ashe blocked one of the firefighter's promotion and punished the other four as well. In August 2000, a federal magistrate issued a permanent injunction against Ashe to prevent him "from taking adverse employment action against most city firefighters because of their political beliefs." The mayor could have settled the suit with minimal damage at any time, but he angrily refused to do so. The jury decided that Ashe had acted illegally and therefore awarded restitution and damages to the city employees. Thus, even though not a few of Victor Ashe's supporters feared that losing a federal civil rights suit would seriously hurt any future political ambitions, the mayor would not be moved.[35]

The Danny Mayfield imbroglio, many believed, was even more revealing of Ashe's temperament. A native of Camden, New Jersey, Daniel Anthony (Danny) Mayfield came to Knoxville to attend Knoxville College, where he met his wife Melissa (Missy). In 1997 at the age of twenty-eight, he staged a stunning political upset in the sixth councilmanic district by defeating Ashe-supported incumbent Bill Powell. "Danny's election was a slap at me," the mayor later—and characteristically—remembered. The young and dynamic preacher and community organizer was sworn into office wearing an African robe.

For all his energy, however, at most Mayfield was but a minor irritant on a city council that for the most part did the mayor's bidding. And when in 1999 Mayfield announced that he would enter the mayor's race against Ashe, no one gave him any chance of winning ("I beat him in every African American precinct," the mayor later boasted). But Mayfield had crossed Ashe, and for that transgression there could be no forgiveness.[36]

Thus when Mayfield died of cancer on March 21, 2001, there was considerable speculation as to whether the mayor would exact his political retribution from even beyond Mayfield's grave. As it became increasingly clear that Danny Mayfield's courageous battle against cancer would not be won, many wondered who the city council would name to serve the remainder of Mayfield's term. A number of people, for a variety of motives, called for the council to appoint Mayfield's widow to the seat. And while Ashe was a eulogist at the memorial service for Danny Mayfield at the Greater Warner Tabernacle AME Zion Church and was quoted as having said that he was impartial regarding the empty council seat, which was "completely up to council members," rumors abounded that the mayor had no intention of allowing his pliant council to vote for Missy Mayfield. Virtually ignored was the fact that a large number of African Americans considered Mayfield too brash and confrontational and opposed the naming of his widow to complete his councilmanic term.

In the end, the mayor and the more conservative black leaders had their way. In a stormy city council meeting on April 3, 2001, the council named not Missy Mayfield but Raleigh Wynn (age seventy-seven) to serve the remainder of Danny Mayfield's term. Clearly Ashe once again had bent the majority of the council to his will or, as the lone Mayfield supporter on the city council claimed, the mayor was "pulling strings to deny the appointment of Melissa Mayfield to complete her late husband's expired term." The one dissenter charged that there was "no question" that the seven-to-one council vote "came from the mayor's office." Immediately a petition for Ashe's recall was circulated, but that effort ultimately came to naught.[37]

And yet, even though many Knoxvillians charged that as mayor Victor Ashe's political style was arrogant and tyrannical, those same citizens were forced to concede that the city's political history proved that a strong mayor was necessary in the fractious and often intensely conservative city. Moreover, many of the mayor's harshest critics had to admit that Ashe seemed "dictatorial" when they disagreed with his decisions but "courageous" when they agreed with him. Indeed, many of the same citizens who had accused Ashe of demagoguery and insisted that he should be recalled were some of his most steadfast defenders when he stood up to the city council and the rank and file of the police department on the extremely sensitive and contentious issue of a civilian police review board.

In spite of the fact that Knoxville saw its first African American police officer in 1882 (Atlanta did not have any black policemen until 1947), relations between the Knoxville Police Department and the city's African Americans could best be characterized as mutually suspicious. In June 1913 a race riot was barely averted when a black man was accused of killing a white police officer. And the major riot of 1919 almost surely was touched off by a white policeman's false arrest of Maurice Mayes. Throughout the twentieth century, Knoxville's African Americans were convinced that some of the city's police officers belonged to the local klavern of the Ku Klux Klan, a suspicion that historian Kenneth Jackson later found to have been true in the early 1920s, but those rumors continued as late as the 1980s.[38]

In 1983, the police department's internal affairs division investigated charges of police brutality against African Americans and recommended policy reforms in the department, but little or nothing actually was done. In the late 1990s, however, alleged incidents and charges became so common that they no longer could be ignored. On June 4, 1997, police officers killed James Woodfin while in the process of serving a misdemeanor warrant (police claimed that Woodfin had fired first, while sitting on the toilet). Then, on October 17 of the same year, Juan Daniels was shot to death by police officers when he charged at them with a knife (Daniels was a severely troubled man who was also blatantly intoxicated). On December 14, police investigating a domestic disturbance beat a handcuffed suspect (one officer accused of the beating as well as others who attempted to cover up the incident were dismissed). Finally, on January 9, 1998, Andre Stenson died in police custody after being apprehended when he tried to flee from a traffic stop. Stenson, on parole, allegedly was stopped by police for driving without his headlights on at 8:20 P.M. Running from police, he was struck with a pistol, wrestled to the ground, and sprayed with mace, at which time he suddenly expired. An autopsy revealed that Stenson had a preexisting heart condition and had died as a result of excessive stress. Police claims that Stenson was "high" on cocaine (the medical examiner found no traces of cocaine in his system) and that cocaine had been found in Stenson's automobile (a claim later proved to be false) only made the already volatile situation even worse. Indeed, *Metro Pulse* newspaper probably was not exaggerating when it said that "Knoxville could well be on the verge of a racial crisis."[39]

As one might expect, the city council meeting held less than a week after Andre Stenson's death was filled to overflowing, with well over 500 people in the council meeting room, which held only 310 on the main floor (an additional 136 could fit into the balcony). For years many blacks and a few whites had called for a civilian review board to probe certain activities of the police department. At the January 13 meeting, however, those calls had become angry demands, with some threatening economic retaliation if such a board was not created and even the moderate African American spokesman Rev. Harold Middlebrook stating that "nothing short of a civilian review board is going to satisfy us." In response, at that meeting Ashe appointed a nine-person commission, headed by prominent and respected attorney Bernard Bernstein (of the firm Bernstein, Stair, and McAdams), to investigate the need for some form of police review board. But even that did not appear to quell the general anger and frustration of the African American community. Indeed, a later WBIR-TV and University of Tennessee poll revealed that 81 percent of Knoxville's black citizens thought they possessed "too little" power, and Raleigh Wynn (who had been appointed as a community ombudsman by the Bernstein Commission) reported that he received seven to eight complaints per week about Knoxville police officers.[40]

Unquestionably Mayor Ashe was in an extremely difficult position. Knoxville Police Chief Phil Keith and a vast majority of the rank-and-file police officers opposed the creation of any type of civilian review board. Moreover, not a few whites were outraged at the possibility that the mayor and council would "give in" to what they considered to be a roomful of noisy and ill-mannered blacks. And although the deaths of Woodfin, Daniels, and Stenson had been (to use *Metro Pulse's* description) "perplexing," some whites pointed out that none of the three men had been in line for a model citizenship award. Finally, as pointed out by University of Tennessee administrator and *News-Sentinel* columnist Theotis Robinson, most Knoxville whites simply were uncomfortable talking about racial issues.[41]

At the same time, a poll showed that nearly 100 percent of blacks and 64 percent of whites favored the creation of some form of police review board, as did the city's one daily paper and its "alternative" weekly, along with the Knoxville Ministerial Association and a fair number of respected and prominent members of the progressive business elite.[42]

Not surprisingly, the Bernstein Commission unanimously recommended the establishment of what it called a Police Advisory and Review Commission. The mayor supported the recommendation, but a majority of the city council balked, claiming either that a majority of Knoxvillians opposed it or that such a body would just be more bureaucracy. Only Danny Mayfield, who had been calling for a review board since his 1997 election, and Carlene Malone (an uncompromising and obstreperous representative from the Fourth District) favored the Bernstein Commission recommendation. Interestingly, Mayfield and Malone had been the mayor's harshest critics, while those council members who stood against him on the issue of the police review board on most occasions had been Ashe's most pliable and dependable allies.[43]

Sidestepping the city council, Ashe created the Police Advisory and Review Commission by executive order. "It cost me the support of the rank and file police department," the mayor later admitted. At the same time, however, those Knoxvillians who had castigated the mayor for what they said was his despotic political style on this issue applauded his vision and his courage. In the next mayoral election, Ashe carried every precinct that contained a majority of African American voters. "It was the toughest time I had as mayor," Ashe later confessed. In all, despite criticisms of Ashe's political style, he had shown genuine leadership in a city so bereft of it historically.[44]

The Downtown Dilemma

But even as Knoxvillians and their leaders wrestled with the complicated issues of city finance, economic development, urban growth, annexation, neighborhoods, and race, the major dilemma of how to resuscitate a struggling downtown appeared insoluble. This is not to say that there were no ideas or plans, for from the years immediately prior to the World's Fair of 1982 until the closing months of Victor Ashe's mayoral administration there had been probably close to a dozen plans put forth by numerous commissions and appointed bodies. And yet very few of those efforts had yielded any substantial fruits. As one frustrated observer put it, "Every three or four months, some grandiose plan with millions of dollars comes along, and this is going to be the savior of downtown, and nothing ever happens."[45]

Even more galling was the fact that, as Knoxville seemed mired and helpless, nearby midsize cities appeared to be reviving their downtowns. Asheville, North Carolina, appeared to be veritably throbbing with activity, with downtown festivals, arts, and a lively and diverse center city population. In a feature story on Asheville, Knoxville's *Metro Pulse* claimed that the North Carolina mountain city "seems deliberately calculated to ruin all the cherished complacency of Knoxville's municipal fatalists, who say that Knoxville's just too small and too remote to ever have a vibrant urban life."[46]

And if Asheville's robust downtown made Knoxvillians envious, the virtual revolution in Chattanooga made them enraged and ill. Once very much like Knoxville in its heavy industrial base and downtown stagnation and unattractiveness, Chattanooga more than once had been referred to as "the armpit of the South." But since 1984, when the Lyndhurst Foundation (funded principally by local Coca-Cola money) had launched the "Chattanooga Venture" project to build a broadly based coalition of all Chattanoogans that would come up with a Vision 2000 plan for the city, Chattanooga had lured businesses, tourists, and residents into the center city with a bold and innovative facelift, a downtown baseball park, and a stunning aquarium. In the five years since the aquarium's opening in 1992, 128 retail businesses and restaurants had been established in the downtown and free electric shuttle buses began bringing Chattanoogans downtown again. Back in Knoxville, one envious letter-writer complained that "Knoxville is talking about projects, while Chattanooga has done them," and another moaned, "I am so tired of hearing the question, 'why can't Knoxville be more like Chattanooga?'"[47]

Struggling to understand why other midsize cities had outpaced Knoxville in downtown renewal and the general embracing of new ideas, Knoxvillians characteristically turned on one another, blaming each other for the city's failures. Frank Cagle, then managing editor of the *News-Sentinel,* believed that much of the fault lay with the city's leaders, asserting, "There is a belief within the heart of hearts of many of Knoxville's leaders that change is not a good thing." Cagle urged those leaders "to do something, even if it's wrong." But one former leader blamed the community itself, maintaining that it was "*terribly* passive." And Sherry Kelly Marshall, former executive director of Partnership for Neighborhood Improvement, maintained that what held Knoxville back was a kind of mass negative psychology: "I have never seen a community that is against so many things and in favor of so few."[48]

Over many years, however, the walls and moats of mutual suspicion and distrust had been erected between the city's many neighborhoods, interests, classes, and races, thus making cooperation and even simple dialogue extremely difficult. Fearful that any interest or neighborhood or class or race would gain some favor or benefit, many Knoxvillians simply opposed all ideas for civic progress. Thus when James O. Kennedy, the CEO of Chattanooga's Chamber of Commerce, told Knoxvillians that a city must build a consensus that will then "forge a vision" of what that city will become, many enthusiastically applauded but left in disbelief. Indeed, it is instructive to note that when a Pittsburgh developer told a luncheon held to celebrate Knoxville's 210th anniversary that the "most important thing is to get the public engaged at the very beginning," the guests at the event were there by invitation only. Looking back over the city's history as chronicled in these pages, one would be surprised by anything else.[49]

Perhaps no single individual has had more influence on American urban planning in the second half of the twentieth century than has Jane Jacobs (1916–   ). Her enormously influential book *The Death and Life of Great American Cities* (1961) maintained that American cities had failed because they had allowed themselves to become geographically segmented, zoned into single-function parts (commercial, residential, etc.). Instead, Jacobs argued that successful cities would be "organic," should be diverse composites of residential, retail, offices, entertainment, etc. or, as she put it, "mixed-use" in the urban fabric. Unflinching in the face of criticism from traditional planners, she retorted that "some men tend to cling to old intellectual excitements, just as some belles, when they are old ladies, still cling to the fashions and coiffures of their exciting youth."[50]

It was easier, however, to talk about Jane Jacobs's ideas than to make them work. Prior to the opening of the World's Fair in 1982 just a few blocks west of the downtown core, a collection of national planners and consultants had recommended that after the fair closed, the sixty-seven-acre site should be developed according to Jacobs's mixed-use model (up to 1,200 residential units, festive retailing, etc.). But, as noted earlier, Kyle Testerman had discouraged mixed-use development on the fair site and for nearly fifteen years the area had languished as a rarely used park.

Once Ashe had gotten the city's financial house in order, he began to push for the construction of a major new convention center on the site, a facility that would be more than double the size of the more modest center that was built for the World's Fair, with a projected cost of $160 million. Ashe used a combination of political arm-twisting and acumen to get the city council to approve a 19-cent increase in the property tax rate, a new 3 percent city tax on hotel and motel rooms, and the movement of another 19 cents out of the city's operating budget. The very impressive structure opened on Friday, October 18, 2002, on time and under budget. "This puts us on an even footing . . . with other cities that have fine convention centers," the mayor boasted. "The future is before us, and it is unlimited."[51]

Over a year before the formal opening, at the center's "topping out" ceremony on July 9, 2001, Ashe gloated, "On those who said it wouldn't happen: THEY WERE WRONG!" Indeed, even before the convention center had opened, Knoxville Sports Corporation's dynamic head Gloria Ray had lined up two major events: the AAU Junior Olympics and the American Bowling Congress, the latter projected to bring in around 50,000 participants and companions. Even then, the predictable army of naysayers mocked the mayor's bloated rhetoric and brayed that the new convention center would not be able to attract enough events to pay the $2 million annual operating expenses.[52]

What even the harshest critics overlooked, however, was whether or not Jane Jacobs's concept of mixed-use areas would be used to surround the new convention center with related and nonrelated activities. For what the site needed in addition to bookings was *bodies:* men and women who would patronize and support the hoped-for stores, restaurants, and clubs in-between the conventions. No one said it more clearly than the authors of the Urban Land Institute's 1998 report on redeveloping the World's Fair site: "The strategy is simple: more residents, office workers, and visitors walking around downtown." The city's Public Building Authority enthusiastically agreed, stating that, in order for the convention center to be successful, there must be nearby "amenities." And yet conventioneers alone would not be able to support those crucial "amenities." Thus the success of Knoxville's beautiful and even opulent convention center depended as much on a larger vision of downtown revival than just more tourists, a vision that would require more than publicly financed studies and initiatives. As Ashe understood, government could carry redevelopment and progress only so far before opposition would mount.[53]

This was clearly the case in the fierce battle over a new baseball park for Knoxville's minor league team, the Knoxville Smokies. Around 1915 Col. William Caswell donated land in East Knoxville for a public park, which in 1953 became the site for Bill Meyer Stadium. By the mid-1990s, the ballpark had become sadly run down and the surrounding neighborhood mainly populated by African Americans. With attendance plummeting except on special promotional nights, the team's owner demanded that the city and county combine forces to purchase a better site and build a new ballpark. As with many major and minor league sports franchises, lurking behind the demand was the threat to abandon the city and move elsewhere.

As city and county governments bickered over where to locate a new stadium and how much each would be required to pay, political opposition once again arose (as it had about the convention center) over the use of public money to build a facility that would enrich private interests. As he had done to build the convention center, Ashe probably could have used his political muscle to fashion an agreement and build a new ballpark. But in this instance, he chose not to do so. The Smokies left Knoxville and Bill Meyer Stadium at the end of the 1999 season, relocating to a new $19.4 million stadium twenty miles away in Sevier County (where the club enjoyed record attendance figures and Sevier County collected almost triple the projected tax revenues). Once the team had left, Ashe pushed for and got a beautiful public park where the run-down ballfield used to be. Again, however, mixed-use planning seems to have been ignored or forgotten.[54]

An initiative that produced more positive results was the 1990 opening of the Knoxville Museum of Art on the western edge of the World's Fair site. By the late 1970s, the private Dulin Gallery of Art on Kingston Pike in exclusive West Knoxville had outgrown its modest facilities. Eager to make use of the fair site, in 1985 Mayor Kyle Testerman offered the gallery free real estate on the fair site and $1 million if it would relocate. Yet even with prominent attorney Caesar Stair III in charge of fundraising, the necessary funds to construct a new building and purchase a permanent art collection were slow in coming. Then, on Christmas Eve 1987, Knoxville-based mobile home manufacturer Jim Clayton pledged $3.25 million, enough to finish the building but leaving nothing to cover operations. Clayton's generosity obviously gave him the respectability he wanted among Knoxville's elite, and to date the museum has drawn respectable crowds, especially for its exhibits such as those of the works of August Rodin, Andy Warhol, and Ansel Adams. Still grappling to find its identity, the Knoxville Museum of Art has tried to serve as both a window for national and international art and a repository for the region's creative talents.[55]

If downtown renewal was going to have any chance of succeeding, interesting but piecemeal projects such as the convention center, the new baseball stadium, or the Knoxville Museum of Art would have to be enveloped into a broad, comprehensive, mixed-use vision for Knoxville's center city. In spite of persistent calls for more residential units in the downtown area, between 1990 and 1998 the city approved the demolition of 618 housing units in the central business district while at the same time issuing only 652 housing permits in the district. Thus by 1997 downtown Knoxville had only 788 residential units, which housed 1,387 people (Chattanooga had nearly triple that number). Meanwhile, suburban sprawl continued westward and northward where, according to University of Tennessee architecture professor Mark Schimmenti, it "eats up our resources, our time, and leads us into a one-dimensional existence." Clearly something would have to be done.[56]

Thus, in spite of the fact that since the 1970s a groaning shelf of comprehensive downtown redevelopment plans had been created and for the most part ignored, in 1998 the Public Building Authority issued invitations to private developers to submit proposals for still another comprehensive plan. The only firm to respond to the invitation was Worsham Watkins International, which in late June unveiled its astoundingly bold plan before a gasping, almost overwhelmed audience of a thousand business, political, and media leaders at the Tennessee Theatre.[57]

The Worsham Watkins plan called for 3.3 million square feet of new commercial and residential space, including a glass-encased 140,000-square-foot shopping mall on top of the present Henley Street, a 33-story spired office tower, a 10-screen cineplex, a new 415-room Marriott Hotel, a 5,500-seat amphitheater, a complete renovation of (and possible dome over) Market Square, and four new parking garages. Worsham Watkins estimated that the total cost would be approximately $600 million, of which $310 million would come from private investments and $290 million would come from public funds (including $160 million for the convention center on the World's Fair site that already was underway plus $130 million for the parking garages and infrastructure modifications). In all, the redevelopment would be called "Renaissance Knoxville," which, one observer commented, had "a nice ring to it." One local newspaper called the Worsham Watkins vision "a one-time opportunity to catapult KNOXVILLE into the ranks of American cities that are on the ascent," while the other newspaper commented that "in the last 18 years, too often Knoxville has been a city of diminishing expectations" and called for the Worsham Watkins plan to "move forward today."[58]

As with almost every idea for change in Knoxville in the past century, opposition surfaced immediately. Participants in the Internet discussion group K2K (Knoxville 2000) complained that the Worsham Watkins plan was still another example of top-down initiatives that ignored any grass roots notions or ideas. Downtown property owners, especially those on Market Square, were angered that they had not been consulted. Worse, in their opinion, was the Worsham Watkins recommendation that the city seize Market Square property by eminent domain and then lease it to Worsham Watkins, who would then subcontract development to another private developer. As usual, critics attacked the spending of public funds for the enrichment of the few (Worsham Watkins's "management fees," for example, were expected to reach $33 million) and predicted that the developers would not be able to line up the necessary $310 million in private investments to bring the plan to life. At the same time, still other opponents picked apart pieces of the project, attacking the mall over Henley Street as "an imitation of a plastic Disneyland" and claiming that the cineplex (a projected major "draw" to visitors) would never be built because Knoxville was already "overscreened." Finally, the coup de grâce was delivered when Mayor Victor Ashe publicly began to express doubts. Within a year, the Worsham Watkins plan was scaled back and then lay moribund, as *Metro Pulse* put it "a victim of [the planners'] own excesses and . . . Ashe's unwillingness to support them." At the end, the imaginative Worsham Watkins plan for Knoxville's downtown renewal could not swim against the cultural tide of conservatism, doubt, fearfulness, envy, and negativism. As one editorial writer put it, "the past 20 years are littered with abortive downtown redevelopment proposals," all of them victims of resistance to change.[59]

By the dawn of the new millennium, downtown Knoxville's problem no longer was its physical unattractiveness, for the city under both the Testerman and Ashe administrations had done a good deal of sprucing up until significant parts of downtown actually looked fairly pleasant. Rather, the central problem, as it had been for decades, was *people:* people to patronize the sagging retail establishments and mostly marginal restaurants; people to support entertainment events; and people on the streets to give the city a bustling and safe feeling. Ashe's magnificent convention center certainly would help, but it was situated on the western edge of the downtown, four blocks from the main center city artery (Gay Street) and separated from the downtown proper by multilaned Henley Street that discouraged east-west pedestrian traffic. Moreover, even the convention center's most ardent and vocal supporters never claimed that conventioneers alone could keep downtown businesses going.

Not atypically, some Knoxville leaders hoped for a "quick fix" to the dearth of warm bodies on the downtown streets. For their part, Worsham Watkins International and the Knoxville Area Chamber Partnership (founded in March 1998 and headed by former journalist, political adviser to Lamar Alexander, and head of a successful public relations firm Tom Ingram) championed the notion of a planetarium and educational center that would attract visitors in the same way that Chattanooga's immensely successful aquarium was doing. Patterned after New York City's new Rose Center for Earth and Space at the city's American Museum of Natural History, Universe Knoxville, as it was dubbed, promised to draw 1.1 million visitors per year to downtown Knoxville, where they would spend $23.4 million on the site and (it was hoped) millions more in nearby businesses.[60]

Realizing that Knoxville's traditional opposition to change would smother Universe Knoxville if he did not move aggressively, Ingram tried to build at least the illusion that the project had broad popular support. Downtown businesses were urged to put "YES! Universe Knoxville" signs on their business windows and marquees and to place the same message on fax coversheets, newsletters, e-mail messages, and store receipts. Individual supporters were encouraged to speak with friends, relatives, and associates and to inundate county commissioners with pro-Universe telephone calls, letters, etc. Civic clubs were asked to request the "Super Chamber" to provide speakers for meetings and luncheons. Thus, Ingram almost certainly reasoned, what he lacked in raw numbers might be overcome by sheer noise. "I see very little will to do anything in this community," he said, but the "Super Chamber" CEO would give it his best.[61]

And at first it appeared as if Ingram's strategy would work. On April 22, 2001, the *News-Sentinel* threw its not inconsiderable support behind Universe Knoxville, and the next day the county commission appropriated $200,000 to get the ball rolling. "Planetarium clears first hurdle," exulted the *News-Sentinel*. Later 150 business leaders, almost all of them from West Knoxville, attended an early morning pep rally for Universe Knoxville sponsored by Pilot Oil

Corporation's Jim Haslam. If downtown Knoxville needed a major entertainment destination and anchor for other tourist-related businesses, maybe Universe Knoxville was it.[62]

It was not. Tied as it was to Worsham Watkins's Renaissance Knoxville, when that project declined, enthusiasm for Universe Knoxville waned as well. As it was for the overall Renaissance Knoxville plan, the necessary private money (estimated at between $116 million and $150 million) was frustratingly elusive, the predictable opposition charged that the optimistic feasibility study was wrong and that the city would be saddled with an unsuccessful project and a huge debt, and Victor Ashe was less than enthusiastic to increase the city's debt service beyond what his convention center already would do. A frustrated Tom Ingram lamented that "Knoxville is a very difficult place to deal with in terms of economic development." More serious, however, was the fact that Ingram had tried to out-muscle the mayor and, as has been shown earlier, for such a transgression there could be no forgiveness or mercy. Not only did Ashe block Ingram at almost every turn, but in mid-2002 the mayor announced that the city would not renew its contract with the Super Chamber, and therefore essentially would starve the Knoxville Area Chamber Partnership by refusing to make the city's annual $145,000 contribution. When new county executive Mike Ragsdale finally pronounced a eulogy for what one editorial writer once had called a "silver bullet tourist attraction," it came as no surprise that the angry and politically impotent Ingram stormily quit the Super Chamber, leaving it in the hands of the less controversial Mike Edwards. Earlier Ragsdale had observed that Knoxville was "a community of missed opportunities." Yet even as still another opportunity was suffering wounds that would turn out to be fatal, Portland, Oregon, consultant Crandall Arambula and others were hired to produce still one more downtown master plan.[63]

While the public's attention was concentrated on the large and visible initiatives and failures such as the convention center, the justice center, Renaissance Knoxville, Universe Knoxville, and Market Square, below the proverbial radar screen some increasingly important changes were taking place in the downtown core. At first a trickle and then a modest but steady stream of mostly young professionals, many of whom had never heard of Jane Jacobs, were eschewing suburban sprawl for lofts, condominiums, town houses, free-standing houses, and apartments in the center city. Dubbed by the magazine *Knoxville City View* "urban pioneers," these individuals and couples engaged the services of imaginative architects and developers such as Kristopher Kendrick (probably the first of the developer-pioneers, who had spurred the revival of the badly run-down Old City neighborhood), Buzz Goss and Cherie Piercy-Goss, David Dewhirst, Joan Allen, Wayne Blasius, Adam Cohen, and others to design and build their new homes on the urban frontier. Part developer and part missionary, Dewhirst (who lives with wife Tracy and young daughter in a beautiful loft on North Gay Street) says that to some people, living in the downtown core "is more pleasant than a vehicle-oriented lifestyle. When you live downtown, you can walk every place [and] you see people, you bump into them, you talk to them"[64]

Pioneers searched for center city enclaves with all the inventiveness and energy that Sherlock Holmes and Dr. Watson searched for evildoers. Some found them in the new condominiums of Volunteer Landing overlooking the Tennessee River. Others hunkered in lofts fashioned out of the old Sterchi Brothers Furniture Store or Fowler's Furniture Store or in other downtown nooks and crannies. And while the movement was primarily financed by private developers, banks, investors, and homeowners, the city government helped through the institution of flexible building codes (without which many of the old buildings could not have been refitted for residential use), tax abatements, assistance in securing federal historic preservation tax incentives and low-interest loans, reduced fees for plan reviews and permits, low- or no-cost parking for the new residents, and beefed-up police on the streets. "Knoxville is desperate for this," reported Jon Clark, who with his wife Mandy built a 1,700-square-foot loft on the top floor of a building on Market Square. "We saw downtown as the opportunity to invest, not only to benefit ourselves, but also to benefit the community."[65]

In sum, an increasing number of people were coming to the conclusion that a downtown residential movement in the long run would have more of an impact on center city revitalization than either tourism or more businesses. Indeed, one survey reported that each person who lived in the downtown core spent *twenty-five times* more money in the center city than the average visitor. And one 2002 estimate expected that within two years the downtown residential population would double.[66]

But would that be enough people to turn the center city around? Necessary retail establishments such as grocery stores had abandoned the downtown core decades ago and showed no signs of a desire to return until the critical mass of residents increased significantly (the closest Kroger grocery store was 2.3 miles away). Moreover, the downtown population of "undesirables" was visible and occasionally annoying. Knoxville's homeless population (which had increased by 30 percent between 1986 and 1996) tended to congregate from the "hobo village" under the Henley Street Bridge to the Knox Area Rescue Ministries and the Salvation Army facility on North Broadway just a few blocks from downtown. Prostitutes plied their trade on the "ho stroll" near the intersection of Broadway and Central. Perhaps worst of all, parts of the city appeared empty and forbidding after dark. Thus while an increasing number of bold and imaginative "pioneers" were opting to live downtown rather than in the suburban sprawl, it was by no means clear that this migration would be strong enough to effect a revolution in the central core. The *News-Sentinel* put it best when it wrote in a feature story on downtown residents, "Wanted: more urban dwellers." To many, they were Knoxville's salvation.[67]

Knoxville at the New Millennium

The last decades of the twentieth century were not good times for America's cities. Financial difficulties, center city deterioration, racial troubles and white flight, increased crime and drug use each tested the imagination and courage of urban economic, social, and political leaders as well as city residents themselves. In all, as the nation's cities approached a new millennium, prospects appeared bleak.

Knoxville faced all of those troubles—and more. For decades feelings of lethargy and negativism as well as a kind of mass intellectual and cultural paralysis had frustrated and routed even the most courageous and visionary pied pipers. With their hopes often dashed, many Knoxvillians became despondent and apathetic, believing that the city had lost the will and the strength to control its own destiny.

And yet, while one could not deny that Knoxville and its citizens faced a myriad of problems, at the same time the *magnitude* of those difficulties did not appear to be insurmountable. The Appalachian city had emerged from the Butcher debacle psychologically shaken but hardly seriously wounded. Although a victim of anti-change ideology, a combative political environment, and his own personal excesses, Mayor Kyle Testerman had stabilized the city's post-fair finances and produced a plan for downtown resurgence that was both practical and visionary. For his part, Victor Ashe's four-term administration, the longest uninterrupted mayoralty in the city's history and certainly a testament to his political sagacity, brought a period of much-needed governmental consistency, improved city finances, applauded physical improvements and beautification (especially new and refurbished city parks), an inclusive political style, and (twenty years after the closing of the World's Fair) at last a use for the fair site in the form of a magnificent convention center. Race relations still were far from good, but a larger African American middle class was emerging, and a police review board at least seemed to show the city's good intentions. To be sure, much of Ashe's success can be attributed to the fact that he dominated a weak and pliable city council, thus severely imbalancing the local government's checks and balances. With the exception of the strong and independent Carlene

Malone (Fourth District) and the brief tenure of Danny Mayfield (Sixth District), the council almost invariably gave the mayor what he wanted. Thus while Ashe's long tenure was a scandal-free, productive, and generally good one, the very strong mayor–very weak council form of local government did not auger well for a city whose citizens were so suspicious of governmental power, elites, and new ideas.[68]

And yet, so many times before there had been wondrous opportunities. As other American cities foundered, was Knoxville's destiny in the future or already behind it?

Epilogue

Cas Walker died. After being a noisy, quarrelsome, retrogressive force in Knoxville politics for roughly forty years, on September 25, 1998, he went quietly to meet his Maker. True to the last, he had spent his final years hawking a supposed health salve and his rambling, self-congratulatory, and nearly incoherent autobiography. After a brief funeral that was attended by only two currently serving elected officials, he was laid to rest in Woodlawn Cemetery.[1]

Commenting on Walker's demise, twice mayor Kyle Testerman said that "Cas' death brings down the curtain on a very significant portion of [the] history of Knoxville politics." To be sure, his opposition could spell the death of many a proposal for progress in Knoxville, for, as university official and newspaper columnist Theotis Robinson explained, as a political combatant "he could be mean as a snake." Just as often, however, Walker's opposition had been able to slow but not to stop other ideas, such as the Market Square Mall project, fluoridation, a new downtown library, zoning restrictions, a new city-county building and the 1982 World's Fair, to name but a few. Indeed, perhaps it was Cas Walker as a symbol of a general *culture of opposition* that Testerman believed—or hoped—had come to an end.[2]

Whether it had or not was a question Knoxvillians had yet to answer as they greeted the new millennium. Could they break the grip of pessimism, negativism, and a general culture of opposition that had infected much of the elite and non-elite as well? As Williams Arant Jr., senior vice president of SunTrust Bank, put it, "For twenty years, Knoxville has struggled as if it had some kind of *disease*. [There] was always *something*, some obstacle, that got in the way, . . . a sort of *complex* that we need to break through." Would Cas Walker's death symbolize the end of that culture or would it survive him as powerfully as it had preceded him?[3]

In order to answer that question, however, Knoxvillians first would have to deal with other issues and answer other questions. To begin with, could the city's various neighborhoods, interests, and constituencies put aside their petty bickering and come together to fashion a collective vision for Knoxville and then be able to summon up the collective will to breathe life into that vision? This had never been done before, in part because the city had evolved as a cluster of mutually suspicious and often competing peoples and in part because Knoxville's leaders more often than not had discouraged such collective urges and movements. Indeed, even the city's leadership was fractured into competing interests, geographical sections, and even leadership groups themselves (Leadership Knoxville, Leadership Community Action Committee, neighborhood associations, etc.). To be sure, they might occasionally celebrate a UT athletic triumph by singing "Rocky Top" until their adenoids nearly fell out, but even those moments of merrymaking were not participated in by everyone.

Then in May 1999 approximately 150 community leaders were invited to a meeting at the Ijams Nature Center to witness the birth of a somewhat different sort of "visioning" initiative. Conceived by Laurens Tullock (former city director of development and in 1999 president of the Cornerstone Foundation of Knoxville) and bankrolled by seventeen corporate sponsors (including Baptist Health System, St. Mary's Hospital, Clayton Homes, the *News-Sentinel*, TVA, and the Haslam Family Foundation), the gathering was a top-down effort to bring people from Knox County and eight surrounding counties together to discuss common challenges and opportunities. A ninety-person steering committee was selected by a group headed by Knoxville Area Chamber Partnership head Tom Ingram, Lynne Fugate (former vice president for community development at First American Bank) was hired as executive director, and consultant Gianni Longo of American Communities Partnership (who had worked on similar projects in Chattanooga, Kingsport, Birmingham, New Haven, and Washington, D.C.) was brought aboard as consultant, at $124,000 plus expenses. Dubbed "Nine Counties One Vision" by its creators, the project looked like just one more top-down effort to move the region in directions that its elite wanted it to go.[4]

But it was not. In February–March 2000, twenty citizens' meetings were held throughout the region to solicit the public's ideas and suggestions on ways in which the nine counties could work together in order to move forward. Over 3,600 people attended those meetings, where they agreed on 48 general objectives and offered 8,827 separate ideas and suggestions, not a few of them bold and even visionary. For the most part the elite stayed away, correctly feeling that their presence would stifle open conversation and give the appearance that the whole initiative was being manipulated from above, which it was not. Few of those who attended expected that all the people's ideas would be adopted. On the other hand, perhaps they believed that, for the first time in Knoxville's history, they had been heard and taken seriously.[5]

Thus the first question Knoxvillians in the post-Walker era had to answer was whether the various constituencies of the city could work together toward a common end. Ever-present cynics lamented that the real name for the project should be "One County, Nineteen Visions." And yet many citizens seem to have sensed that the time was ripe for new ideas and that their collective will this time might turn back timid leaders and their intransigent fellow Knoxvillians.[6]

If Knoxvillians were to work together to break the crust of the city's cultural paralysis, mutual suspicion and envy, and aversion to change, at the very least they would have to respect the city's various constituencies and be more tolerant of the region's increasing diversity. As noted earlier, many Knoxvillians had become convinced that this could be accomplished only by putting an end to top-down pronouncements and instead actually *listening* to all of Knoxville's citizenry.

But this would not be easy. In the past, even the most progressive city leaders had preferred to institute change and reforms from above. Knoxville's citizens, in their view, were hopelessly reactionary and could never be depended upon to support new ideas. Throughout the twentieth century, therefore, most of the business-political elite supported changes in the city's government that would not *include* more Knoxvillians in the decision-making process but would instead *exclude* more of the general populace from participating in decisions. General plebiscites, such as a vote on whether or not to host a World's Fair in 1982, were studiously avoided, fearing that the voters, "dungforks gleaming in the sun," as H. L. Mencken once put it, would follow popular demagogues like Lee Monday or Cas Walker not forward but backward.

Those who felt themselves to be most impotent were the city's African Americans. Urban renewal and the construction of Neyland Drive (running along the Tennessee River on the southern edge of the downtown) had displaced hundreds of black families and businesses who had had no voice in those decisions. Later, in the late 1990s, the public housing project College Homes (built in 1940) was razed, to be replaced by a "more traditional" looking neighborhood of single-family and duplex rental and occupant-owned units. To be sure, both areas were marked improvements over what had been there before, but the point was that few African Americans had participated in the decisions to reconstruct these neighborhoods. Zimbabwe Matavou, president of the Black Business/Contractors Association, certainly overstated the case when he opined that urban renewal "was the worst thing to happen to black folk in Knoxville since slavery." But even Victor Ashe, who in his long term of office as mayor had attempted to improve conditions for Knoxville's blacks, lamented, "If I could repeal anything from the last fifty years, that [urban renewal] along with the location of Neyland Drive would be it."[7]

And other African American neighborhoods continued to struggle with poverty, physical deterioration, drugs, and crime. "We can't even get the city to clean our streets," complained one resident of Martin Luther King Jr. Avenue. "This place would depress the pope." And Dennie Littlejohn, a member of the board of Neighborhood Housing and Commercial Services, mourned, "Black people who could afford to get out did." In frustration, Dewey Roberts, president of the Knoxville branch of the NAACP, asserted that, in spite of the many improvements and initiatives intended to help Knoxville's African Americans, racism still existed, even though "white people deny it." In order to get all Knoxvillians to work together, considerable energy and sensitivity would have to be expended to bring the city's skeptical African Americans "inside the tent."[8]

Barely noticed were significant increases among Knoxville's other minorities. Barely numbering 2,000 people in 1990, by 1998 the city's Latino population had more than doubled. Latinos and Latinas could be found in all of Knoxville's socioeconomic classes and possessed so much purchasing power that a local Spanish language newspaper *(Mundo Hispano)* and a local radio station were established to serve the growing community, and Latinos offered the city a richer texture that the comparatively homogeneous and bland city had not had before. At the same time, Knoxville's Asian and Middle Eastern populations increased as well. On a more somber note, however, while "hate crimes" against African Americans declined in the city, offenses against Middle Easterners increased, especially after the September 11, 2001, attacks on the World Trade Center and the Pentagon. If growing ethnic diversity was making Knoxville a more interesting and enriched city, at the same time the attacks and their aftermath presented challenges for those who would bring residents together to establish and work for common goals.[9]

In the eyes of many Knoxvillians, the most serious issue to be addressed was the city's changing economic picture. Once dependent on non-durable-goods manufacturing and government jobs, Knoxville had seen those two sectors decline significantly in the 1980s and 1990s, as some large manufacturing firms moved their operations to Mexico (Jim Robbins Seat Belts, Levi Strauss, etc.), where wages were even lower than East Tennessee's. At the same time, government cutbacks meant losses of jobs in Oak Ridge, and at TVA, the University of Tennessee, etc. From 1983 to 1996, the percentage of Knoxville workers in manufacturing declined from 21.5 percent to 15.7 percent, while government jobs went from 21.1 percent to 17.8 percent of all jobs. And from October 1996 to October 1997, the city lost an additional 3,100 jobs. As late as 2003, however, four of the five top employers in metropolitan Knoxville still were government institutions (the U.S. Department of Energy, the University of Tennessee, Knox County Schools, and the City of Knoxville).[10]

Sectors that did grow included services, retail, hospitals (which more than doubled in jobs between 1980 and 1990), technology, and tourism. In tourism, retail, and much of the service sector, however, wages were lower and benefits were rare. As it had in the past, Knoxville would pay dearly for its unwillingness to welcome new types of enterprises. By the time some of the more progressive business leaders tried to lure high tech companies by establishing a "technology corridor" in West Knox County, it may have been too late, what investment adviser Paul Fain labeled a "failed dream, . . . a great idea that never happened." In addition, sufficient venture capital was lacking, and efforts by a new school superintendent to make Knox County schools "internationally competitive" so as to attract new industry became mired in political warfare between the frustrated and impolitic superintendent, the elected school board, and a county commission ever suspicious of anyone who challenged its prerogatives. The ultimate result was a series of debilitating lawsuits and an ambivalent citizenry that was not certain that it wanted to pay for a "world class" school system. Initiatives from the top, when they came at all, clearly had proved insufficient, and it seemed as if full citizen participation would be necessary in order to deal with Knoxville's changing economy.[11]

One interesting—and somewhat surprising—outcome of the public meetings sponsored by Nine Counties One Vision was the discovery that a large number of people who did not live in the city proper wanted to see a resurgence of downtown Knoxville. Most of those respondents, however, rarely *went* downtown and certainly didn't want to *live* downtown. Even as the center city was experiencing modest gentrification, between 1990 and 2000 upscale suburban enclaves in West Knox County increased in population by over 50 percent. West Town Mall, redesigned to resemble an old-time downtown (what University of Tennessee professor Paul Ashdown dubbed a "pseudo reality"), averaged almost 25,000 visitors per day, few of whom ever shopped—or even went—downtown. In 2002 Turkey Creek Mall opened—one million square feet of developed space to cater to affluent West Knox County shoppers. Indeed, some people even attested that Turkey Creek Mall was so large that they actually had to *drive* from one parking space to another in order to "do the mall."[12]

Many people explained that they did not shop downtown because it lacked free parking (West Town Mall claimed to have 6,760 parking spaces). At the same time, however, comparatively few people patronized Knoxville Area Transit's free "shop and ride" service, which was instituted in 1990. Indeed, the service was used mostly by people in public housing (the "projects"), hardly the men and women downtown retailers hoped would reinvigorate center city shopping. Yet when people who participated in Nine Counties One Vision's meetings were asked to list what they considered to be the area's most important needs, a light-rail mass transit system ranked a shocking second in the number of public responses. Although it was far from clear whether East Tennesseans were willing to live in or even patronize a rejuvenated downtown Knoxville, it did seem as if they *wanted* the center city to survive and prosper. In order for it to do so, however, Knoxville's citizens would have to work together to make that dream a reality. Whether they could do that was by no means clear by the dawn of the new millennium.[13]

In the long run, the most serious problem that Knoxvillians would have to face was one they preferred not to think about at all. By 2002 the city had the eighth worst air quality of all United States cities, and between 1997 and 1999 there were an astounding ninety-four days in which it was *unhealthy to breathe at all* in Knox County. Sulfur dioxide, carbon dioxide, and nitrogen oxide emissions were among the highest in the nation. Visibility in the nearby Smoky Mountains was roughly one-third of what it ought to have been, and acid rain posed a growing threat to plants, birds, fish, amphibians, and some mammals—including humans. First Creek, Second Creek, and Third Creek, which drained water from the downtown area into the Tennessee River, were rich in fecal bacteria and urban runoff, and health authorities warned Knoxvillians not to eat large fish that were caught in the Tennessee River. Did Knoxville's citizens have the will and collective self-discipline to address an environment that was, according to *News-Sentinel* journalist Fred Brown, "as healthy as dwelling in a dustbin"? In one of the most beautiful locations in the country, could Knoxvillians work together to stop contaminating their own home place?[14]

In order to accomplish all—or any—of these things, Knoxvillians would have to do considerably more than talk about their common opportunities and challenges. In short, they would have to begin thinking as citizens of a *city*, not as their rural ancestors had thought. They would have to embrace a new system of values that, at crucial times, would put the good of the whole community above their own individual self-interests. Then, armed with new ways of thinking and a new sense of civic and personal responsibility, they would have to rise up on their hind legs and shout down the cynics and naysayers. In truth, if Knoxville was the way it was because their forebears had wanted it so, then *they* must summon the will to make a new city.

It would not be easy. In 1999 alone, some 8,000 bags of illegally dumped trash littered the empty lots and roadways, hideous and appalling reminders that at least some Knoxvillians had not become truly urban. Just as police officers are adept at catching criminals but for the most part are unable to prevent crimes, so also a veritable legion of additional city employees would not be enough to remove the mountain of crud that greeted the city's citizenry every day. Instead, a new kind of urban thinking would be necessary, one that was grounded more in a hopeful future than in a pre-urban past.[15]

In September 1994, *USA Today* called together a group of mayors and others who worked in America cities to discuss the question "Can our cities survive?" What was striking was the extent to which the 1994 gathering differed from the lamentations of the mayors who in 1971 had appeared before the House Ways and Means Committee.[16] In 1971 the consensus of the mayors seemed to be that only massive amounts of federal dollars would rescue America's cities from most of their problems.[17]

In 1994, however, the mayors, while certainly welcoming fiscal injections from Washington, spent most of their time calling for a new sense of values and personal responsibility from their citizens. Probably Minneapolis mayor Sharon Sayles Belton spoke for them all when she said,

> I absolutely think that public officials and elected officials ought to be involved in the discussion about values. I don't think that we should use our laws and ordinances to dictate values, but I think we have to talk about them.
>
> We've been talking about four basic values in Minneapolis. . . . We've been talking about the community value of education, of work, . . . of self-respect . . . about personal responsibility. No free lunch. You've got to make some contribution to society if you expect something is going to change for you.[18]

In sum, Knoxville was a city. Now it was time to *think* like a city.

On January 27, 2000, approximately sixteen months after the death of Cas Walker, six hundred people gathered in the ballroom of the Hyatt Regency Hotel to honor Pilot Oil Corporation president Jim Haslam. Radio talk show host Hallerin Hilton Hill was the master of ceremonies, and tributes included remarks by former senator Howard Baker and the song "Captain of the Team," which was composed by Hill and sung artfully by Bill Arant. In a characteristically gracious acceptance of the plaudits of the assemblage, the person *Metro Pulse* had described as Knoxville's "most conspicuous philanthropist" quoted Winston Churchill in a call to arms that was pure Haslam: "Never give up!"[19]

The event marked Haslam's stepping down from the chairmanship of Leadership Knoxville, an organization he had formed in 1984 to identify and educate present and future Knoxville leaders and to "quit letting *outside* forces decide where we're going." But the evening also was intended as a show of support for Haslam himself who, after twenty-eight years of serving as the chairman of the Public Building Authority, in mid-1999 had been unceremoniously ousted by the county commission, a move that some people interpreted as secretly instigated by Knox County sheriff Tim Hutchinson in return for Haslam's support of still another failed effort at unified government for the city and county. Although Haslam himself never commented publicly on his removal, many believed that he had been hurt personally by the act, which one person described as "about as crudely handled as a banana republic coup." On the evening of January 27, however, much of that was forgotten as James Haslam II basked in the deserved applause of his fellow citizens.[20]

Coming as they did so close together, the death of Cas Walker and the honoring of Jim Haslam appeared to stand as clear-cut choices for Knoxvillians. On one hand, they could follow the spirit of Walker, of fierce opposition to change and new ideas. On the other hand, they could follow the example of Haslam, of advocating change not as an option but as a crucial necessity. Indeed, even when these changes made Haslam nervous, as they often did, he could embrace them. And while those choices were never as simple or as black-and-white as they sometimes appeared to be, in the end those were the two paths the people of Knoxville were free to tread.

In some important ways, of course, the choice was a false one. In the year 1190, while leading his army across a stream during the Third Crusade, the fully armored Emperor Frederick I (better known to us as Frederick Barbarossa) fell from his horse and drowned. Without the emperor to lead them, many of his troops simply melted away and thus failed to reinforce the army of Richard the Lion-Hearted. Jerusalem remained in the hands of Saladin.

For decades those who would change the city of Knoxville yearned and searched for a leader, a person who would lead them across the many streams. At last, however, many came to realize that the power to alter their city rested not with any leader but with themselves. In that sense, both Walker and Haslam were *symbols,* representations of the directions in which Knoxville could go. It was they themselves who would have to face the blinding sunlight and frightening shadows in the days that lay ahead of them. Rather than fashion a mythical past to explain their present, as had the tragic Jay Gatsby, Knoxvillians needed to understand clearly from whence they came. And then they should turn around, and move on—together. For as Oliver Wendell Holmes so succinctly put it, "What lies behind us and what lies before us are tiny matters compared to what lies within us."

Notes

Preface

1. F. Scott Fitzgerald, *The Great Gatsby* (New York: Charles Scribner's Sons, 1925, 1953 ed.), 46–47, 60–63, 66, 88–89. For the critic's observation see *Harper's,* February 1999, 18. Not surprisingly, one of Ralph Lauren's (né Lifshitz) literary heroes is Jay Gatsby. *New York Times,* January 20, 2003.

2. Mary U. Rothrock, ed., *The French Broad–Holston Country: A History of Knox County, Tennessee* (Knoxville: East Tennessee Historical Society, 1946); Lucile Deaderick, ed., *Heart of the Valley: A History of Knoxville, Tennessee* (Knoxville: East Tennessee Historical Society, 1976). See also Betsey Beeler Creekmore, *Knoxville,* 3rd ed. (Knoxville: Univ. of Tennessee Press, 1976).

Chapter 1

1. *Progressive Knoxville 1904: A Pictorial Review of the City* (Knoxville: Russell Harrison, 1903).

2. For some examples of boosterism, see H. M. Branson, *Annual Hand Book of Knoxville, Tennessee, for the Year 1892* (Knoxville: Tribune Office, 1892), 15–16; *Knoxville Sentinel,* July 19, 22, 23, 1904. For a later example see *This Week in Knoxville and East Tennessee* 1, no. 2 (September 11–17, 1927).

3. Daniel E. Sutherland, ed., *A Very Violent Rebel: The Civil War Diary of Ellen Renshaw House* (Knoxville: Univ. of Tennessee Press, 1996), 184, 190. Ellen's sister Fannie married Thomas O'Conner, a Confederate veteran who made a fortune in real estate, railroad bonds, banking, and coal mining (with leased convict labor). He died in a gun battle with a longtime business associate on the street outside the Mechanics' National Bank in 1882. See Lucile Deaderick, ed., *Heart of the Valley: A History of Knoxville, Tennessee* (Knoxville: East Tennessee Historical Society, 1976), 589.

4. Father Abraham Ryan to Miss Canny, Sept. 12, 1865, quoted in Noel C. Fisher, *War at Every Door: Partisan Politics and Guerrilla Violence in East Tennessee, 1860–1869* (Chapel Hill: Univ. of North Carolina Press, 1997), 158.

5. For a good discussion of East Tennessee prior to the Civil War see Charles Faulkner Bryan Jr., "The Civil War in East Tennessee: A Social, Political, and Economic Study," Ph.D. diss., Univ. of Tennessee, 1978, chap. 1. See also Stanley J. Folmsbee, Robert E. Corlew, and Enoch L. Mitchell, *Tennessee: A Short History* (Knoxville: Univ. of Tennessee Press, 1969), 163–66.

6. On Knoxville's elite see Karen Thornton, "The Elite of Knoxville, Tennessee, in the Age of Jackson" (unpub. student paper, Univ. of Tennessee; in possession of author).

7. On railroads see Mary U. Rothrock, ed., *The French Broad–Holston Country: A History of Knox County, Tennessee* (Knoxville: East Tennessee Historical Society, 1946),

108–12. On the city's secession vote see *Knoxville Daily Register,* June 11, 1861. On southern orientation of Knoxville's economy see W. Todd Groce, *Mountain Rebels: East Tennessee Confederates and the Civil War, 1860–1870* (Knoxville: Univ. of Tennessee Press, 1999), 4–10. On First Presbyterian Church see Rothrock, *French Broad–Holston Country,* 144. For McAdoo's statement see William Gibbs McAdoo Diary, Dec. 12, 1860, in Special Collections, Hoskins Library, University of Tennessee. For an illuminating study of the secession crisis in the Knoxville area see DeAnna Davis, "The Secession Crisis in the Knoxville, Tennessee, Region" (unpub. graduate student paper, Univ. of South Carolina, 2003; in possession of the author).

8. Percy M. Pentecost, "A Corporate History of Knoxville, Tennessee, before 1860" (M.A. thesis, Univ. of Tennessee, 1946), 85–86.

9. The best study of the Battle of Knoxville is Maury Klein, "The Knoxville Campaign," *Civil War Times Illustrated* 10 (Oct. 1971): 4–10, 42.

10. Klein, "Knoxville Campaign," 4. For an excellent book on Knoxville during the Civil War see Digby Gordon Seymour, *Divided Loyalties: Fort Sanders and the Civil War in East Tennessee* (Knoxville: Univ. of Tennessee Press, 1963). For the context see Thomas L. Connelly, *Civil War Tennessee: Battles and Leaders* (Knoxville: Univ. of Tennessee Press, 1979), 79–80.

11. I am indebted to Dr. Kathleen Zebly-Liulevicius for allowing me to see her unpublished work on pardons in Tennessee. See her "Rebel Salvation: The Story of Confederate Pardons," Ph.D. diss., Univ. of Tennessee, 1998.

12. Rothrock, *French Broad–Holston Country,* 141–47. A good survey of the 1867 flood is in *Metro Pulse,* March 21, 2002. On funds raised by the East Tennessee Relief Association see Thomas William Humes, *The Loyal Mountaineers of Tennessee* (Knoxville: Ogden Brothers and Co., 1888), 396–97.

13. Susanna Delfino, *Yankees del Sud: Svilutto Economico e Trasformazioni Sociali nel Sud degli Stati Uniti, 1790–1860* (Milan: Franco Ageli Libri, 1987). See also C. Vann Woodward, *Origins of the New South, 1877–1914*, vol. 9 of *A History of the South,* ed. Wendell Holmes Stephenson and E. Merton Coulter (Baton Rouge: Louisiana State Univ. Press, 1951).

14. Grady, "The New South," in *Words That Made American History,* ed. Richard N. Current and John A Garraty (Boston: Little, Brown, 1962), 2:24–31. For an excellent analysis see Paul M. Gaston, *The New South Creed: A Study in Southern Mythmaking* (New York: Alfred A. Knopf, 1970) and Harold E. Davis, *Henry Grady's New South: Atlanta, A Brave and Beautiful City* (Tuscaloosa: Univ. of Alabama Press, 1990).

15. William J. MacArthur Jr., *Knoxville's History: An Interpretation* (Knoxville: East Tennessee Historical Society, 1978), 30. One example of the city's strong Unionist sentiment was the statue of a Union soldier erected in Knoxville's National Cemetery, the largest Union monument in the South. Jack Neely and Aaron Jay, *The Marble City: A Photographic Tour of Knoxville's Graveyards* (Knoxville: Univ. of Tennessee Press, 1999), 47.

16. Don H. Doyle, *New Men, New Cities, New South: Atlanta, Nashville, Charleston, Mobile, 1860–1910* (Chapel Hill: Univ. of North Carolina Press, 1990). On Knoxville's postwar elite, I am indebted to DeAnna Davis, whose unpublished research on the city's elite informed much of the following analysis.

17. Gray Cemetery (after the 1890s called "Old Gray") was established in 1850 and named by Henrietta Reese after Thomas Gray, the English poet who wrote "Elegy Written in a Country Churchyard." The first burial was that of William Martin, who was killed at

a Fourth of July celebration when a cannonball accidentally blew off his arm. *Metro Pulse,* June 1, 2000.

18. On "parvenus" statement see Sutherland, ed., *A Very Violent Rebel,* xviii. On Cowan see Rothrock, *French Broad–Holston Country,* 401–2.

19. On Dickinson see *Knoxville Journal and Tribune,* July 19, 1901; Rothrock, *French Broad–Holston Country,* 411–12; William J. MacArthur Jr., *Knoxville: Crossroads of the New South* (Knoxville: East Tennessee Historical Society, 1982), 58.

20. On Temple see Fred Arthur Bailey, "Oliver Perry Temple, New South Agrarian" (M.A. thesis, Univ. of Tennessee, 1972); Rothrock, *French Broad–Holston Country,* 496–97; *Knoxville Journal and Tribune,* Nov. 3, 1907.

21. For pallbearers for Dickinson and Temple see *Knoxville Journal and Tribune,* July 19, 1901; Nov. 3, 1907.

22. On Sanford see *Knoxville Journal and Tribune,* Oct. 28–29, 1902; Rothrock, *French Broad–Holston Country,* 479–80; MacArthur, *Crossroads of the New South,* 61–62. For the attack on Sanford see *Knoxville Chronicle,* June 5, 1886. On Albers see *Knoxville Journal and Tribune,* Nov. 11, 1910; Deaderick, *Heart of the Valley,* 485. On Woodruff see Rothrock, *French Broad–Holston Country,* 507. On William Chamberlain see *Knoxville News-Sentinel,* April 17, 1917.

23. On Luttrell see *Knoxville Journal,* Nov. 21, 1933; Rothrock, *French Broad–Holston Country,* 441–42. For a fine analysis of Luttrell's banking practices see Kathleen A. Johnston, "The City of Tomorrow with the Spirit of the Past: Bankrolling the Industrial Development of Knoxville, Tennessee" (M.A. thesis, Univ. of Tennessee, 1994), esp. 9, 45–49, 54–56, 60–62.

24. On Tyson see Rothrock, *French Broad–Holston Country,* 498–99. On McGhee Tyson's death see *Metro Pulse,* June 1, 2000. On Tyson's father-in-law see Rothrock, *French Broad–Holston Country,* 447–48; *Knoxville Journal and Tribune,* May 6, 1907.

25. *Knoxville Daily Chronicle,* Aug. 11, 1875. For Richmond newspaper's 1871 statement see Robert Corlew, *Tennessee: A Short History,* 2nd ed. (Knoxville: Univ. of Tennessee Press, 1990), 365. By the mid-twentieth century, it was almost impossible to tell which of Knoxville's elite families had been antebellum, transitional, or new. For example, Edward J. McMillan, the head of Standard Knitting Mills, was described as coming from an "old family." His father had come to Knoxville in 1870. See "The Conservatives of Knoxville," *Fortune,* July 1952, 111; Deaderick, *Heart of the Valley,* 568.

26. Chamber of Commerce, *Knoxville, Tenn.: A City Unsectional and Cosmopolitan* (Knoxville: Chamber of Commerce, 1890), 29; Daniel Jansen, "Knoxville's Jobbing Industry" (unpub. student paper, Univ. of Tennessee, 1990), 11; *Knoxville Tribune,* April 21, 1881; *City Directory 1906* (Knoxville: G. M. Connelly, 1906), 5.

27. Chamber of Commerce, *A City Unsectional,* 14–16, 29; Ellwood Oakley Dille, "Knoxville, Tennessee, as a Wholesale Trade Center," Ph.D. diss., Ohio State Univ., 1942, 26–27; *Knoxville Tribune,* April 20, 1881; *Goodspeed's History of Hamilton, Knox, and Shelby Counties of Tennessee* (Nashville: Goodspeed, 1887), 850–51.

28. *Knoxville Market Annual* (Knoxville, 1908), 3–5, 24; Chamber of Commerce, *A City Unsectional,* 29; Knoxville Board of Trade, *Knoxville, Tennessee: The Queen City of the Mountains* (Knoxville: Board of Trade, 1907), 23; MacArthur, *Knoxville's History,* 46. On Briscoe and Carhart see Jansen, "Knoxville's Jobbing Industry," 15, 21–24. For trade volume see *City Directory 1909* (Knoxville: Knoxville Directory Co., 1909), 5.

29. Blaine A. Brownell, *The Urban Ethos in the South, 1920–1930* (Baton Rouge: Louisiana State Univ. Press, 1975), 4–5. Commerce still far exceeded manufacturing in dollar volume. See Board of Trade, *Queen City,* 23.

30. J. B. Killebrew, *Introduction to the Resources of Tennessee* (Nashville: Tennessee Bureau of Agriculture, 1874), 444.

31. On Chamberlain see John Hope Franklin, *Reconstruction: After the Civil War* (Chicago: Univ. of Chicago Press, 1961), 94–96; Rothrock, *French Broad–Holston Country,* 313; Deaderick, *Heart of the Valley,* 32. Not long after founding the Knoxville Iron Company, Chamberlain relocated to Chattanooga, although his brother William P. Chamberlain remained in the city and Hiram retained several business interests in Knoxville. James W. Livingood, *Hamilton County,* Tennessee County History Series 33 (Memphis: Memphis State Univ. Press, 1981), 57; Gilbert E. Govan and James W. Livingood, *The Chattanooga Country, 1540–1962: From Tomahawks to TVA* (Chapel Hill: Univ. of North Carolina Press, 1963), 295–96. On Mechanicsville see Metropolitan Planning Commission (MPC), *Mechanicsville, Lonsdale, Beaumont Small Area Study* (Knoxville: MPC, 1976).

32. Knoxville Woolen Mills Records, 1884–1914, in Special Collections, Hoskins Library, University of Tennessee; Branson, *Annual Hand Book,* 51; W. M. Goodman, ed., *Souvenir History of Knoxville, The Marble City and Great Jobbing Market* (Knoxville: Knoxville Engraving, 1907), 2–3; Board of Trade, *Queen City,* 2.

33. Board of Trade, *Queen City,* 2–3; *Knoxville News-Sentinel,* special supplement, Feb. 28, 1999; MacArthur, *Crossroads of the New South,* 56, 94; Goodman, *Souvenir History of Knoxville,* 27.

34. *Knoxville Market Annual,* 3–5; *The Statistics of the Population of the United States . . . Ninth Census (June 1, 1870); Tenth Census of the United States, 1880; Eleventh Census of the United States, 1890.* See also Board of Trade, *Queen City,* 1. Between 1880 and 1887, capital invested in manufacturing increased an astounding 464 percent.

35. *Knoxville Market Annual* (Knoxville, 1908), 3–5, 24. On housing see *Commercial and Industrial Survey of Knoxville, Tennessee,* compiled for the Chamber of Commerce (Knoxville, 1939).

36. On Fort Sanders see Knoxville Heritage, Inc., *Fort Sanders Walking Tour* (Knoxville: Knoxville Heritage, 1977).

37. In 1890, excluding Tennessee, of the top twenty states of origin of Knoxville's population, nine were northern (Ohio, New York, Pennsylvania, Indiana, Illinois, Michigan, Massachusetts, Wisconsin, and Minnesota). See Branson, *Annual Hand Book,* 18.

38. Alrutheus Ambush Taylor, *The Negro in Tennessee, 1860–1880* (Washington, D.C.: Associated Publishers, 1941), 27, 30–35, 141–42. Other Knoxville businesses that employed large numbers of African Americans include the Knoxville Rolling Mills, Knoxville Foundry and Machine Co., and Knoxville Leather Co. Taylor, *Negro in Tennessee,* 142. For more on black migration to Knoxville see Stephen V. Ash, *A Year in the South: Four Lives in 1865* (New York: Palgrave Macmillan, 2002), 56. In 1864 some of the in-migrating African Americans were organized as the U.S. Colored Heavy Artillery, part of the town's garrison force. Ash, *Year in the South,* 56.

39. For a good survey of Knoxville's African Americans see Robert J. Booker, *Two Hundred Years of Black Culture in Knoxville, Tennessee, 1791–1991* (Virginia Beach: Donning, 1993), esp. 17–39. On black voting see Booker, *Black Culture in Knoxville,* 59; *Knoxville Chronicle,* July 17, Oct. 17, 1880, and April 7, 17, 21, May 30, June 5, 1885; *Knoxville Journal,* February 15, 1888; Joseph H. Cartwright, *The Triumph of Jim Crow:*

Tennessee Race Relations in the 1880s (Knoxville: Univ. of Tennessee Press, 1976), esp. 11–27; Lester C. Lamon, *Blacks in Tennessee, 1791–1970* (Knoxville: Univ. of Tennessee Press, 1981), 48. On police see Levi Strauss Foundation, *Project Change* (Executive Summary Release, Nov. 1995), n.p. On black voting percentage and 1894 gerrymandering see *Clinton Weekly Gazette,* Oct. 17, 1894, quoted in Gordon M. McKinney, "Southern Mountain Republicans and the Negro, 1865–1900," *Journal of Southern History* 41 (Nov. 1975): 512. On 1912 gerrymandering as well as black businesses and professionals at the turn of the century see Robert J. Booker, *Heat of a Red Summer* (Danbury, Conn.: Rutledge Books, 2001), 62.

40. Especially good on Republican strategy is Vincent P. DeSantis, *Republicans Face the Southern Question: The New Departure Years, 1877–1897* (Baltimore: Johns Hopkins Univ. Press, 1959).

41. On Yardley see Booker, *Black Culture in Knoxville,* 62–63; Rothrock, *French Broad–Holston Country,* 324–25; *Metro Pulse,* Feb. 21, 2002. In 1868 Yardley helped to organize Knoxville's black fire department. *Knoxville News-Sentinel,* March 17, 1985.

42. *Knoxville Daily Tribune,* Dec. 29, 1877. On Lawrence see *Knoxville Daily Tribune,* Dec. 24, 1887; Booker, *Black Culture in Knoxville,* 63–64. An excellent account of African American political involvement in Knoxville is Sally Ripatti, "Black Political Involvement in Late-Nineteenth Century Knoxville" (unpub. student paper, Univ. of Tennessee, 1976; in possession of author).

43. Ripatti, "Black Political Involvement," 10–18. See also *Knoxville Daily Tribune,* July 14, 1888. On gerrymandering see *Clinton Weekly Gazette,* Oct. 17, 1894, quoted (complete with ward totals) in McKinney, "Southern Mountain Republicans and the Negro," 512.

44. For German and Irish immigrants see *Metro Pulse,* Dec. 9, 1999. For material on Sevier County see Smoky Mountain Historical Society, *The Gentle Winds of Change: A History of Sevier County, Tennessee, 1900–1930* (Sevierville: Smoky Mountain Historical Society, 1986), 3–4, 82–83.

45. For deaths see a photocopy of Sevier County's 1882 report to the state in Smoky Mountain Historical Society, *In the Shadow of the Smokies* (Sevierville: Smoky Mountain Historical Society; 1985), 733–34. The most common cause of deaths of children was diphtheria. See also Smoky Mountain Historical Society, *Gentle Winds of Change,* 205–6. For Sevier County disqualifications see C. E. Allred et al., *Tennessee, Economic and Social, Part II* (Knoxville: Univ. of Tennessee Extension Service, 1929), 202. Of Knox County's draftees 15.3 percent were disqualified. Allred et al., *Tennessee, Economic and Social,* 202.

46. Smoky Mountain Historical Society, *Gentle Winds of Change,* 131, 142–43.

47. Allred et al., *Tennessee, Economic and Social,* 49, 51, 143. For Sevier County physicians see Smoky Mountain Historical Society, *Gentle Winds of Change,* 199. For the Tennessee Valley's rural and urban population growth and the percentage of valley residents living in cities see William Bruce Wheeler and Michael J. McDonald, "The Communities of East Tennessee, 1850–1940: An Interpretive Overview," East Tennessee Historical Society's *Publications,* 58–59 (1986–87), 27, and TVA Department of Regional Planning, *The Population of the Tennessee Valley* (Knoxville: Tennessee Valley Authority, 1937), 27, 31–32, 40, 43.

48. On crime see *Knoxville Daily Journal,* March 27, July 1, Dec. 1–2, 1885; Deaderick, *Heart of the Valley,* 34–35, 38. On prostitution see James B. Jones Jr., "Municipal Vice: The Management of Prostitution in Tennessee's Urban Experience. Part II: The Examples of Chattanooga and Knoxville, 1838–1917," *Tennessee Historical Quarterly* 50 (summer 1991): 116–17. See also *Knoxville Daily Journal,* April 4, 1885. On the South Central Avenue area

see *Metro Pulse,* Dec. 9, 1999. On "cocaine schools" (drug dens) see Booker, *Heat of a Red Summer,* xv. For criticism of the city's unwanted image see *Knoxville Chronicle,* Feb. 10, 1881. In reply, the pro-farmer *Knoxville Daily Tribune* (Oct. 14, 1881) referred to some Knoxvillians as "stuck up city folk."

49. The best treatment of the three Knoxville expositions is Robert D. Lukens, "Portraits of Progress in New South Appalachia: Three Expositions in Knoxville, Tennessee, 1910–1913" (M.A. thesis, Univ. of Tennessee, 1996). President Theodore Roosevelt visited the 1910 exposition, at which he stated that the people of East Tennessee were "more purely native American than in any other part of our country." *Knoxville Journal and Tribune,* Oct. 8, 1910. The 1910 exposition also was the first time that most Knoxvillians had seen a "flying machine," or "aeroplane." *Knoxville Sentinel,* Sept. 6, 1910; Joseph Wood Krutch, *More Lives Than One* (New York: William Sloane Assoc., 1962), 31–35. Oliver later admitted to having had a well-stocked private bar at the "dry" 1910 exposition. Lukens, "Portraits of Progress," 73.

50. On health see *Knoxville Daily Journal,* March 8, 1885. On paving see MacArthur, *Crossroads of the New South,* 64; Nancy E. Davidson, "The Life and Death of Gay Street" (unpub. student paper, Univ. of Tennessee, 1986; in possession of author). On foul streets, Russell Briscoe, address at Sequoyah Branch of the Knoxville–Knox County Public Library, 1972. On "wretched state" see *Knoxville Sentinel,* May 5, 1904. On hogs running free in the streets see *Knoxville Daily Tribune,* Sept. 18, 1881.

51. For a fine study of the municipal water issue see Jennifer E. Brooks, "'One Grand United Hymn': Boosterism in Knoxville, Tennessee, at the Turn of the Century" (M.A. thesis, Univ. of Tennessee, 1991), esp. 45–50, 56–58. On water wagons see Davidson, "Life and Death of Gay Street," 2. A board of health was established in 1873 and a sanitation commission in 1874, but their roles appear to have been limited. MacArthur, *Crossroads of the New South,* 64. On the permanent water company see Brooks, "Boosterism in Knoxville," 43; *Knoxville Daily Journal,* May 2, 1885. On controversy over the bond issue in 1904 see *Knoxville Sentinel,* May 21, June 17, 20, July 9, 19, 26, 1904. On corrupt politics see *Knoxville Sentinel,* May 5, 1904, in which it was claimed that "thousands of votes were bought, openly and above board" and that up to two-thirds of Republican votes (mostly cast by African Americans) were purchased. See also *Knoxville Chronicle,* July 17, Oct. 17, 1880. On Oliver's frustration see MacArthur, *Crossroads of the New South,* 96.

52. See Knoxville Woolen Mills Records, 1884–1914, Special Collections, Hoskins Library, Univ. of Tennessee. See also Lawrence D. Tyson, *President's Report, Knoxville Woolen Mills, Jan., 1905* (Knoxville: S. B. Newman and Co., 1905), esp. 1–4. In 1904 the principal stockholders were C. M. McGhee (553 shares), Oliver P. Temple (164), William P. Chamberlain (146), James Van Deventer (128), E. T. Sanford (126), L. D. Tyson (84), C. M. McClung (36), C. M. Cowan (36), and A. J. Albers (30). For more on Oliver see Deaderick, *Heart of the Valley,* 48–49, 590.

53. On the sweeping of rural East Tennessee into the market economy see Joe Cummings, "Community and the Nature of Change: Sevier County, Tennessee, in the 1890s," *East Tennessee Historical Society's Publications,* 58–59 (1986–87): 63, 73. On the earlier reliance on wheat see Groce, *Mountain Rebels,* 11–12. On urging East Tennessee farmers to diversify see *Knoxville Daily Chronicle,* Aug. 11, 1881. On rural hard times see Cummings, "Sevier County," 71–75. On underselling of Knoxville manufacturers see C. M. McClung and Co., *Catalog* (1907).

54. Paul H. Bergeron, *Paths of the Past: Tennessee, 1770–1970* (Knoxville: Univ. of Tennessee Press, 1979), 84.

55. Ibid.; Deaderick, *Heart of the Valley,* 106–7. On Heiskell's defense see *Knoxville Sentinel,* Feb. 9, 1907. For the best treatment of the prohibition controversy in Knoxville see Roger Dale Posey, "Anti-Alcohol City: Social, Economic, and Political Aspects of Knoxville, Tennessee, 1870–1907" (M.A. thesis, Univ. of Tennessee, 1982).

56. For the 1893 protest see MacArthur, *Crossroads of the New South,* 74. For the 1905 abortive streetcar boycott see Lukens, "Portraits of Progress," 26; for the 1913 lynch mob see Matthew Lakin, "'A Dark Night': The Knoxville Race Riot of 1919," *Journal of East Tennessee History* 72 (2000): 3. For Tyson's 1911 comment see *Knoxville Sentinel,* Sept. 12, 1911. On Cansler see Charles W. Cansler to the Honorable Tom C. Rye (governor of Tennessee), Feb. 1918, in "Document," *Journal of Negro History* 57 (October 1972): 407–14. On the NAACP chapter see Lakin, "'A Dark Night,'" 3.

57. The most authoritative treatment of the riot is Lakin, "'A Dark Night,'" 1–29. But for an excellent setting of the stage, see Booker, *Heat of a Red Summer.* See also Lester C. Lamon, "Tennessee Race Relations and the Knoxville Riot of 1919," *East Tennessee Historical Society's Publications* 41 (1969): 67–85. For the oral history on casualties see Lakin, "'A Dark Night,'" 24–25. On blacks fleeing the city see *Chicago Defender,* Sept. 6, 1919. Mayes's attorney was the venerable William Francis Yardley. Mayes was executed in 1922 in spite of strong circumstantial evidence that he was not guilty. In 2001, Knoxville mayor Victor Ashe petitioned Tennessee governor Don Sundquist for a pardon for Mayes, an effort that may have been initiated by Booker. *Knoxville News-Sentinel,* July 13, 2001.

58. William C. Ross, *A Scrapbook for My Grandchildren* (New York: G. P. Putnam's Sons, 1941), 47–48. For the failure of Knoxville wholesalers to overcome post–World War I conditions see Dille, "Knoxville Wholesaling," 32–43.

59. Deaderick, *Heart of the Valley,* 109, 115. On the 1917 annexation see MacArthur, *Crossroads of the New South,* 98, 108. On the Rotary Club see MacArthur, *Crossroads of the New South,* 102.

60. For two interesting analyses of Progressivism see Robert H. Wiebe, *Businessmen and Reform: A Study of the Progressive Movement* (Cambridge: Harvard Univ. Press, 1962), and Gabriel Kolko, *The Triumph of Conservatism: A Reinterpretation of American History, 1900–1916* (Glencoe, Ill.: Free Press, 1963).

61. Deaderick, *Heart of the Valley,* 111–12.

62. For commission graft and corruption see *Knoxville News,* May 9, 20, 25, 29, July 13, Aug. 8, 25, Sept. 20, Oct. 25, 1922; Brownell, *Urban Ethos in the South,* 34. For costs added by annexation see MacArthur, *Crossroads of the New South,* 108. The 1917 annexation brought much of what is now referred to as East Knoxville into the city, including most of Magnolia Avenue. The street was named by banker–mill owner and Park City mayor Hardy Bryan Branner (1851–1938), who named the street after his mother, Magnolia Branner.

63. For election fraud see *Knoxville News,* April 1, Aug. 8, 1922. On change of government see *Knoxville Sentinel,* March 4, 1923; Deaderick, *Heart of the Valley,* 113–14; City Council Minute Book 10 (1923); Brownell, *Urban Ethos in the South,* 107. For Meeman's statement see *Knoxville News,* Oct. 1, 1923.

64. On Morton and Fulton see Deaderick, *Heart of the Valley,* 525–27, 580–81; MacArthur, *Crossroads of the New South,* 102, 108, 110, 167, 171.

65. The best source on Brownlow is his own autobiography, from which most of this treatment is drawn. See *The Autobiography of Louis Brownlow: A Passion for Anonymity* (Chicago: Univ. of Chicago Press, 1958), esp. 152–208.

66. Brownlow, *A Passion for Anonymity,* 190–97. For Brownlow's accomplishments see Brownell, *Urban Ethos in the South,* 34; MacArthur, *Crossroads of the New South,* 110.

67. Brownell, *Urban Ethos in the South,* 34; Brownlow, *A Passion for Anonymity,* 190–97; Lee S. Greene, Professor Emeritus of Political Science, University of Tennessee, interview by the author, Feb. 15, 1977.

68. Greene, interview, Feb. 15, 1977.

69. Brownlow, *A Passion for Anonymity,* 190.

70. Ibid., 197.

71. On debt see Rothrock, *French Broad–Holston Country,* 184–85.

72. Population and age distribution can be found in *Fifteenth Census of the United States, 1930.* Building permit figures are from the records of the Knoxville building inspector, which are summarized in reports for 1934 in the TVA Technical Library, Knoxville (as are statistics on telephone installations and membership in civic organizations). Home owner-ship data are from the abstract of the *Fifteenth Census, 1930,* 436. Fully 40.6 percent of the homes in the city were owned in 1930, up 0.2 percent from 1920. County figures show an even greater stability, with 45.6 percent of families owning their own homes in 1930 (47.3 percent of white families and 32.6 percent of black families). These figures are higher than for families in Shelby, Hamilton, or Davidson counties in 1930 and 8.5 percent higher than the state's average. As for illiteracy, 4.7 percent of Knox Countians were illiterate in 1930, down from 6.9 percent in 1920 and fourth lowest of any county in the state. Surrounding counties all had higher illiteracy figures in 1930: Union (9.9 percent), Anderson (8.1 percent), Blount (6.8 percent), Roane (7.8 percent), Sevier (9.3 percent), Rhea (6.3 percent), and Loudon (8.0 percent).

73. Mutual Development Co., *Talahi* [promotional literature] (Knoxville, 1929).

74. The *Fourteenth Census of the United States Taken in 1920* and *Fifteenth Census, 1930* indicate that the racial composition of central Knoxville changed rapidly in the 1920s:

Ward	White Population, 1920–30	Black Population, 1920–30
1	-29.19%	+247.25%
2	-19.24	+4.17
3	-67.89	+98.00
4	-9.56	+10.32
5	-77.88	+41.84
6	-29.66	+15.18
7	-14.93	+32.30
8	-27.28	+18.78
9	-15.69	+40.30

75. TVA Report on Population of Knoxville, 1934, TVA Technical Library, Knoxville.

76. Real Estate Assessment by Wards from Tax Books of County Assessor by TVA, 1934, TVA Technical Library, Knoxville. For employment statistics see *Fifteenth Census of the United States: 1930. Population,* 4:1512, 1533–35. On population density see T. J. Woofter Jr., *Negro Problems in Cities: A Study* (Garden City, N.Y.: Doubleday, Doran and Co.), 79.

77. *Fifteenth Census: 1930. Population,* 4:1512.

78. The Knoxville klavern records, including fragmentary membership records, are in the Knox County Klan Number 14 Papers, Emory University. To our knowledge, the Knoxville klavern's membership records are the only such records that have been preserved. The statistical observations made here derive from an analysis of membership applications, which contain applicants' names, addresses, occupations, religions, ages, and number of years in Knox County. See also Kenneth T. Jackson, *The Ku Klux Klan in the City, 1915–1930* (New York: Oxford Univ. Press, 1967), 59–65.

79. For the 2,000-member estimate see *Knoxville Journal,* Sept. 16, 1923. For the Klavern's political influence see *Knoxville Journal,* Sept. 23, 1923.

80. Klingrapp's Quarterly Report, first quarter 1928, Knox County Klan Number 14, Emory University; K. Ramsey to C. B. Lee, May 12, 1930, Knox County Klan Number 14, Emory University.

81. Dabney's list of accomplishments and reforms is too long to list here. His papers are in Special Collections, Hoskins Library, University of Tennessee. For a partial list see William Bruce Wheeler, "Three Knoxville Teachers," address honoring James Haslam II, Jan. 27, 2000, on videotape and available from Leadership Knoxville. On the ousting of Humes see James Riley Montgomery, Stanley J. Folmsbee, and Lee Seifert Greene, *To Foster Knowledge: A History of the University of Tennessee, 1794–1970* (Knoxville: Univ. of Tennessee Press, 1984), chap. 6. On Dabney see Montgomery, Folmsbee, and Greene, *To Foster Knowledge,* 132–55.

82. For Lowell's comment see Henry F. May, *The End of American Innocence: A Study of the First Years of Our Own Time, 1912–1917* (New York: Alfred A Knopf, 1959), 57.

83. On general atmosphere see Bobby Eugene Hicks, "The Great Objector: The Life and Public Career of Dr. John R. Neal," *East Tennessee Historical Society's Publications* 41 (1969): 33–66; James R. Montgomery, "John R. Neal and the University of Tennessee: A Five-Part Tragedy," *Tennessee Historical Quarterly* 32 (Summer 1979): 214–34; Ray Ginger, *Six Days or Forever?: Tennessee v. John Thomas Scopes* (Boston: Beacon, 1958), 79, 212.

84. The best treatment of this period in the university's history is Stephen D. Chandler, "Cleaning House: The U.T. Faculty Firings of 1923" (M.A. thesis, Univ. of Tennessee, 1998). For Dougherty's and the board member's comments see Chandler, "Cleaning House," 38–39, 41. As dean, Hoskins earlier had threatened a student with expulsion for an article he had written in the school newspaper critical of the state legislature. See Krutch, *More Lives Than One,* 54–56. He also tried to discourage students from dancing the Charleston on the grounds that it "causes injuries, fallen arches, large ankles and stomach trouble." See *Orange and White,* Feb. 18, 1926, quoted in Christopher Bryan Scott, "Between Good Clean Fun and the Flapper: College Youth at the University of Tennessee during the 1920s" (unpub. senior honors thesis, Univ. of Tennessee, 1995), 17.

85. Montgomery, "John R. Neal," 228–33. For Will Rogers's comment see Chandler, "Cleaning House," 23.

86. Charles P. White, "Banking Developments, 1811–1976," in Deaderick, *Heart of the Valley,* 377–78.

87. Ibid., 387–88.

88. On building permits see "Building Permits in Knoxville, 1923–1933," unpub. TVA report, 1934, table 11A, TVA Technical Library, Knoxville. The number of houses built between 1930 and 1934 was but 823, one-third the number of homes constructed during the preceding five-year period. On telephone disconnections see data furnished to TVA by E. F. Garratt, district manager of the Southern Bell Telephone Company in "Telephone

Facilities and Services, Knoxville, 1924–1934," TVA Technical Library, Knoxville. Knox County civic clubs experienced a similar decline in membership. See "Membership of Selected Social and Civic Clubs, Knoxville," (TVA report, 1934), TVA Technical Library, Knoxville. Though the births and deaths per 1,000 population were lowest for Knoxville of any large city in the state, the low growth rate of population clearly points to significant out-migration, both to the county and beyond. For example, in 1935 in the combined areas of Anderson, Campbell, Claiborne, Granger, and Union counties, there were 4,817 persons who had lived in nonfarm residences outside those counties in 1930.

89. All figures are for March 1939, from *Commercial and Industrial Survey of Knoxville, Tennessee,* for the Chamber of Commerce (Knoxville, 1939), n.p. Technically the "Henley Street Bridge" is the "Henley Bridge." In 1964 it was renamed the "George R. Dempster Bridge," but the new name never caught on. See Knoxville *News-Sentinel,* April 21, 2002. On the contractor, Sam Bolt, conversation with the author, Jan. 15, 2003. On Lucille Thornburgh see *News-Sentinel,* July 29, 1995; *Metro Pulse,* Nov. 12, 1998, and July 18, 2002. For a distressing portrait of Knoxville's poor neighborhoods in 1937, see the comments of Swiss writer Annemarie Schwarzenbach in *Metro Pulse,* Dec. 7, 2000.

90. Lyndon E. Abbott and Lee S. Greene, *Municipal Government and Administration in Tennessee,* Bureau of Business and Economic Research, study no. 5 (Knoxville: Univ. of Tennessee, Div. of Univ. Extension, 1939), 113.

91. Ibid., 29; *Commercial and Industrial Survey,* n.p.

92. Of the dwellings considered residential structures, 12.4 percent were more than forty years old in 1934. Of 25,851 dwelling units, nearly 30 percent were classed as "too crowded." Nearly 40 percent of the dwelling units rented for under $15 per month and one-fourth were without gas or electricity. Abbott and Greene, *Municipal Government,* 29.

93. A survey of whites fleeing or being removed from the area's rural regions is found in Michael J. McDonald, "Appalachian Stereotypes and Quality of Life Variance: TVA's Norris Dam Population Removal Problems," unpub. paper presented to the Southern Regional Science Association, April 1976.

94. Charles S. Johnson, comp., "The Negro Population of the Tennessee Valley Area," unpub. report by TVA, CWA, and Fisk Univ., 1934, TVA Technical Library, Knoxville, 2:106–7; Lorin A. Thompson, "Urbanization, Occupational Shift and Economic Progress," in *The Urban South,* ed. Rupert B. Vance and Nicholas J. Demerath (Chapel Hill: Univ. of North Carolina Press, 1954), 48–49.

95. Johnson, "Negro Population," 2:113.

96. Charles H. Houston and John P. Davis, "TVA: Lily-White Reconstruction," *The Crisis* 41 (Oct. 1934): 290–91, 311; John P. Davis, "The Plight of the Negro in the Tennessee Valley," *The Crisis* 42 (Oct. 1935): 294–95, 314–15.

97. The 1930 homicide rate for African Americans was 78 per 100,000 black population as opposed to a white homicide rate of 14 per 100,000 white population. Johnson, "Negro Population," 1:148. On high crime rate and juvenile delinquency among the city's blacks see Johnson, "Negro Population," 1:168, 2: 88–89. On occupations of blacks arrested and convicted of crimes in Knoxville in 1931 and 1932 see Johnson, "Negro Population," 1:164. On percentage of females who were heads of households see ibid., 2: 64–70. Knoxville public schools for blacks had only eleven grades. Johnson, "Negro Population," 1: 16. Illiteracy in Knoxville for blacks was nearly three times that for whites. Johnson, "Negro Population," 1: 16. On low standard of living for the city's blacks see William J. Durbin, "Household Equipment Survey, Knoxville, Tennessee 1934," unpub. TVA-CWA Project 76B, TVA Technical Library, Knoxville. Durbin surveyed 13,505

Knoxvillians (2,296 of whom were black). Also on standard of living and employment, in 1934 Johnson sampled 101 families in Ward Five, an area with a heavy concentration (94.99 percent in 1930) of blacks. See Johnson, "Negro Population," 1:177.

98. Between 1930 and 1940 black population in Knoxville declined from 17,093 to 16,106, a net loss of 987. Taking natural increase into account, the out-migration would be significant indeed.

99. Caroline Bird, *The Invisible Scar* (New York: D. McKay, 1966).

Chapter 2

1. John Gunther, *Inside U.S.A.* (New York: Harper and Brothers, 1946), xvi.

2. Ibid., 761.

3. Ibid., 910.

4. *Knoxville Journal,* June–Aug. 1946; *Knoxville News-Sentinel,* June 1, 1946.

5. *Knoxville News-Sentinel,* June 1, 1946. On Lucy Templeton see Deaderick, *Heart of the Valley,* 612–13. It is generally believed by Knoxvillians that Gunther's attack was responsible in part for the establishment of the Dogwood Arts Festival. See *Metro Pulse,* March 19, 1998. For the festival's inauguration see Betsy B. Creekmore, *Knoxville: Our Fair City* (Knoxville: Greater Knoxville Chamber of Commerce, 1984), 29.

6. From 1946 to 1950 Americans purchased some 21 million automobiles, 20 million refrigerators, and 5.5 million electric stoves. As for television, in 1947 all of 7,000 Americans owned television sets, whereas by 1950 over 7 million did—with "TVs" selling at a rate of 70,000 per day.

7. George Brown Tindall, *The Emergence of the New South, 1914–1945,* vol. 10 of *A History of the South,* eds. Wendell Holmes Stephenson and E. Morton Coulter (Baton Rouge: Louisiana State Univ. Press, 1967), 695–703. For the Georgia veterans see *Knoxville Journal,* Dec. 10, 1941. For mechanization see Jack Temple Kirby, *Rural Worlds Lost: The American South, 1920–1960* (Baton Rouge: Louisiana State Univ. Press, 1987), 54–55, 77–78, 334–37.

8. For percentage of Knoxville's workforce employed in textiles see Patricia Brake Howard, "Knoxville's Rosies: The Impact of World War II on Women Production Workers of Knoxville, Tennessee," Ph.D. diss., Univ. of Tennessee, 1988, 23. On Holston Mills see Beverly Buster, "The Holston Mill Strike of 1939" (unpub. senior honors paper, Univ. of Tennessee, 1983).

9. On contracts see Patricia Brake Howard, "Tennessee in War and Peace: The Impact of World War II on State Economic Trends," *Tennessee Historical Quarterly* 51 (spring 1992), 53–54. On ALCOA see Russell Dean Parker, *More Than Metal: ALCOA and Alcoa; A Study in Progressive Paternalism* (Maryville, Tenn.: Privately published, 1997), 141. On Oak Ridge (Clinton Engineer Works) see Charles W. Johnson and Charles O. Jackson, *City behind a Fence: Oak Ridge, Tennessee, 1942–1946* (Knoxville: Univ. of Tennessee Press, 1981) and William E. Cole, "Urban Development in the Tennessee Valley," *Social Forces* 26 (Oct. 1947): 68. For Oak Ridgers as "furriners," see "The Conservatives of Knoxville," *Fortune,* July 1952, 114. On TVA see Don McBride, "TVA and National Defense," 1975, unpub. TVA report, TVA Technical Library, Knoxville.

10. On income see Paul H. Bergeron, Stephen V. Ash, and Jeanette Keith, *Tennesseans and Their History* (Knoxville: Univ. of Tennessee Press, 1999), 281. In 1943 Knoxville ranked 89th of 132 U.S. cities over 100,000 population in per-capita buying income.

Comparably sized cities with less buying power than Knoxville included Chattanooga; Reading, Pa.; Miami, Fla.; and Savannah, Ga. On women see Howard, "Knoxville's Rosies," 43, 252. War plants paid three times the salaries of domestic workers. *Knoxville News-Sentinel,* May 14, 1943.

11. Florence Cope Bush, *Dorie: Woman of the Mountains* (Knoxville: Univ. of Tennessee Press, 1992), 223–24.

12. Deaderick, *Heart of the Valley,* 392–96 and tables 9 and 10.

13. In 1946 the city's percentage of Knox County's retail sales was 93.64 percent. By 1950 it had decreased to 90.32 percent.

14. Deaderick, *Heart of the Valley,* 120.

15. Ibid., 230.

16. Ibid., 118.

17. Howard, "Knoxville's Rosies," 149–64. On blacks see Howard, "Tennessee in War and Peace," 62. Roughly 80 percent of the women employed at Rohm and Haas wanted to keep their jobs after the war. Howard, "Knoxville's Rosies," 151.

18. Howard, "Knoxville's Rosies," 252; Howard, "Tennessee in War and Peace," 62. On UT enrollment see Milton M. Klein, *Volunteer Moments: Vignettes of the History of the University of Tennessee, 1794–1994,* 2nd. ed. (Knoxville: Univ. of Tennessee, 1996), 58. For 1946 unemployment see *Knoxville News-Sentinel,* Nov. 6, 1946. For the fear that Knoxville would not be able to absorb all the returning veterans as well as the rural-to-urban migrants, see *Knoxville News-Sentinel,* Jan. 13, 1946.

19. *Knoxville Journal,* Dec. 17, 1950; *Knoxville News-Sentinel,* Oct. 1, 1950.

20. *Knoxville News-Sentinel,* Oct. 1, 1950. For an interesting discussion of these trends nationally see Howard P. Chudacoff, *The Evolution of American Urban Society,* 5th. ed. (Englewood Cliffs, N.J.: Prentice Hall, 2000), 267–73, and Kenneth T. Jackson, *Crabgrass Frontier: The Suburbanization of the United States* (New York: Oxford Univ. Press, 1985), 231–45.

21. On homicide see *Knoxville Journal,* April 14, 1948. For other data see *Knoxville News-Sentinel,* Oct. 1, 1950.

22. *Knoxville News-Sentinel,* Oct. 1, 1950.

23. "The Conservatives of Knoxville," *Fortune,* July 1952, 110.

24. David Madden, *Bijou* (New York: Crown Publishers 1976), 63–64. Many of the houses had been there nearly that long. Of the dwelling units in Ward One (the boundaries of which were Gay Street, the Tennessee River eastward to Ferry, and Cumberland Avenue), 25 percent had been built before 1885. Knoxville Housing Authority, "Real Property Inventory and Low Income Housing Area Survey of Knoxville, Tennessee," WPA Project 665-44-3-11 (Knoxville: City of Knoxville, 1939), 3:52.

25. Cormac McCarthy, *Suttree* (New York: Random House, 1979), 66–67.

26. Edith Foster Howard, "Riverfront: The Protection of Municipal Waterfronts in Tennessee," *University of Tennessee Record,* Extension Series 25, no. 1 (March 1949), 22.

27. Knoxville Housing Authority, "Real Property Inventory," 19, 21, 23, 24; 42 (chart 7); block tabulation, Ward 9, 60.

28. Ibid., 23; pt. 3, 52.

29. Ibid., 38 (chart 5), 42 (chart 7), 45 (chart 9). For Johnson's statement see *Knoxville News-Sentinel,* May 8, 1964.

30. For Cash's quip see David R. Goldfield, "Urbanization in a Rural Culture: Suburban Cities and Country Cosmopolites," in *The South for New Southerners,* ed. Paul D. Escott and David R. Goldfield (Chapel Hill: Univ. of North Carolina Press, 1991), 83. For *Fortune* see "The Conservatives of Knoxville," 110.

31. On Kennerly see *Knoxville Journal,* Oct. 31, 1939; Nov. 6, 1943; Deaderick, *Heart of the Valley,* 546–47. His faction often was referred to as "the Mynatt-Kennerly machine," after Kennerly and W. W. "Jud" Mynatt. Although a veteran of the Spanish-American War, Kennerly's informal title of "General" (which he liked) came from his position as U.S. Attorney for the Eastern District of Tennessee, 1917–21. On McNew see Ray H. Jenkins, *The Terror of Tellico Plains* (Knoxville: East Tennessee Historical Society, 1978), 52. On Bass and Webb see Greene, interview, Feb. 8, 1977. On Knoxville voting, from 1868 to 1976 Knoxville voted for a Democratic presidential candidate only five times, three of them for Franklin D. Roosevelt.

32. On Dempster's opinion of Walker see Todd A. Baker, "Politics of Innovation," Ph.D. diss., Univ. of Tennessee, 1968, 115. For *Fortune's* opinion see "The Conservatives of Knoxville," 110.

33. Deaderick, *Heart of the Valley,* 519–21; MacArthur, *Crossroads of the New South,* 165.

34. Donald G. Thompson, "Edward J. Meeman: The Knoxville Years" (M.A. thesis, Univ. of Tennessee, 1974), 66, 75; *Knoxville News-Sentinel,* Oct. 9, 1929; Deaderick, *Heart of the Valley,* 520–21; MacArthur, *Crossroads of the New South,* 165. On the mayor-manager law see *Knoxville Journal,* March 21, 1946. On taxes see George R. Dempster, "What a Businessman Hopes to Accomplish as Mayor," *American City* 67 (Jan. 1952): 103; "The Conservatives of Knoxville," 110.

35. *Knoxville Journal,* Nov. 3, 1939.

36. The best treatment of Smith can be found in Edgar H. Miller Jr., "The *Knoxville Journal*: A Historical Study" (M.S. thesis, Univ. of Tennessee, 1994), esp. 44, 61–67, 76–79, 85, 105–11. But see also Deaderick, *Heart of the Valley,* 605–6; *Knoxville News-Sentinel,* Nov. 10, 1955; George Fritts, retired realtor and keen observer of Knoxville politics, interview by the author April 8, 1977. Many believe that the "local businessman" whom Smith tried to get to run for mayor was Pilot Oil Corporation president James A. Haslam, an assertion that Haslam will neither confirm nor deny. James A. Haslam II, interview by the author, Aug. 13, 2002.

37. Walker's much-anticipated autobiography, *My Life History: A True Living Legend* (Knoxville: Volunteer Printing, 1993), is disappointing. Better are *Knoxville News-Sentinel,* Sept. 26–27, 1998; Jan. 21, 2001; *Metro Pulse,* July 30, 1998; Walker lecture to history class, Univ. of Tennessee, July 3, 1980. See also summary of his career in *Knoxville Journal,* Dec. 17, 1971; *Knoxville News-Sentinel,* Dec. 28, 1969.

38. Walker lecture, July 3, 1980. On chicken hurling see Walker, *My Life History,* 120.

39. On "Digger O'Dell" see *Metro Pulse,* July 30, 1998; Walker, *My Life History,* 102–3. Since the publication of the first edition of this book, literally hundreds of people have volunteered "Cas Walker stories." We apologize for not being able to use them all.

40. In 1974 Walker owned 22 markets, 19 other businesses, 73 parcels of Knoxville real estate, and a 600-acre farm in Blount County. *Knoxville Journal,* July 8, 1974; *Knoxville News-Sentinel,* Dec. 28, 1969.

41. *Knoxville Journal,* Oct. 22, 27, 31, Nov. 2, 3, 1939.

42. Cas Walker, interview by the author, Feb. 21, 1977.

43. Ibid.

44. For election results see *Knoxville News-Sentinel,* Nov. 7, 1941. For opposition to parking meters and the three-dollar license fee see *Knoxville News-Sentinel,* Oct. 23, 29, 1941. On the hiring of drunks and little girls see Walker, *My Life History,* 100, and Walker interview by the author, Feb. 21, 1977.

45. For anti-administration intentions see *Knoxville News-Sentinel,* Oct. 22, 1942. For the mayoralty controversy see *Knoxville News-Sentinel,* Nov. 7, 21–22, 28, Dec. 9, 14, 1941; Jan. 2, 1942. For Mynatt's resignation and the selection of Webb see *Knoxville News-Sentinel,* Nov. 21–22, 28, 1941.

46. For Walker's attack on the property tax assessments for the rich, see *Knoxville News-Sentinel,* Oct. 20, 23, 27, 1943; *Knoxville Journal,* Nov. 4, 1943. In 1943 Walker attacked Claude Reeder of Reeder Chevrolet for settling a tax bill of over $75,000 for $10,000. *Knoxville News-Sentinel,* Oct. 20, 1943. For Walker's recollections of the break with Dempster and his attacks see Walker interview by the author, Feb. 21, 1977, and Miller, "The *Knoxville Journal,*" 111. For attempts by Walker's enemies to turn black and white labor voters against him see *Knoxville News-Sentinel,* Oct. 13, 25, 1943.

47. *Knoxville Journal,* Nov. 3, 1943; Walker interview, Feb. 21, 1977.

48. For election results see *Knoxville News-Sentinel,* Nov. 16, 1945. The *News-Sentinel* had backed Mynatt.

49. For problems see *Knoxville News-Sentinel,* Jan. 4, 5, 7, 10, 13, 14, 16, 20, 1946.

50. For the "state of emergency" pronouncement see *Knoxville News-Sentinel,* Jan. 31, 1946. For Morton's plans see *Knoxville News-Sentinel,* Jan. 3, 5, 6, 16, 20, 26, 28, 1946. For the comparison to Nashville see *Knoxville News-Sentinel,* Jan. 21, 1946.

51. On spot rezoning see *Knoxville News-Sentinel,* Jan. 10, 15, 16, Feb. 5, 1946. On Morton's budget see *Knoxville News-Sentinel,* Jan. 20, 1946. Morton's budget actually was 5.5 percent higher than the 1945 budget. But his proposal to spend the 1945 surplus of approx. $163,000 raised the percentage to 8.02 percent.

52. *Knoxville News-Sentinel,* Feb. 16, March 1, 1946. On Walker's budget and tax cut see *Knoxville News-Sentinel,* March 1, 1946.

53. *Knoxville News-Sentinel,* Feb. 7, 1946.

54. Ibid., March 20, 1946.

55. Ibid., Nov. 25, 1946. On Citizens Protective League see ibid., March 22, Nov. 14, 1946. On Chavannes see ibid., Nov. 25, 1946. On the comparison to Brownlow see ibid., Nov. 19, 1946.

56. *Knoxville News-Sentinel,* Nov. 2, 15, 16, 18, 20, 24, Dec. 1, 1946. For a sampling of organizations supporting recall see *Knoxville News-Sentinel,* Nov. 19, 1946.

57. *Knoxville News-Sentinel,* Nov. 20, 23, Dec. 1, 1946.

58. Ibid., Nov. 23, 27, 1946.

59. For election results see ibid., Dec. 4, 1946. Chavannes bested Walker by 9,937 votes to 5,673.

60. *Knoxville Journal,* June 19, 1974. Walker's statement on progress was made while opposing the proposed city-county building. *Knoxville Journal,* June 20, 1974.

61. On wartime Oak Ridge see Charles W. Johnson and Charles O. Jackson, *City behind a Fence : Oak Ridge, Tennessee, 1942–1946* (Knoxville: Univ. of Tennessee Press, 1981).

62. *Knoxville News-Sentinel,* Aug. 7, 1945.

63. Ibid., Aug. 10, 1945.

64. Ibid., Aug. 14, 1945.

65. Ibid., Aug. 15, 1945.

66. Ibid., Aug. 16, 1945.

67. Many excellent studies of this aspect of the 1920s exist. A few are Paul Carter, *Another Part of the Twenties* (New York: Columbia Univ. Press, 1977); Don Kirschner, *City and Country: Rural Responses to Urbanization in the 1920s* (Westport, Conn.: Greenwood, 1970); Stanley Coben, *Rebellion against Victorianism: The Impetus for Cultural Charge in 1920s America* (New York: Oxford Univ. Press, 1991); Lynn Dumenil, *The Modern Temper: American Culture and Society in the 1920s* (New York: Hill and Wang, 1995). On the Scopes Trial see Edward Larson, *Summer for the Gods: The Scopes Trial and America's Continuing Debate over Science and Religion* (New York: Basic Books, 1997). Still useful is Ginger, *Six Days or Forever?* (1958). Perhaps iron-ically, one of the best critiques of modernity was Knoxvillian Joseph Wood Krutch's *The Modern Temper: A Study and a Confession* (New York: Harcourt Brace, 1957).

68. For 1891 law see Forrest Marion, "Blue Laws, Knoxville, and the Second World War" (unpub. student paper, Univ. of Tennessee, n.d.; in possession of author), 3. For early Knoxville theaters see John Kyle Thomas, "Of Paramount Importance: American Film and Cultural Home-Rule in Knoxville, 1872–1948," Ph.D. diss., Univ. of Tennessee, 1990, 14–28; MacArthur, *Crossroads of the New South,* 143; Booker, *Black Culture in Knoxville,* 94–95; *Metro Pulse,* Oct. 22, 1998.

69. Knox County Association of Baptists, *Minutes,* Oct. 16–17, 1934, quoted in Thomas, "Of Paramount Importance," 166.

70. On *Snow White* see Thomas, "Of Paramount Importance," 155. On the 1938 arrests see Thomas, "Of Paramount Importance," 167. The ordinance stated that theaters could show films on Sundays if the films were of a religious or moral nature, a permit was secured, and the proceeds donated to charities. In the case of the Tennessee Theater, the manager had failed to secure a permit.

71. For the unofficial poll see Thomas, "Of Paramount Importance," 166. For the 1938 referendum see *Knoxville News-Sentinel,* Nov. 7, 9, 1938. For the supporters of repeal see Thomas, "Of Paramount Importance," 169–70.

72. For the 1943 results see *Knoxville News-Sentinel,* Nov. 19, 1943. For Gunther's com-ment see *Inside U.S.A.,* 761.

73. For the 1946 effort see *Knoxville News-Sentinel,* Feb. 20, March 6, 7, 1946. For the legislative end run see Thomas, "Of Paramount Importance," 174–76.

74. On the Baron incident see Bergeron, Ash, and Keith, *Tennesseans and Their History,* 291; Montgomery, Folmsbee, and Greene, *To Foster Knowledge,* 226; conversation between former history professors John Muldowny and Lawrence Silverman, June 25, 2002. For Baron's career see *Directory of American Scholars,* 6th ed., vol. 1, *History* (New York: R. R. Bowker, 1971), 30.

75. Montgomery, Folmsbee, and Greene, *To Foster Knowledge,* 26.

76. Montgomery, Folmsbee, and Greene, *To Foster Knowledge,* 226. On the panty raid see *Knoxville News-Sentinel,* May 19, 1952, and Sharon Seal, "May 19, 1952" (unpub. stu-dent paper, Univ. of Tennessee, 1990; in possession of author).

77. Muldowny-Silverman conversation, June 25, 2002.

78. Much of the material on Mildred Doyle comes from former judge David Creekmore (Jan. 20, 2000) but also from Kellie Wilkinson McGarrh, "Hangin' In Tough: The Life of Superintendent Mildred E. Doyle, 1904–1989," Ed.D. diss., Univ. of Tennessee, 1995, and obituary and memorials in *Knoxville News-Sentinel,* May 7, 9, 1989.

79. For Hoffmeister's compliment see *Knoxville News-Sentinel,* May 9, 1989.

80. For Chilhowee Park and the university see Booker, *Black Culture in Knoxville,* 137–38. On the golf course see *Knoxville News-Sentinel,* May 21, 1952. For King's remark (made in a Knoxville College commencement address) see *Metro Pulse,* June 14, 2001; Levi Strauss Foundation, *Project Change,* 10–11.

81. For the 1952 Southern Historical Association convention see C. Vann Woodward, *Thinking Back: The Perils of Writing History* (Baton Rouge: Louisiana State Univ. Press, 1986), 89–90; John Herbert Roper, *C. Vann Woodward, Southerner* (Athens: Univ. of Georgia Press, 1978), 168–69; *Context* (Univ. of Tennessee faculty and staff newsletter), March 29, 1996.

Chapter 3

1. *Knoxville News-Sentinel,* March 24, 1957. The review reported that Dr. Soper "says carefully that no parody on Knoxville is intended. But leave us not play ostrich." A subsequent article was even less circumspect, saying that in the play "local political shenanigans get a working over." *Knoxville News-Sentinel,* April 3, 1957.

2. Alonzo Hamby, *The Imperial Years: The United States Since 1939* (New York: Weybright and Talley, 1976), 181–82.

3. William E. Leuchtenberg, *The Unfinished Century: America since 1900* (Boston: Little, Brown, 1973), 680, 724.

4. Ibid., 717.

5. Hammer and Associates, *The Economy of Metropolitan Knoxville,* a report prepared for Metropolitan Planning Commission (Washington, D.C., 1962), 35, table 16. Hereafter cited as Hammer Report. See also *Knoxville News-Sentinel,* Jan. 1, 19, Feb. 10, June 5, 1954; March 12, 1956. On the decline of the textile industry, see Jack Neely's excellent "When Knoxville Was the 'Underwear Capital of the World,'" in *Metro Pulse,* July 18, 2002.

6. Hammer Report, 29, 36, and tables 14 and 16. For aluminum stockpiles see *Knoxville News-Sentinel,* Jan. 1, 1954. On competition from Reynolds and Kaiser see Parker, *More Than Metal,* 145.

7. Hammer Report, 35.

8. Ibid., 29, 91–92, and tables 14 and 34.

9. Ibid., 100, table 37. In 1959 Knoxville had 33 percent of its labor force earning under $3,000. The national figure was 15 percent.

10. *Knoxville News-Sentinel,* Jan. 3, 1957. Bass served on city council from 1956 to 1959. Deaderick, *Heart of the Valley,* Appendix F, 646.

11. David Dickey (director of industrial development, Knoxville Chamber of Commerce), "Preliminary Recommendations for the Industrial Development Program," in Industrial Sites File, Metropolitan Planning Commission (MPC), 1960.

12. Baker, "Politics of Innovation," 71–72.

13. Ibid., 71–72, 314. State law mandated that an industrial bond referendum had to garner the support of at least 75 percent of those voting.

14. Hammer Report, 154–57 and table 43.

15. Ibid., 154–57, 214, 231–33, and table 43. For earlier studies that reached the same conclusion see Colonna and Pate, "Knoxville–Knox County Industrial Sites Survey, 1957"; MPC, "Knox County Industrial Land Needs, 1959"; Chamber of Commerce Committee

of 100, "Sites for Industry Study, 1959"; Chamber of Commerce Staff Study, 1960, all in Knoxville MPC Industrial Sites Committee File.

16. The story is from Don Mirts, one of the Knoxville business leaders present when Clement made his statement, in a conversation with the author at a 1992 meeting of the board of directors of Leadership Knoxville, and corroborated by Betty Mirts, July 10, 13, 2002. The incident was not mentioned in Lee Greene's biography of Clement (*Lead Me On: Frank Goad Clement and Tennessee Politics* [Knoxville: Univ. of Tennessee Press, 1982]).

17. Tennessee State Planning Commission, *Population in Tennessee, Publication #376* (Nashville: State Planning Division, 1970), 12, 15, and table 6; Hammer Report, 62, 67, and table 26. For Akron "joke" see Phillip J. Obermiller, *Appalachian Odyssey: Historical Perspectives on the Great Migration* (Westport, Conn.: Praeger, 2000), xii. Between 1940 and 1960, over 7 million people left Appalachia. Obermiller, *Appalachian Odyssey,* xii.

18. Hammer Report, 62–63. For the aging population see Real Estate Research Corp., *Trends, Conditions and Forecasts of Knoxville's Economy . . .* (Knoxville: MPC, June 1969), 31. For comparative unemployment see statistics from Tennessee Department of Employment Security, quoted in Hammer Report, 64.

19. Hammer Report, 64.

20. Real Estate Research Corp., *Trends, Conditions and Forecasts,* 33. For national trends see Chudacoff, *Evolution of American Urban Society,* 263.

21. Hammer Report, 77.

22. Hammer and Associates, *Knoxville's CBD* (Atlanta: Hammer and Assoc., 1955), 6, in MPC files. See also Larry Smith and Co., "Market Square Development Feasibility Study," report prepared for MPC, Nov. 30, 1960, in MPC files, 8; Deaderick, *Heart of the Valley,* 125. For West Hills see Michael E. Weaver, "A History of West Hills" (unpub. student paper, Univ. of Tennessee, 1986; in possession of author), 1–3.

23. Hammer and Associates, *Knoxville's CBD,* 41 and table 9.

24. Deaderick, *Heart of the Valley,* 125.

25. *Knoxville News-Sentinel,* July 20, 1961; Feb. 11, 1962; April 4, 1981.

26. Ibid., Sept. 16, 1956; Aug. 17, 1958.

27. Larry Smith, "Market Square," 8; *Knoxville News-Sentinel,* May 18, 1954; Sept. 19, 20, 1956; Feb. 7, April 26, 1959. All these shopping centers were "strip centers," and by 1970 Knoxville was the only city of its size in the U.S. without a *major* suburban shopping mall. MacArthur, *Knoxville History,* 64.

28. *Knoxville News-Sentinel,* Jan. 16, 1950.

29. Ibid., Oct. 10, 1954.

30. Hammer and Associates, *Knoxville's CBD,* 47–49; A. J. Gray, "Center City Major Studies and Project Proposals, 1930–1973," report to the Center City Task Force, May 1974, in MPC files; *Knoxville News-Sentinel,* March 4, 1956.

31. *Knoxville News-Sentinel,* Feb. 7, 1959.

32. Hammer and Associates, *Knoxville's CBD,* downtown map.

33. On Rich's announcement see *Knoxville News-Sentinel,* Jan. 18, 1954. For the location of the removed buildings and accompanying photographs see *Knoxville News-Sentinel,* March 7, 1954.

34. *Knoxville News-Sentinel,* June 2, 1954; Deaderick, *Heart of the Valley,* 130–31. It was claimed that the Miller's parking garage would be "the largest under one roof in Tennessee."

35. Hammer and Associates, *Knoxville's CBD,* 7.

36. "The Conservatives of Knoxville," 110.

37. *Knoxville News-Sentinel,* July 4, 1954. For the Market House fire and the cigarette see Baker, "Politics of Innovation," 290.

38. On James Whitman "Jack" Dance see Deaderick, *Heart of the Valley,* 512–13. On his importance to downtown development see Deaderick, *Heart of the Valley,* 129–30; Gray, "Center City Major Studies," 11. On related topics see *Knoxville News-Sentinel,* Feb. 22, 1957; Feb. 11, 1959.

39. *Knoxville Journal,* May 6, 1958.

40. On the "super shopping center" see *Knoxville News-Sentinel,* July 31, 1958. See also Gray, "Center City Major Studies," 7.

41. MPC, "The Downtown Knoxville Story," 1965, in MPC files. See also Gray, "Center City Major Studies," 4. To get everyone in line, the project used a "joint venture agreement," which required 100 percent of the merchants to sign on before the project could be undertaken.

42. *Knoxville News-Sentinel,* Feb. 1, 1959; Gray, "Center City Major Studies," 4.

43. Gray, "Center City Major Studies," 4–5. For the origins of the Market House, see *This Week in Knoxville* 13 (Oct. 26, 1939), 13. For an excellent albeit brief history of Market Square see *Metro Pulse,* Nov. 6, 2003.

44. MPC, "The Downtown Knoxville Story." See also Gray, "Center City Major Studies," 5. On Walker see Baker, "Politics of Innovation," 112.

45. Baker, "Politics of Innovation," 3–4.

46. MPC, "The Downtown Knoxville Story." See also Gray, "Center City Major Studies," 5. On Walker see Baker, "Politics of Innovation," 112. It was rumored that other merchants were not unhappy to see Walker's store go, since they did not want what some people called "country people" or "Cas Walker voters" rubbing elbows with shoppers the DKA hoped to attract. Baker, "Politics of Innovation," 112.

47. MPC, "The Downtown Knoxville Story"; Gray, "Center City Major Studies," 5.

48. MPC, "The Downtown Knoxville Story"; Gray, "Center City Major Studies," 5.

49. For Lois Reagan Thomas's comment see Tony Mary, "Gay Street: The Heart of Knoxville" (unpub. student paper, Univ. of Tennessee, 1986; in possession of author), 7.

50. The best account of the Walker-Cooper brawl can be found in Deaderick, *Heart of the Valley,* 309–10. The *Journal* photograph of the incident also appeared in the *Miami Herald, Life, Newsweek,* and a newspaper in East Berlin with the caption "Democracy in Action."

51. *Knoxville News-Sentinel,* March 7, April 3, 1956. For Martin's recollection see Deaderick, *Heart of the Valley,* 310. Before he stepped between the two men, Martin apologized to WBIR's listeners and took the program off the air. For the "most embarrassing" designation see *Metro Pulse,* Nov. 4, 1999.

52. On O'Connor see Deaderick, *Heart of the Valley,* 587–88, 646. On Friedman see Deaderick, 524–25, 646–47; Wendy Lowe Besmann, *A Separate Circle: Jewish Life in Knoxville, Tennessee* (Knoxville: Univ. of Tennessee Press, 2001), 96, 109–12; *Metro Pulse,* March 15, 2001. For Friedman's comment see Baker, "Politics of Innovation," 113. Although evidence is slender, it is generally believed that Friedman suggested the term "New Deal" to Franklin D. Roosevelt during a 1932 visit to then-governor Roosevelt in Albany. Deaderick, *Heart of the Valley,* 525.

53. *Knoxville News-Sentinel,* Jan. 14, 29, April 4, 1959.

54. Ibid, Feb. 23, April 6, 1959.

55. Baker, "Politics of Innovation," 70. For one example of Walker's opposition see *Knoxville News-Sentinel,* March 1, 1959.

56. Deaderick, *Heart of the Valley,* 127; *Knoxville News-Sentinel,* Feb. 28, April 6, 7, 8, 1959.

57. *Knoxville News-Sentinel,* April 10, 1959.

58. Baker, "Politics of Innovation," 312. Legal sales of alcoholic beverages were approved in 1961. Also voted down by voters in the next decade were an increase in the city tax rate, an increase in the mayor's salary, the expansion in the number of municipal court judges, the relaxing of residency requirements for police officers and firefighters, on the power of the city council to set the work week for police officers. Baker, "Politics of Innovation," 319. In fairness to Knoxville voters, from 1805 to 1992, city-county government unification proposals were turned down by voters in the United States at a ratio of four to one. See Janet Ward, "Can Two Live as Cheaply as One?" *American City and County,* February 1992, 30.

59. Every reader has her or his preferred study of the Civil Rights Movement. This author's favorite is Taylor Branch's *Parting the Waters: America in the King Years, 1954–63* (New York: Simon and Schuster, 1988). On the 1950s, see Stephanie Coontz, *The Way We Never Were: American Families and the Nostalgia Trap* (New York: Basic Books, 1992).

60. Douglas R. Jones, "An Abstract of an Opinion Poll on Attitudes of White Adults and Desegregation in the Public Schools of Knoxville, Tennessee," Ph.D. diss., Peabody College, 1958, quoted in Hugh Davis Graham, *Crisis in Print: Desegregation and the Press in Tennessee* (Nashville: Vanderbilt Univ. Press, 1967), 295–96. For the Chuck Berry incident see Berry, *Chuck Berry: The Autobiography* (New York: Harmony, 1987), 136.

61. For the newspapers see Graham, *Crisis in Print,* 32, 48. In Tennessee, the *Chattanooga Times, Nashville Tennessean,* and *Memphis Commercial Appeal* all avoided endorsing the *Brown* decision. Graham, *Crisis in Print,* 34, 37, 39, 41. For *Goss* see *Josephine Goss et al. vs. Board of Education of City of Knoxville,* 186F. Supp. 559 560; *Westlaw 2001,* 560.

62. Deaderick, *Heart of the Valley,* 258–59; Graham, *Crisis in Print,* 195.

63. The best treatment is Merrill Proudfoot, *Diary of a Sit-In* (Chapel Hill: Univ. of North Carolina Press, 1962). Also valuable are Valentina Tate, "Knoxville College after Brown" (unpub. student paper, Univ. of Tennessee, 1986; in possession of author); Judy R. Effler, "Standing Up By Sitting Down: The Knoxville Sit-Ins" (unpub. student paper, Univ. of Tennessee, 1986; in possession of author); *Context* (Univ. of Tennessee faculty and staff newsletter), March 29, 1996.

64. Effler, "Standing Up By Sitting Down," 3.

65. Ibid., 3–8; *Context,* March 29, 1996; Booker, *Black Culture in Knoxville,* 138–42. On Urban League see J. Harvey Kerns, *Social and Economic Conditions in Knoxville, Tennessee, As They Affect the Negro* (Atlanta: Urban League, 1967), 50. On UT Hospital see *Context,* March 29, 1996.

66. Adrian Wheatley, "Sit-In at Knoxville Lunch Counters" (unpub. student paper, Univ. of Tennessee, 2001; in possession of author), 12.

Chapter 4

1. *Knoxville News-Sentinel,* Dec. 6, 1987.

2. Kyle Testerman, interview by the author, Jan. 22, 1981. Plans for downtown redevelopment went back at least as far as 1930, one of the first being the Harlan Bartholomew plan. See Haworth and Anderson, Inc., "Knoxville International Energy Exposition: Environmental Impact Statement—Draft" (Spokane, Wash.: Haworth and Anderson, Dec. 1976), 1.

3. Testerman, interview, Jan. 22, 1981.

4. For city expenditures see Robert B. Pettengill and Jogindar S. Uppal, *Can Cities Survive?: The Fiscal Plight of American Cities* (New York: St. Martin's Press, 1974), 10, 18, 27, 39.

5. *General Revenue Sharing,* Hearings before the Committee on Ways and Means, House of Representatives, 92nd Cong., 1st Sess., in Pettengill and Uppal, *Can Cities Survive?* 7–8 and *passim.*

6. For San Francisco–Palo Alto–Berkeley, see Sir Peter Hall, *Cities in Civilization* (New York: Pantheon Books, 1998), 423–54.

7. Hammer and Associates, *Economy of Metropolitan Knoxville,* 16–17, 26–27, 30–31, 64–68; Real Estate Research Corp., *Trends, Conditions and Forecasts,* 40–42, 53.

8. White, "Banking Developments," in Deaderick, *Heart of the Valley,* 379–89.

9. Testerman, interview, Jan. 22, 1981.

10. *Knoxville News-Sentinel,* Oct. 23, 1960; *Knoxville Journal,* Dec. 29, 1960; May 4, 1968; Greene, interview, Feb. 15, 1977; Baker, "Politics of Innovation," 70, 111, 220.

11. George Fritts (realtor and keen observer of Knoxville politics), interview by the author, April 8, 1977; Leonard Rogers, interview by the author, January 17, 1981; Baker, "Politics of Innovation," 319–20.

12. Kerns, *Social and Economic Conditions in Knoxville,* 2, 52.

13. Lamon, *Blacks in Tennessee,* 107–11. In Oct. 1967 the *Knoxville News-Sentinel* reported on a forty-seven-year-old African American man with a college degree who was working as a porter. Lamon, *Blacks in Tennessee,* 111. On one writer's comment about protests, see John Grisham, *The Street Lawyer* (New York: Dell, 1998), 284.

14. A. J. Gray, "Report to the Center City Task Force, May 1974," in MPC files; Downtown Knoxville Association, *The Downtown Knoxville Story* (Knoxville: DKA, 1965).

15. Stone and Webster Engineering Co., "Site Proposal for the New National Accelerator Laboratory" (preliminary site survey for the city of Oak Ridge, June 1965), 106. For an excellent study of suburbanization in the United States, see Kenneth T. Jackson, *Crabgrass Frontier: The Suburbanization of the United States* (New York: Oxford Univ. Press, 1985). For a decidedly different view, see Coontz, *The Way We Never Were.* By 1970, 37.6 percent of Americans lived in suburbs (31.4 percent in central cities and 31.0 percent in rural and small towns).

16. Pettengill and Uppal, *Can Cities Survive?* 7–8.

17. Stone and Webster, "Accelerator Site Proposal," 106, 124.

18. *Knoxville News-Sentinel,* Nov. 16, 1980; Testerman, interview, Jan. 22, 1981.

19. Real Estate Research Corp., *Trends, Conditions and Forecasts,* 187. In this period, UT students were exceedingly sensitive about the general image of the university. In 1964 a group of students protested the American Broadcasting Company's decision to film a segment of the

popular folk music television show *Hootenanny* on the campus, fearful that ABC's requirement that students wear calico, checkered shirts, and denim might reinforce some people's notions of the university as a haven for hillbillies. See Deanna Bowman, "Hootenanny" (unpub. student paper, Univ. of Tennessee, 2001; in possession of author), 7–8.

20. John D. Photiadis has observed this pattern in Cleveland, Ohio. See his *West Virginians in Their Own State and in Cleveland, Ohio: Summary and Conclusions of a Comparative Social Study*, Appalachian Center Information Report 3 (Morgantown: West Virginia Univ., 1970).

21. For statistics on birthplaces, occupations, lengths of residence in Knoxville, and home ownership, see Voter Registration Books, Knox County Election Commission. For correlation of these areas to social problems see Knoxville–Knox County Community Action Committee, *Poverty in Knoxville and Knox County* (Knoxville, 1973), 23. It is interesting to note that most areas housing Appalachian in-migrants, whether of lower- or middle-class character, have a strikingly low percentage of blacks. See Knoxville–Knox County Community Action Committee, *Poverty in Knoxville and Knox County*, 14. One disturbing aspect of the populations of Wards Thirty-Six and Forty is that the areas appear to be failing over the past decades to hold their young populations, another indication of the city's inability to absorb even its own skilled population. See Voter Registration Books, Knox County Election Commission.

22. Walker's power bases were identified through analysis of council election returns from 1941 through 1957. See *Knoxville News-Sentinel,* Nov. 7, 1941; Nov. 5, 1943; Nov. 2, 1945; Dec. 4, 1946 (recall election); Nov. 7, 1947; Nov. 8, 1957.

23. Walker, interview, Feb. 21, 1977. On strength see *Knoxville Journal,* Nov. 8, 1963; Nov. 3, 1967.

24. Rogers, interview, Jan. 17, 1981.

25. *Knoxville News-Sentinel,* March 1, 1981; Rogers, interview, Jan. 17, 1981; Haslam, interview, Aug. 14, 2002.

26. Testerman, interview, Jan. 22, 1981; Haslam, interview, Aug. 14, 2002. On Rogers's reelection and the Citizens Group see *Knoxville News-Sentinel,* Nov. 1, 3, 15, 17, 1967; Baker, "Politics of Innovation," 114.

27. On "floating wards," so named because the voters "floated" to whoever paid the highest for their votes, see *Knoxville News-Sentinel,* April 19, 1959.

28. *Knoxville News-Sentinel,* March 1, 1981; Rogers, interview, Jan. 17, 1981.

29. Rogers, interview, Jan. 17, 1981; Haslam, interview, Aug. 14, 2002. According to Robert Booker, Rogers was incapable of pronouncing the word "Negro," which usually came out as "Niggra." In frustration, one African American told the mayor, "Think of your *knee!*" Robert Booker, interview by the author, July 28, 2003.

30. Rogers, interview, Jan. 17, 1981; *Knoxville Journal,* Nov. 15, 1971. On falling out with Walker see *Knoxville News-Sentinel,* Nov. 1, 15, 1967.

31. Rogers, interview, Jan. 17, 1981; Testerman, interview, Jan. 22, 1981.

32. Rogers, interview, Jan. 17, 1981.

33. Ibid. See also *Knoxville News-Sentinel,* Nov. 1–4, 1971; *Knoxville Journal,* Nov. 1–4, 11, 17, 1971.

34. Rogers, interview, Jan. 17, 1981.

35. Garry Wills, "How Nixon Used the Media, Billy Graham, and the Good Lord to Rap with Students at Tennessee U.," *Esquire,* Sept. 1970, 119–22, 179–80; *Metro Pulse,* May 18,

2000; Diana M. Stultz, "The Billy Graham Crusade" (unpub. student paper, Univ. of Tennessee, 1986; in possession of author); Rogers, interview, Jan. 18, 1981.

36. The University of Tennessee was hardly an activist campus. But there were some stirrings. Early in 1969, the Student Government Association sued the university over a policy that the administration had to approve all speakers that student groups wished to bring to campus (the students won). In that same year, women protested dormitory curfews, and again the university was forced to back down. Then, in 1970, some students and faculty protested the appointment of Dr. Edward Boling as the university's president, one student going so far as to challenge Boling to an arm-wrestling contest, the winner to be named president (some remember it as a challenge to a lemon pie fight). Around 2,000 students showed up for that piece of guerilla theater, and campus police arrested 22 of them. See *The Daily Beacon* (UT's student newspaper), Feb. 4–8, 12, 1969; *Metro Pulse,* May 18, 2000; Elizabeth Guenther, "Love Is in the Air: A Chronicle of Events at the University of Tennessee during the Week of February 7–14, 1969" (unpub. student paper, Univ. of Tennessee, 1995; in possession of author). One of the arrested protesters, Dr. Charles Reynolds of the Religious Studies Department, was denied tenure by the board of trustees, but the board reversed itself in 1974. Reynolds, interview by the author, Sept. 30, 2002.

37. *Knoxville Journal,* Nov. 5, 19, 1971.

38. *Knoxville News-Sentinel,* March 1, 1981.

39. For biographical information see ibid., Dec. 6, 1987.

40. Testerman, interview, Jan. 22, 1981.

41. Metropolitan Planning Commission and East Tennessee Development District, *General Plan, 1990* (Knoxville: MPC, 1970); Testerman, interview, Jan. 22, 1981.

42. Testerman, interview, Jan. 22, 1981.

43. Guy Smith IV, interview by the author, Dec. 29, 1981.

44. Ibid.

45. Baker, "Politics of Innovation," 73, 97.

46. On the ribbon cutting, Robert Booker, presentation to the East Tennessee Historical Society, Oct. 27, 2002. On UNICEF, see Smith interview, Dec. 29, 1981.

47. Smith, interview, Dec. 29, 1981; *Knoxville News-Sentinel,* Nov. 21, 1975. On July 18, 1983, the *Knoxville Journal* reported that the mayor had been in his cups when he made his election night outburst.

48. Testerman, interview, Jan. 22, 1981.

49. When the garbage collectors represented by the American Federation of State, County, and Municipal Employees went on strike on July 1, 1974, the mayor responded by firing all three hundred of them and then offered to rehire all those who would return to work under the old contract (about half did so). Testerman then hired some new workers, asked other municipal employees to help out, and went out himself on the garbage trucks on well-photographed collections. On July 12, the mayor announced that the strike was over. Tom Schaffler, "Knoxville—July, 1974" (unpub. student paper, Univ. of Tennessee, 2001; in possession of author), 2–4.

50. On Tyree's four-year campaign, see Smith, interview, Dec. 29, 1981. On critic's view of Tyree's apparent sincerity, Dr. Joe Dodd, conversation with author, March 24, 1979.

51. In a receiving line, Rev. Mull, who is blind, reached out to grasp Tyree and accidentally placed his hand on Tyree's wife's breast. "This ain't the mayor, Lady Mull," the preacher said to his own wife. Some maintain the story is apocryphal, although Tyree admits that it did occur.

52. *Knoxville News-Sentinel,* Nov. 26, 1968.

53. On West Town Mall see *Metro Pulse,* Dec. 10, 1998. At present West Town Mall has grown to almost 1.4 million square feet, 130 stores and restaurants, 7,000–8,000 parking spaces, and between 10 and 15 million shoppers per year.

54. Knoxville–Knox County Community Action Committee, *Poverty in Knoxville and Knox County,* 23.

55. Earl Ramer, interview by the author, Aug. 15, 1979. In 1959 only 21 percent of city voters and 13.8 percent of county voters voted for metropolitan government.

56. The vote in the county was 14,391 (38 percent) for, 23,196 (62 percent) against. *Knoxville News-Sentinel,* November 8, 1978. On Walker's comment, Ramer, interview, Aug. 15, 1979.

57. On Knoxville city council's endorsement of the Tellico Dam, see *Knoxville News-Sentinel,* July 14, 1965. On Timberlake, see William Bruce Wheeler and Michael J. McDonald, *TVA and the Tellico Dam, 1936–1979: A Bureaucratic Crisis in Post-Industrial America* (Knoxville: Univ. of Tennessee Press, 1986), chap. 7. On the increasing dependence on automobiles, see Mark Schimmenti, in *Metro Pulse,* Dec. 10, 1998.

58. Address by George Siler, Univ. of Tennessee, Aug. 15, 1979; address by Carroll Logan, Univ. of Tennessee, July 8, 1980; Joe Dodd, *World Class Politics: Knoxville's 1982 World's Fair, Redevelopment and the Political Process* (Salem, Wis.: Sheffield, 1988), 7.

59. Sandra Lea, *Whirlwind: The Butcher Banking Scandal* (Oak Ridge, Tenn.: J. Lord, 2000), 11–12. Additional Butcher biographical material was found in 1980 in the Public Relations Office of the United American Bank, now defunct, and in the clipping file of the *Knoxville News-Sentinel* and the McClung Historical Collection. On the Southern Industrial Banking Corp., see *Knoxville News-Sentinel,* April 30, 1995.

60. On the struggle to acquire the United American Bank see White, "Banking Developments," in Deaderick, *Heart of the Valley,* 398–400; Lea, *Whirlwind,* 20–22; *Knoxville Journal,* Oct. 25, 1983.

61. *Knoxville Journal,* Oct. 24, 1983.

62. Ibid.; Lea, *Whirlwind,* 2–8, 56–60. Butcher's gubernatorial bid was almost fatally hurt by the scandals surrounding Democratic governor Ray Blanton's term and by the fact that the supporters of Bob Clement, whom Butcher and defeated in the Democratic primary, secretly supported Alexander.

63. Siler address, Aug. 15, 1979.

64. On the financing, see Lea, *Whirlwind,* 63, 84–85. On entertaining the Carters, see *Knoxville Journal,* Oct. 24, 1983.

65. Dodd, *World Class Politics,* 9–10, 29–34, 48. In a 1981 interview for the *Christian Science Monitor,* Tyree confessed that he opposed a referendum because he "knew it would be voted down." Quoted in Dodd, *World Class Politics,* 49.

66. For opponents see *Knoxville News-Sentinel,* March 11, 1976; June 1, 1979; Leon Ridenour (chair, Citizens for a Better Knoxville) to John Cole (regional environmentalist, Economic Development Administration), June 11, 1979, copy in possession of author; Dodd, *World Class Politics,* esp. 45; Regional Urban Design Assistance Team (RUDAT) hearings, March 24, 1979, in possession of Joe Dodd.

67. For statistics see Lea, *Whirlwind,* 147–69. See also *Metro Pulse,* May 8, 1997.

68. Lea, *Whirlwind,* 179; Haworth and Anderson, "Environmental Impact Statement," 6. Since some people visited the fair site many times (season tickets were sold to locals), the 11,127,786 was the number of *visits,* not the number of *visitors.*

69. On public money see Dodd, *World Class Politics,* 115. On highway improvements see Eddie Shaw (Commissioner, Tennessee Department of Transportation) to Jake Butcher, Oct. 18, 1976, in Haworth and Anderson, *Environmental Impact Statement,* 303–4. On sports see *Metro Pulse,* May 8, 1997.

70. Dodd, *World Class Politics,* 119–26; Lea, *Whirlwind,* 75, 183–84.

71. On hotel, motel, and camping facilities, see the 1975 estimate by Haworth and Anderson in "Environmental Impact Statement," 268.

72. Income by census tract was obtained from the MPC in 1979. See the MPC map of census tracts with average family incomes. See also Knoxville–Knox County Community Action Committee, *Poverty in Knoxville and Knox County,* 20.

73. Knoxville–Knox County Community Action Committee, *Poverty in Knoxville and Knox County,* 20.

74. For the remark on a "back-to-the-city movement," see University of Tennessee Graduate School of Planning Research Center, "A Housing Market Study for Lower Second Creek Redevelopment Plan," quoted in MPC, *Knoxville's Center City: Data and Technical Information Report* (Knoxville: MPC, August 1981), 14. For RUDAT report, see *After Expo* (Knoxville: RUDAT, March 1979).

75. For slippage of central business district's retail trade, see MPC, *Knoxville's Center City,* 124–25.

76. MPC, *Knoxville's Center City,* 9–10, 12, 16, 24, 121–22.

77. Ibid., 9–10.

78. William Greider, "The Education of David Stockman," *Atlantic Monthly,* Dec. 1981, 30.

Chapter 5

1. *Knoxville Journal,* Nov. 7, 1983; Lea, *Whirlwind,* 179; Dodd, *World Class Politics,* 130. One of the best accounts of the fall of the Butcher empire is *Nashville Tennessean* and *Knoxville Journal, Borrowed Money, Borrowed Time: The Fall of the House of Butcher* (a collection of articles published in both papers between Oct. 24 and Nov. 12, 1983, and published in booklet form Nov. 18, 1983).

2. *Knoxville Journal,* Nov. 7, 1983. Later FDIC officials admitted that the $90 million figure was much too low—probably closer to $377 million, including $211 million in unsecured loans to Butcher family members and friends (Jake's brother-in-law alone owed $33 million to UAB). *Knoxville Journal,* Nov. 7, 1983; Lea, *Whirlwind,* 185, 261; Dodd, *World Class Politics,* 136–37. For auditor's comment see Lea, *Whirlwind,* 412.

3. Dodd, *World Class Politics,* 131; Lea, *Whirlwind,* 201–13. Jake Butcher was indicted for bank fraud on Nov. 13, 1984. Lea, *Whirlwind,* 403.

4. Probably the best summary of the Butchers' tactics can be found in *Knoxville Journal,* Oct. 24–Nov. 12, 1983, reprinted in *Borrowed Money, Borrowed Time,* 3–40. For the party story see *Knoxville Journal,* Oct. 24, 1983, and Lea, *Whirlwind,* 119.

5. On Suite 2136 see *Knoxville Journal,* Oct. 28, 1983. For the eventual resolution of the SIBC mess, see *Knoxville News-Sentinel,* April 30, 1995. Of the $62.7 million ultimately recovered, SIBC depositors finally received $27.6 million. All the depositors with holdings under $5,000 received all their money back.

6. Jake and C. H. Butcher Jr. were convicted of multiple counts of bank fraud and tax evasion and were sentenced to twenty and twenty-five years, respectively, in federal prison. Jake ultimately served six years and C. H. was paroled after having served seven years. Neither returned to the Knoxville area.

7. In the 1982 gubernatorial race, Alexander charged that Tyree's campaign was being financed by Jake Butcher. Later it was learned that United American Bank had loaned Tyree $500,000, money that in 1983 the ex-mayor was having great difficulty repaying. Interestingly, it also was later revealed that C. H. Butcher Jr., had secretly backed Alexander, a fact the governor appears to have forgotten when he made his accusations. Lea, *Whirlwind,* 175–77. For Testerman's remark see *Knoxville News-Sentinel,* Dec. 19, 1975.

8. *Knoxville News-Sentinel,* April 28, 1984.

9. For Testerman's formal announcement see *Knoxville Journal,* Sept. 7, 1983. On Testerman and Fairfield see *Knoxville Journal,* Sept. 9, 1983; *Knoxville News-Sentinel,* Aug. 25, Sept. 28, 1983. For a summary of the Testerman-Fairfield conflict see the guest column by A. J. "Flash" Gray in *Knoxville News-Sentinel,* Oct. 9, 1984.

10. Testerman carried 19,403 of the 30, 877 votes cast (33.2 percent of the registered voters), with the closest opponent garnering but 7,403. *Knoxville News-Sentinel,* Sept. 28, 1983.

11. For council election see *Knoxville Journal,* Nov. 2, 1983. Perhaps the biggest surprise was the ousting of three-term councilman and vice mayor M. T. "Tee" Bellah, possibly seen by voters as not combative enough to stand up to Testerman. On relations with city council see *Knoxville Journal,* Dec. 2, 1984; *Knoxville News-Sentinel,* July 22, 1987. For Sansom's comment see *Knoxville News-Sentinel,* Dec. 6, 1987.

12. *Knoxville News-Sentinel,* Sept. 28, 1983. On park see *Knoxville News-Sentinel,* Sept. 9, 1984. For critique of Testerman's plan for the fair site, see *Knoxville News-Sentinel,* Sept. 9, 1984.

13. On Whittle see UT *Daily Beacon,* Feb. 4–5, 1969; *Knoxville News-Sentinel,* Dec. 6, 1987; Oct. 3, 1994; *Metro Pulse,* Feb. 1, 2001; Edward Earl Cook, "13–30 Corporation: A Case Study in Innovative Magazine Publishing" (M.S. thesis, Univ. of Tennessee, 1983). Like Testerman, Whittle in part fell victim to his own ambitious dreams. The company collapsed in 1994, and the downtown headquarters now houses the federal court.

14. For Testerman's accomplishments see *Knoxville News-Sentinel,* Aug. 27, Dec. 6, 1987. On downtown redevelopment see Downtown Task Force, *Downtown Knoxville Plan* (Knoxville: MPC, 1987) and Downtown Task Force, *Downtown Knoxville: The Next Big Step* (Knoxville: MPC, n.d.).

15. *Knoxville News-Sentinel,* Jan. 14, 1986; Jan. 22, Dec. 6, 1987.

16. For a few examples of the extent to which Kyle and Janet Testerman's "dirty laundry" (including the private detective hired by Janet) was made public, see *Knoxville News-Sentinel,* Jan. 14, Dec. 5, 18, 1986; Jan. 25, 1987; *Knoxville Journal,* Jan. 14, Dec. 5, 1986.

17. For Ashe's lineage see Deaderick, *Heart of the Valley,* 326–27 488–89. Victor Ashe's grandfather Gregory Ashe served as alderman from 1892 to 1893. Deaderick, *Heart of the Valley,* 643. His uncle Edward Joseph Ashe was president of Standard Knitting Mills and his father and mother, Robert L. and Martha Ashe, at one time owned 30 percent of WBIR radio and television stations.

18. For the West Knoxville Sertoma Club comment, see *Knoxville News-Sentinel,* July 22, 1987.

19. *Knoxville News-Sentinel,* Aug. 19, 27, Sept. 23, 30, Oct. 1, Nov. 4, 1987.

20. For Lyons's statement see *Knoxville News-Sentinel,* Nov. 4, 1987. For his part, Testerman joined the law firm of Lockridge and Becker. See *Knoxville News-Sentinel,* Feb. 6, 1988.

21. William Lyons, interview by the author, Sept. 11, 2002.

22. On business vs. homeowners, Lyons, interview, Sept. 11, 2002; Haslam, interview, Aug. 14, 2002. Interestingly, a public opinion poll cosponsored by the University of Tennessee and WBIR-TV revealed that neighborhood goals and concerns were almost identical in Knoxville's black and white neighborhoods: improved streets, parks and recreation, more police officers on the streets, etc. *Knoxville News-Sentinel,* July 19, 1998. Founded in 1965, the Community Action Committee generally worked with people who lived, worked, or volunteered in poorer neighborhoods. Barbara Kelly, executive director of CAC, conversation with the author, Dec. 24, 2002.

23. Clearly such a progressive business group exists (called by one of its probable members "the stakeholders"), although the number may not be accurate and membership is impermanent. While no one this author interviewed admitted to belonging to such a group, others believe that at one time or another James Haslam II (Pilot Oil), William Sansom (H. T. Hackney), William Arant (First Tennessee Bank, then SunTrust), William Baxter (Holston Gases), Larry Martin (First Tennessee Bank), Sam Furrow (auctioneer and investor-developer), Pat Wood (realtor), Edward Boling (UT president, 1970–86), Harry Moskos (editor, *Knoxville News-Sentinel,* to 2001), Richard Ray (ALCOA), among others, may well have been in such a group.

24. Lyons, interview, Sept. 11, 2002.

25. *Knoxville News-Sentinel,* Nov. 4, 1987.

26. Ibid. For African Americans see *Knoxville News-Sentinel,* May 24, 1985; July 21, 1998; Levi Strauss Foundation, "Knoxville, Tennessee: Opportunities for Racial Unity in the 21st Century," in *Project Change.*

27. Lyons, interview, Sept. 11, 2002, interview with Ashe, Oct. 4, 2002. At the end of his mayoral term, Ashe explained to his successor, William Haslam, that city council members were "like children who must be attended to at all times." Ashe did. *Knoxville News-Sentinel,* Nov. 23, 2003.

28. *Knoxville News-Sentinel,* Nov. 23, 2003; *Metro Pulse,* Oct. 12, 1995.

29. Lyons, interview, Sept. 11, 2002; Victor Ashe, interview by the author, Oct. 4, 2002.

30. Since 72.2 cents of every dollar collected in sales taxes in both city and county was designated for the school system, what the city and county would fight over was the remaining 27.8 cents. If that was collected in the city of Knoxville, then the city could keep the 27.8 cents. See *Knoxville News-Sentinel,* Aug. 27, 2000. For reference to "toy towns" see *Metro Pulse,* May 7, 1998.

31. *Metro Pulse,* Sept. 6, 2000.

32. For an excellent survey of the metro government controversy, see William Lyons and John M. Scheb II, "The Rejection of Consolidated Government in Knox County, Tennessee," *State and Local Government Review* 30 (spring 1998): 92–105. For Furrow's role see *Knoxville News-Sentinel,* April 12, 1998. For Ashe's denial that he secretly opposed consolidation, Ashe, interview, Oct. 4, 2002. But Lyons guesses that Ashe did oppose unification. Lyons, interview, Sept. 11, 2002. The 1996 referendum was the fourth time consolidation had been rejected, after previous rejections in 1959, 1978, and 1983.

33. On state law, Ashe's and Schumpert's putative support, the appointment of a twelve-person planning committee, and Leuthold's comments see *Metro Pulse,* May 7, 1998;

Aug. 26, 1999. For the *Metro Pulse* contest, see *Metro Pulse,* May 6, 1999. Runners-up included former Ashe press secretary and political consultant George Korda, Knoxville police chief Phil Keith, UT President Joe Johnson, county commissioner Mary Lou Horner, and "Super Chamber" CEO Tom Ingram.

34. *Metro Pulse,* Nov. 18, 1999; Jan. 6, Aug. 3, 2000; *Knoxville News-Sentinel,* Jan. 16, July 27, Aug. 20, 27, Sept. 6, 2000. At the same meeting at which the city council declared an impasse, it approved the annexation of fifty additional parcels. The agreement ultimately was negotiated by county commissioner Frank Leuthold and city information director Gene Patterson. *Metro Pulse,* Dec. 14, 2000; *Knoxville News-Sentinel,* Dec. 31, 2000. For the commission's fear of the three-judge panel, John Schmid, interview by the author, Dec. 26, 2002.

35. *Knoxville News-Sentinel,* July 27, 2000; *Metro Pulse,* Dec. 21, 2000; Jan. 17, 2002.

36. On Mayfield see *Knoxville News-Sentinel,* May 2, 1999; *Metro Pulse,* April 6, Sept. 7, 2000. For Ashe's statements, Ashe, interview, Oct. 4, 2002.

37. *Knoxville News-Sentinel,* April 8, 2001; *Metro Pulse,* April 5, 12, 2001. For anger directed at city council and Ashe and for demands for the mayor's recall, see *Knoxville News-Sentinel,* April 8, 2001; *Metro Pulse,* April 12, 2001. Much of the criticism of Raleigh Wynn was unfair. Born in Knoxville in 1924, Wynn was a veteran of World War II, a graduate of Tennessee State University (where he played football), a college and high school football coach, a recipient of a master's degree from UT, a junior high school principal, and in 2001 the vice president and athletic director at Knoxville College. *Knoxville News-Sentinel,* April 15, 2001. For the conservative black leadership's distrust of Mayfield, Booker, interview, July 28, 2003.

38. For 1882 black police officers see Levi Strauss Foundation, "Knoxville, Tennessee." For 1913 and 1919 see Lakin, "'A Dark Night,'" 3, 8–9. For KKK see Kenneth T. Jackson, *The Ku Klux Klan in the City, 1915–1930* (New York: Oxford Univ. Press, 1967), 62. For 1980s rumors see *Knoxville Journal,* Nov. 10, 1983.

39. *Knoxville Journal,* Nov. 10, 1983. For the 1997–98 incidents see *Knoxville News-Sentinel,* Jan. 14, 1998; *Metro Pulse,* Feb. 26, March 5, 1998.

40. For city council meeting see *Knoxville News-Sentinel,* Jan. 14, 1998. For member of the Bernstein Commission see *Knoxville News-Sentinel,* July 19, 1998. Beginning on July 19, the *News-Sentinel* published a perceptive four-part series, "The Racial Divide." One of its conclusions was that "Racism is a fact we live with every day." See *Knoxville News-Sentinel,* July 26, 1998. Also, on July 23 WBIR-TV aired a community forum on the same subject, although it lacked the depth of the newspaper's series. On Raleigh Wynn's claim see *Metro Pulse,* March 5, 1998.

41. On Keith see *Metro Pulse,* Jan. 21, 1999. For "perplexing" see *Metro Pulse,* Sept. 16, 1998. For Robinson see *Knoxville News-Sentinel,* July 27, 1998.

42. For the poll see *Metro Pulse,* July 30, 1998. On the Knoxville Ministerial Association see *Metro Pulse,* Jan. 29, 1998. The *News-Sentinel* became Knoxville's sole daily newspaper after the *Knoxville Journal* published its last issue as a daily on Dec. 31, 1991. The paper had been founded in 1885 by William Rule, who was editor and publisher until his death in 1928. See Ian Winton, "The Death of the *Knoxville Journal:* A Chain Reaction" (unpub. student paper, Univ. of Tennessee 1995; in possession of author), 2. The *Journal* limped along for a while as a weekly newspaper.

43. For the Bernstein Commission recommendation and council's opposition see *Metro Pulse,* July 30, 1998. As soon as he created the Bernstein Commission, Ashe let it be known that he favored a civilian review board, as did Chief Keith. In the city, chief of police was an appointed position that had no political constituency other than the rank-and-file police officers. On the other hand, in Knox County the sheriff was an elected person and therefore had

a voter constituency. Therefore Sheriff Tim Hutchinson was amassing considerable political power, which required nearly everyone running for office in the city or county to beg for his support. See *Knoxville News-Sentinel,* Sept. 27, 1997; Aug. 25, 1999, Sept. 2, Nov. 18, 1999. Ashe probably was the only political figure who could run without Hutchinson's blessing. On Carlene Malone (whom her husband referred to as "a terrorist") see *Metro Pulse,* Dec. 13, 2001. When she first ran for office in 1991, Bill Baxter said, "There's no way that woman will ever be elected. She's from New York." He was wrong. Malone served Knoxville well for ten years on the council, and even Ashe, who probably detested her, admitted that she was "the only person on the council who worked as hard as I did." Ashe, interview, Oct. 4, 2002; *Metro Pulse,* Dec. 13, 2001.

44. In truth, Ashe had been leaning toward a review board since the release of Stenson's medical examiner's report and the contentious council meeting of Jan. 13. See *Metro Pulse,* March 5, 1998. For the mayor's creation of the body by executive order see *Knoxville News-Sentinel,* Sept. 23, 1998.

45. *Knoxville News-Sentinel,* Feb. 6, 2000. For assessments of Ashe's sixteen years as mayor see *Knoxville News-Sentinel,* Nov. 23, Dec. 14, 2003; *Metro Pulse,* Dec. 11, 2003; Victor Ashe, *Sixteen Years of Progress: The Administration of Mayor Victor Ashe* (Knoxville: privately printed, 2003); Ashe to author, Dec. 15, 2003.

46. *Metro Pulse,* Nov. 16, 1995. Knoxville's alternative newspaper implied that Asheville's downtown life was so vigorous because the city was more tolerant and accepting of diversity and alternative lifestyles (gays, lesbians, etc.). As to size, Asheville's 1990 population was 61,607, compared with Knoxville's 165,121.

47. For a perceptive explanation of Chattanooga's success, see *Metro Pulse,* June 26, 1997. For Knoxvillians' comments on Chattanooga, see *Knoxville News-Sentinel,* Dec. 14, 1997; July 5, Aug. 9, 1998; Feb. 13, 2000.

48. *Knoxville News-Sentinel,* May 23, 1998; *Metro Pulse,* Jan. 8, 1998; Nov. 16, 2000.

49. *Knoxville News-Sentinel,* Aug. 9, 1998; Oct. 4, 2001.

50. For a biographical sketch of Jacobs, see *American Women Writers: A Critical Reference Guide* (Detroit: St. James Press, 2000), 2:266–67. For her comment, see *The Columbia World of Quotations* (New York: Columbia Univ. Press, 1996), no. 30400. For a recent reappraisal of Jacobs's thinking, see Steve Belmont, *Cities in Full: Recognizing and Realizing the Great Potential of Urban America* (Chicago: American Planning Assn., 2002), esp. 3–6.

51. Public Building Authority, "Convention Center–Related Private Development" (draft report, December 29, 1999); *Knoxville News-Sentinel,* Jan. 18, July 21, 1998; July 10, 2001; Oct. 13, 2000; Jan. 11, March 8, 2001). Due in large part to new convention centers, cheaper conference and hotel rates, and safer streets, midsize cities were picking up an increasing amount of convention business from traditional convention sites such as New York (down 8.8 percent in the first six months of 2001), Boston (-8.3 percent), Orlando (-9.0 percent), and San Francisco (-13.2 percent). See *USA Today,* July 17, 2001. For the Knoxville Center's opening, see "Celebrating at the Center," an advertising supplement to the *Knoxville News-Sentinel,* Oct. 13, 2002.

52. The author recorded Ashe's statement at the "topping out" ceremony, at which the last girder was set in place, accompanied by what was for Knoxville the indispensable fireworks. On Gloria Ray and on negative opinions, see *Metro Pulse,* March 8, 2001.

53. Urban Land Institute, "Strategies for the Development of a Convention Center and the Redevelopment of the World's Fair Site" (July 27–31, 1998), quoted in Public Building Authority, "Convention Center–Related Private Development."

54. For opposition see *Knoxville News-Sentinel,* Dec. 14, 1997; Jan. 18, March 5, July 21, 1998. For city-county conflict, see *Metro Pulse,* Feb. 19, 1998. For the Smokies' move, see *Sevierville Mountain Press,* Nov. 17, 1998; *Knoxville News-Sentinel,* Jan. 21, June 17, 2001.

55. *Knoxville Journal,* Dec. 30, 1989; Jan. 18, March 20–24, 1990; *Knoxville News-Sentinel,* May 11, June 1, 1990; Sept. 23, Oct. 22, 1991; July 21, 1993; Sept. 12, 1995; *City Works,* vol. 2 (April 1990); *Knoxville Business Review,* Nov. 13, 1989; Mayor's Waterfront Task Force, "Knoxville Waterfront Plan" (Knoxville: MPC, 1988).

56. For housing statistics see Public Building Authority, "Convention Center–Related Private Development," 28. The 2000 census revealed that downtown Knoxville was home to roughly 1,000 fewer residents than it had been in 1990. *Metro Pulse,* Oct. 11, 2001. For Schimmenti's comment, see *Metro Pulse,* March 2, 2000. Schimmenti lived in a condominium in the center city.

57. *Metro Pulse,* July 6, 2000.

58. For the Worsham Watkins plan, costs, and editorial support, see *Metro Pulse,* July 6, 2000; Jan. 20, 2001; *Knoxville News-Sentinel,* July 9, 2000; Feb. 18, 2001.

59. K2K was founded in Oct. 1999 by Buzz Goss and Cherie Piercy-Goss as a "chat room" for "getting together to talk about . . . issues." Not infrequently, the mayor joined in. *Metro Pulse,* May 4, 2000. For attacks on the Worsham Watkins plan, see *Metro Pulse,* July 6, Aug. 3, 24, Sept. 21, Oct. 5, Dec. 21, 2000; May 31, Oct. 11, 2001; *Knoxville News-Sentinel,* Feb. 13, 18, 2001. On Market Square, see *Knoxville News-Sentinel,* July 16, 2000; Feb. 22, March 4, April 1, 2001; *Metro Pulse,* Oct. 19, 2000; March 8, June 7, 2001. In early 1999, developer David Dewhirst allowed the UT School of Architecture to set up a design studio rent-free in a building he owned on Market Square. Many people hoped that this would become the nucleus of a downtown campus, a concept that was warmly supported by University of Michigan dean of architecture Douglas Kelbaugh. But when Dewhirst asked the university for some kind of financial commitment, UT backed out and closed the studio. *Metro Pulse,* Nov. 18, 1999; Feb. 10, April 20, 2000.

60. For Universe Knoxville, see Knoxville Area Chamber Partnership, "Universe Knoxville," a promotional brochure designed by Spectrum Design; *Knoxville News-Sentinel,* April 5, 15, 22, 24, 2001; *Metro Pulse,* April 5, May 3, 2001. The so-called Super Chamber was a merger of the Grater Knoxville Chamber of Commerce, the Downtown Knoxville Association and the Convention and Visitors Bureau and was "strategically allied" with the Knox County Development Corporation. The major force behind its founding clearly was Pilot Oil Corporation's Jim Haslam and a group known as the "Major Issues Committee" (occasionally referred to by its critics as the "twelve white guys"). See *Metro Pulse,* Jan. 29, Aug. 27, 1998; May 4, 2000; *Knoxville News-Sentinel,* Dec. 29, 1998; Edgar Miller, "Not Your Grandfather's Chamber," *Knoxville City View,* August 2002, 44–47.

61. For Ingram's promotional ideas see Knoxville Area Chamber Partnership, "Universe Knoxville."

62. *Knoxville News-Sentinel,* April 22, 24, 2001.

63. On estimated costs see *Knoxville News-Sentinel,* April 24, 2001; *Metro Pulse,* April 5, 2001. For opposition see *Metro Pulse,* May 3, 2001; *Knoxville News-Sentinel,* April 15, May 6, 2001. For Ingram's frustration and Ashe's opposition to the Knoxville Area Chamber Partnership, see Miller, "Not Your Grandfather's Chamber," 44, 46–47. For reference to the "silver bullet" and Arambula see *Metro Pulse,* Nov. 21, 2002. The Universe Knoxville site originally had been earmarked for a new Knox County Justice Center. But political squabbling

between Sheriff Tim Hutchinson, police chief Phil Keith, and Attorney General Randy Nichols appeared to kill that project, although the demise of Universe Knoxville and charges of jail overcrowding may have given it new life. *Knoxville News-Sentinel,* Jan. 19, 2000; Sharon Pound, "Urban Pioneers," *Knoxville City View,* August 2002, 30. For Volunteer Landing see *Knoxville News-Sentinel,* Aug. 20, 1995; *Metro Pulse,* Aug. 31, 2000; Kevin Dubose, assistant director of Knoxville's department of development, conversation with author, Jan. 10, 2003. For other projects see *Metro Pulse,* May 18, 2000; Jan. 11, Oct. 25, Nov. 1, 2001; Jan. 10, 2002. For Ashe's record on downtown residential development see *Metro Pulse,* March 7, 2002.

64. Kristopher Kendrick was a native of Rockwood (in Roane County, approximately forty-five miles west of Knoxville) who started his career as a hairdresser and then moved into real estate and renovation. Imaginative and unorthodox, he became a millionaire "many times over" by being one of the very first to recognize the possibilities in the downtown core. See *Metro Pulse,* Nov. 4, 1994. For Dewhirst and others, see Pound, "Urban Pioneers," 26–30, esp. 28. See also *Metro Pulse,* Oct. 25, Nov. 1, 2001.

65. Pound, "Urban Pioneers," 30. For Volunteer Landing see *Knoxville News-Sentinel,* Aug. 20, 1995; *Metro Pulse,* Aug. 31, 2000; Kevin Dubose, assistant director of Knoxville's department of development, conversation with author, Jan. 10, 2003. For other projects see *Metro Pulse,* May 18, 2000; Jan. 11, Oct. 25, Nov. 1, 2001; Jan. 10, 2002.

66. Mark Ritchie, interview by WATE-TV, Jan. 10, 2003. For estimate see Pound, "Urban Pioneers," 26. Volunteer Landing was part of an upscale development for Knoxville's riverfront, to include restaurants, condominiums, walkways, festive retailing, etc. See *Knoxville News-Sentinel,* June 5, Nov. 5, 1988; Dec. 11, 1989; Feb. 21, July 7, 1991; Sept. 15, 1992; June 2, Nov. 19, Dec. 5, 8, 15, 1993; Aug. 7 1994; Jan. 15, 22, June 22, Aug. 15, Sept. 7, Oct. 30, 1995; April 21, Aug. 25, 1996; April 23, May 21, July 20, 1999; Feb. 16, April 18, 2000; *Metro Pulse,* Feb. 26, 1993; Jan. 27, Aug. 17, 1995; Sept. 17, 1998; *Knoxville Business Review,* Nov. 13, 1989; *Knoxville City View,* March–April 1996. For a more recent analysis, see *Metro Pulse,* Feb. 5, 2004.

67. On Kroger see *Knoxville News-Sentinel,* Feb. 20, 2000. On homeless see Vicki Slagle Johns, "Nowhere to Go: A Professor's Study Finds the Number of Homeless in Knoxville on the Rise," *Tennessee Alumnus* 77, no. 2 (spring 1997): 11–13; *Metro Pulse,* July 23, 1998. As with many of the city's problems, Testerman was among the first to recognize it. Johns, "Nowhere to Go," 11. On prostitutes see *Metro Pulse,* Feb. 17, 2000. For "wanted" article see *Knoxville News-Sentinel,* Feb. 20, 2000. See also "Knoxville 37902" in *Metro Pulse,* Nov. 21, 2002, and summary of the Urban Land Institute's report ("more residents, office workers and visitors walking around downtown") in *Metro Pulse,* Dec. 19, 2002. Fort Sanders, an urban neighborhood separated from downtown by the World's Fair site, was a mixture of upscale gentrification, rental units, and student slum. In the late 1990s a Dallas-based developer began razing structures in order to replace them with more upscale town-houses (over fifty structures were destroyed in 1999 alone). A coalition formed by Mayor Ashe called the Fort Sanders Forum attempted to halt the massive bulldozing. *Metro Pulse,* Sept. 17, 1998; Jan. 27, 2000; *Knoxville News-Sentinel,* Sept. 12, 1999.

68. The most interesting opponent of Ashe on the city council was Carlene Malone (1945–   ), one of the most magnetic political figures in Knoxville's recent history. Born in New York City, she earned a degree in psychology at SUNY Albany before moving with her husband, a UT professor, to Knoxville. After working with her neighborhood organization, in 1991 she announced her candidacy for city council. Malone won and went on to serve three terms on the council. Husband John Malone said his wife "is like a terrorist. She has to blow herself up to get rid of . . . Victor Ashe." *Metro Pulse,* Jan. 13, 2000; Dec. 13,

2001; *Knoxville News-Sentinel,* April 8, 2001. For a positive assessment of Ashe's tenure see *Metro Pulse,* March 7, 2002.

Epilogue

1. *Knoxville News-Sentinel,* Sept. 26, 27, 1998; *Metro Pulse,* Oct. 1, 1998. On the end of Walker's political career, see *Knoxville News-Sentinel,* Jan. 21, 2001. For his autobiography see Cas Walker, *My Life History: A Book of True Short Stories* (Knoxville: Cas Walker, 1993).

2. For Testerman and Robinson see *Knoxville News-Sentinel,* Sept. 26, 1998. In the same issue John Rice Irwin of the Museum of Appalachia claimed that Walker "was the most interesting, talked about, loved and maybe hated individual in this century in East Tennessee."

3. William E. Arant Jr., interview by the author, Oct. 4, 2002.

4. On Nine Counties One Vision see *Knoxville News-Sentinel,* Jan. 9, 16, 19, Feb. 13, 2000; *Metro Pulse,* April 13, 2000. The nine counties were Anderson, Blount, Grainger, Jefferson, Knox, Loudon, Roane, Sevier, and Union. See Nine Counties One Vision, "How We Came to Be the People We Are" (n.p., n.d.; in possession of author).

5. For the statistics see Nine Counties One Vision, *Annual Report 2001* (Knoxville: Nine Counties One Vision, 2001), 1. See also *Metro Pulse,* Jan. 25, 2001; *Knoxville News-Sentinel,* Jan. 28, 2001.

6. Typical of cynics was a letter to *Metro Pulse* from a former Knoxvillian, who wrote that the "people . . . have no say. . . . There's still a lot of cronyism, a lot of *let's just be good ol' boys and maintain the status quo." Metro Pulse,* Jan. 8, 1998. See also *Metro Pulse,* April 13, 2000; Jan. 25, 2001; Jan. 22, 2004. The public co-chairs of Nine Counties One Vision were former television anchor Edye Ellis and retired air force general Fred Forster.

7. On College Homes see George White Jr., "The Heart of the Home: Race and Public Housing Policy in Knoxville, Tennessee," paper presented to the Urban History Association, Sept. 27, 2002; *Knoxville News-Sentinel,* Jan. 18, 1998; *Metro Pulse,* April 9, 1998. For Matavou and Ashe see *Metro Pulse,* Jan. 17, 2002.

8. *Knoxville News-Sentinel,* Jan. 14, 2001. For Littlejohn and Roberts see *Metro Pulse,* Jan. 17, 2002. One promising black-initiated neighborhood improvement effort, the Inner City Community Development, Inc., collapsed in fraud and corruption. *Metro Pulse,* Nov. 2, 2000.

9. On Latinos see *Metro Pulse,* Sept. 2, 1999; Jan. 17, 2002; *Knoxville News-Sentinel,* March 22, 2002; "The Face of Immigration in Tennessee," http://web.utk.edu/~tnlatina/contacts.html; *Sevierville Mountain Press,* Sept. 25, 2003. For hate crimes against middle easterners see *Knoxville News-Sentinel,* Jan. 13, 2003.

10. *Knoxville News-Sentinel,* June 25, 1995; Dec. 31, 2000; *Metro Pulse,* Aug. 31, 2000; July 18, Dec. 19, 2002; Matthew Murray, presentation to Leadership Sevier, Aug. 21, 2002. For 2003 government jobs see *Knoxville News-Sentinel,* April 27, 2003.

11. On the Technology Corridor see *Knoxville News-Sentinel,* Aug. 19, 1984; Arant, interview, Oct. 4, 2002; James Haslam II, presentation at the University of Tennessee, Aug. 17, 1984. The board of the Technology Corridor included Haslam, Arant, and H. T. Hackney president William Sansom. On venture capital see *Knoxville News-Sentinel,* Dec. 10, 2000. On education see *Metro Pulse,* Aug. 17, 2000.

12. For population see *Knoxville News-Sentinel,* March 25, June 10, 2001. For malls see *Metro Pulse,* Sept. 10, 1998; Dec. 19, 2002.

13. On the desire for downtown revival see *Metro Pulse,* Sept. 10, 1998. On parking see *Metro Pulse,* Feb. 28, Sept. 12, 2002. According to the MPC, downtown Knoxville had 16,423 parking spaces, 20,000 short of what was needed. *Metro Pulse,* Sept. 12, 2002. The enthusiasm for light rail owes a good deal to *Knoxville News-Sentinel* editor Harry Moskos, who made that a personal crusade. On rails see *Metro Pulse,* Dec. 3, 1998; Oct. 14, 1999; *Knoxville News-Sentinel,* July 16, 2000; *New York Times,* Nov. 20, 2000.

14. Undoubtedly the best—and most troubling—source on Knoxville's environment is John Nolt et al., *What Have We Done?: The Foundations for Global Sustainability's State of the Bioregion Report for the Upper Tennessee Valley and the Southern Appalachian Mountains* (Washburn, Tenn.: Earth Knows Publications, 1997). See also various issues of the *Hellbender Press,* a regional environmental newsletter, and *Metro Pulse,* July 5, 2001; Dec. 5, 19, 2002; *Knoxville News-Sentinel,* Aug. 18, 2002.

15. On litter see *Knoxville News-Sentinel,* Jan. 9, 2000. For a no-holds-barred description of Knoxville's ugliness see Bill Bryson, *A Walk in the Woods: Rediscovering America on the Appalachian Trail* (New York: Broadway Books, 1998), 114–15. In spite of the fact that Knoxville was far more physically attractive in 2000 than it had been in 1950, patches of startling ugliness remained, as along Clinton Highway.

16. See chapter 4.

17. Uppal, *Can Cities Survive?* 10, 18, 27, 39.

18. *USA Today,* "Seeking Solutions: Can Our Cities Survive?" a forum held Sept. 23, 1994 in the USA Today Building, Rosslyn, Va., transcript in possession of author.

19. For reports on the gala see *Knoxville News-Sentinel,* Jan. 28, 30, 2000. A videotape of the affair, dubbed *A Tribute to "Gem" Haslam,* was produced by the public relations firm Moxley Carmichael. For the planning of the event, Jeannie Dulaney, CEO of Leadership Knoxville, interview by the author, Jan. 13, 2003.

20. The founder of the Leadership Movement was John Gardner of Common Cause, and the first city to establish the program was Philadelphia, in 1959. Jeannie Dulaney, guest lecture at the University of Tennessee, Dec. 4, 2001, notes in possession of author. See *Leadership Knoxville '85,* a brochure describing the program and naming the first steering committee. Haslam was succeeded as chairman by Sam Furrow. On Furrow see *Metro Pulse,* Nov. 28, 2002. On the Public Building Authority see *Knoxville News-Sentinel,* Aug. 25, 29, 1999; *Metro Pulse,* Sept. 2, 1999.

Index